RESEARCHING LIVED EXPERIENCE

SUNY Series in the Philosophy of Education
Philip L. Smith, editor

RESEARCHING LIVED EXPERIENCE
Human Science for an Action Sensitive Pedagogy

Max van Manen

State University of New York Press

For information, address State University of New York Press,
90 State Street, Suite 700, Albany, N.Y. 12207

Library of Congress Cataloging-in-Publication Data

Manen, Max van.
    Researching lived experience: human science for an action
sensitive pedagogy / Max van Manen.
      p. cm. — (SUNY series in the philosophy of education)
Includes bibliographical references.
ISBN 0-7914-0425-0. — ISBN 0-7914-0426-9 (pbk.)
  1. Education—Research. 2. Hermeneutics—Research.
3. Phenomenology—Research. I. Title. II. Series.
LB1028.M2685 1990
370'.7'8—dc20   89-48885
                                         CIP

20 19 18 17 16 15 14

voor mijn moeder

Table of Contents

Preface

This book is an attempt to introduce and explicate a hermeneutic phenomenological approach to human science research and writing. Influenced by the spirit of the European movements as well as by certain North American developments, the text offers a pedagogically grounded concept of research that takes its starting point in the empirical realm of everyday lived experience. The notion underlying this approach is that interpretive phenomenological research and theorizing cannot be separated from the textual practice of writing. Thus, a semiotics inspired dimension is part of this research approach, while the practical nature of the pedagogic lifeworld demands that this form of educational inquiry does not convert into armchair philosophizing or abstract theorizing.

I came to the human sciences, phenomenology and hermeneutics, in my studies of pedagogy in the Netherlands. During the nineteen–sixties the predominant orientation to teacher education was an approach that was called *Geisteswissenschaftliche Pädagogik* in Germany and *Fenomenologische Pedagogiek* in the Netherlands. The German tradition of "human science pedagogy" (the Dilthey-Nohl School) employed an interpretive or hermeneutic methodology and the Dutch movement of "phenomenological pedagogy" (the Utrecht School) was more descriptive or phenomenological in orientation. This text reflects aspects and features derived from both traditions. However, a characteristic of the European approach to pedagogy was its almost total unconcern with questions of method. Those who engaged in interpretive phenomenological research in education (such as Langeveld, Beets, and Bollnow) often wrote sensitively reflective studies of the pedagogic lifeworld that parents and teachers share with their children and students. But questions of method or how to partake in such scholarship were simply not raised. During the late sixties the German hermeneutical pedagogy movement and the Dutch phenomenological tradition declined as a result of certain ideological and social pressures; on the one hand from influences of North American behaviorism, and on the other hand from emerging social critical theories in education in Germany. More recently a resurgence, although in different forms, of the earlier human science impulses is noticeable.

In pursuing this project I have benefitted from discussions with colleagues and friends Ton Beekman, Bas Levering, Antoinette Oberg, Helmut Danner, Robert Burch, Alan Blum and others. And I have been particularly stimulated by the students I have worked with in these past years. Many of them have become good friends and colleagues. I like to mention especially David G. Smith, Vangie Bergum, Carol Olson, Rod Evans, Stefan Baldursson, Kim Krawchenko, Chizuko Maeda, Mikio Fujita, and Stephen Smith who, in their own unique ways, have helped to make the Human Science Pedagogy project such a fascinating endeavour. I thank Geoff Milburn for his confidence and encouragements to publish this text.

The author and publisher wish to express their gratitude to Dr. Phyllis Chesler for granting permission to re-print an extract from *With Child: A Diary of Motherhood* (New York: Crowell, 1979), which appears on pages 72-73 of this book.

CHAPTER 1

Human Science

Introduction

It may be useful to state at the outset what the intention of this book is and what interest a reader may have in it. On the one hand, this text describes a human science research approach, showing a semiotic employment of the methods of phenomenology and hermeneutics. And on the other hand, the text engages the reader in pedagogic reflection on how we live with children as parents, teachers, or educators.

So one may read this work primarily as a methodology, as a set of methodological suggestions for engaging in human science research and writing. But in the human sciences, as conceived in this text, one does not pursue research for the sake of research. It is presumed that one comes to the human sciences with a prior interest of, for example, a teacher, a nurse, or a psychologist. This book attempts to be relevant to researchers in nursing, psychology, and other such professions. But the fundamental orientation in here is pedagogic.

The various examples provided throughout this text will often involve an investigation of the meanings of teaching, parenting, and related pedagogic vocations—not assuming, of course, that teaching and parenting are identical phenomena. And so when we raise questions, gather data, describe a phenomenon, and construct textual interpretations, we do so as researchers who stand in the world in a pedagogic way.

One can distinguish a variety of approaches in the field of the human sciences. A research method is only a way of investigating certain kinds of questions. The questions themselves and the way one understands the questions are the important starting points, not the method as such.

But of course it is true as well that the way in which one articulates certain questions has something to do with the research method that one tends to identify with. So there exists a certain dialectic between question and method. Why then should one adopt one research approach over another? The choice should reflect more than mere whim, preference, taste, or fashion. Rather, the method one chooses ought to maintain a certain harmony with the deep interest that makes one an educator (a parent or teacher) in the first place.

The human science approach in this text is avowedly phenomenological, hermeneutic, and semiotic or language oriented, not just because that happens to be the particular interest or prejudice of the author but rather because pedagogy requires a phenomenological sensitivity to lived experience (children's realities and lifeworlds). Pedagogy requires a hermeneutic ability to make interpretive sense of the phenomena of the lifeworld in order to see the pedagogic significance of situations and relations of living with children. And pedagogy requires a way with language in order to allow the research process of textual reflection to contribute to one's pedagogic thoughtfulness and tact.

Pedagogy is the activity of teaching, parenting, educating, or generally living with children, that requires constant practical acting in concrete situations and relations. The knowledge forms generated by a human science methodology as described in this text are meant to serve the practical aims of pedagogy. The term "human science" is employed more narrowly in this text than it might be encountered elsewhere. Here, "human science" is often used interchangeably with the terms "phenomenology" or "hermeneutics." This usage is not inconsistent with the hermeneutic phenomenological tradition as found in Germany (from about 1900 to 1965) and in the Netherlands (from about 1945 to 1970). The present text intends to be a modern extension of certain aspects of that tradition of "Human Science Pedagogy."

To the extent that the European traditions are sources for this text, an attempt has been made to do a methodological reading of the work of German and Dutch authors. A distinguishing feature of the German *Geisteswissenschaftliche Pädagogik* and the Dutch *Fenomenologische Pedagogiek* has been that there was a marked unconcern with methods and epistemology. Students of outstanding scholars such as Nohl, Litt, Flitner, Bollnow, Langeveld, van den Berg, and Buytendijk were meant to learn the process by osmosis or apprenticeship, which the Germans would sometimes call *Bildung.* Only the most talented succeeded. One said of Dutch scholars who worked in the phenomenological tradition that there was no mediocrity in their research: the work was either very good or very bad. And, of course, only the good studies have survived— which is one criterion of their quality.

In his book *Truth and Method* (1975) the philosopher Gadamer argues that the preoccupation with (objective) method or technique is really antithetical to the spirit of human science scholarship. He shows that the preoccupation of Dilthey or later Husserl to develop an objective human science led them to programs that are alienated from the actual content of the concept of life. The irony in this argument is that the reference to "method" in the title of Gadamer's book, *Truth and Method,* may have contributed to its immense popularity among scholars in North America. At any rate, in this text I hope to show that there is a way to deal with methodological concerns that is decidedly unmethodological in a purely prescriptive or technocratic sense. The fundamental thesis of this approach is that almost anyone who is seriously interested in human science research can benefit from an examination of its methodological dimensions. There is no guarantee, however, that all students of the human sciences will be able to produce work that is "very good." One needs to be constantly on guard against the seductive illusions of technique (Barrett, 1978).

In North America, the field of the human sciences (which includes symbolic interactionism, phenomenological sociology, ethnography, ethnomethodology, critical theory, gender study, semiotics, etc.) consists of approaches to research and theorizing that have certain roots in continental sources while other developments are indigenous to North America. The distinction of "Human" Science versus "Natural" Science is often attributed to Wilhelm Dilthey. Dilthey developed the contrast between the *Naturwissenschaften* (the natural or physical sciences) and the *Geisteswissenschaften* into a methodological program for the latter. For Dilthey the proper subject matter for the *Geisteswissenschaften* is the human world characterized by *Geist*—mind, thoughts, consciousness, values, feelings, emotions, actions, and purposes, which find their objectifications in languages, beliefs, arts, and institutions. Thus, at the risk of oversimplification one might say that the difference between natural science and human science resides in what it studies: natural science studies "objects of nature," "things," "natural events," and "the way that objects behave." Human science, in contrast, studies "persons," or beings that have "consciousness" and that "act purposefully" in and on the world by creating objects of "meaning" that are "expressions" of how human beings exist in the world.

The preferred method for natural science, since Galileo, has been detached observation, controlled experiment, and mathematical or quantitative measurement. And when the natural science method has been applied to the behavioral social sciences, it has retained procedures of experimentation and quantitative analysis. In contrast, the preferred method for human science involves description, interpretation, and self-reflective or critical analysis. We explain nature, but human life we must understand, said Dilthey (1976). Whereas natural science tends to *taxonomize* natural phenomena (such as in biology) and causally or probabilistically *explain* the behavior of things (such as in physics), human science aims at explicating the meaning of human phenomena (such as in literary or historical studies of texts) and at *understanding* the lived structures of meanings (such as in phenomenological studies of the lifeworld).

The starting point of this text is the belief that human science research in education done by educators ought to be guided by pedagogical standards. The fundamental model of this approach is textual reflection on the lived experiences and practical actions of everyday life with the intent to increase one's thoughtfulness and practical resourcefulness or tact. Phenomenology describes how one orients to lived experience, hermeneutics describes how one interprets the "texts" of life, and semiotics is used here to develop a practical writing or linguistic approach to the method of phenomenology and hermeneutics. What is novel to this text is that research and writing are seen to be closely related, and practically inseparable pedagogical activities. The type of reflection required in the act of hermeneutic phenomenological writing on the meanings and significances of phenomena of daily life is fundamental to pedagogic research. Thus, this text has pedagogic ambitions at two levels. It offers a research approach that is fundamental to the process of pedagogy, and it tries to practise what it preaches by orienting itself to questions of pedagogy in the discussion of method.

Why Do Human Science Research?

"Whoever is searching for the human being first must find the lantern," Nietzsche said once (Buytendijk, 1947, p. 22). In this aphoristic reference to the philosopher Diogenes, Nietzsche raised two questions: What does it mean to study the human being in his or her humanness? And, what methodology is required for this kind of study? Diogenes was a Greek philosopher living in the fourth century BC and now known to us as an unconventional thinker of a cutting wit and repartee who taught his fellow citizens largely by pantomimic gesture and example. One day Diogenes was reported to have gone about the city in clear daylight with a lit lantern looking about as if he had lost something. When people came up to ask what he was trying to find he answered: "Even with a lamp in broad daylight I cannot find a real human being," and when people pointed to themselves he chased them with a stick, shouting "it is *real* human beings I want." Of course, most people laughed at this demonstration. But the anecdote survived because it did bring some to reflect on the most original question contained in Diogenes' pantomimic exercise: What is the nature of human being? And what does it mean to ask this question? Diogenes' demonstration was meant as well to jar the moral consciousness of those who settle for easy answers—a human being is not just something you automatically *are*, it is also something you must try to *be*. And apparently Diogenes implied that he had great trouble finding some good examples. The bizarre prop of the lit lamp in bright daylight was his way of saying that he could not "see" any human beings. He felt the need to throw some light on the matter; or perhaps more appropriately, with his lamp Diogenes showed a commitment, not to fancy abstract philosophical discourse, but to practical reflection in the concreteness and fullness of lived life.

From a phenomenological point of view, to do research is always to question the way we experience the world, to want to know the world in which we live as human beings. And since to *know* the world is profoundly to *be* in the world in a certain way, the act of researching—questioning—theorizing is the intentional act of attaching ourselves to the world, to become more fully part of it, or better, to *become* the world. Phenomenology calls this inseparable connection to the world the principle of "intentionality." In doing research we question the world's very secrets and intimacies which are constitutive of the world, and which bring the world as world into being for us and in us. Then research is a caring act: we want to know that which is most essential to being. To care is to serve and to share our being with the one we love. We desire to truly know our loved one's very nature. And if our love is strong enough, we not only will learn much about life, we also will come face to face with its mystery.

The Austrian psychologist, Ludwig Binswanger (1963, p. 173), has shown that the reverse is true as well. We can only understand something or someone for whom we care. In this sense of how we come to know a human being, the words of Goethe are especially valid: "One learns to know only what one loves, and the deeper and fuller the knowledge is to be, the more powerful and vivid must be the love, indeed the passion" (1963, p. 83). I do not suggest that love or care itself is a way or method for knowing, but as Frederik Buytendijk said in his 1947 inaugural lecture, love is foundational for all knowing of human existence. That knowing is not a purely cognitive act is a principle to which we nod occasionally in educational research. Contemporary phenomenologists like the Frenchman Emmanuel Levinas (1981) have attempted to demonstrate the deep philosophical truth of this insight. Especially where I meet the other person in his or her weakness, vulnerability or innocence, I experience the undeniable presence of loving responsibility: a child who calls upon me may claim me in a way that leaves me no choice. Most parents have experienced this moral claim and many ⸺ ⸺nd other educators who are involved in pedago⸺ ⸺elf-forgetful manner have experienced this ⸺s. When I love a person (a child or adult) ⸺es toward the good of that person. So the ⸺s is a sense of the pedagogic Good (van ⸺e I remain sensitive to the uniqueness ⸺tuation.

⸺y is a human science which studies ⸺nology one often uses "subjects" or "in⸺ ⸺ to the persons involved in one's study. But, as V⸺ ⸺uden once said, "individual" is primarily a biological term to classify a tree, a horse, a man, a woman; while the term "person" refers to the uniqueness of each human being. "As persons, we are incomparable, unclassifiable, uncountable, irreplaceable" (1967). One might make a partisan claim for the sphere in which hermeneutic phenomenological research is (or should be) conducted. In the sense that traditional, hypothesizing, or experimental research is largely interested in knowledge that is generalizable, true for one and all, it is not entirely wrong to say that there is a certain spirit inherent in such a research atmosphere. Actions and interventions, like exercises, are seen as repeatable; while subjects and samples, like soldiers, are replaceable. In contrast, phenomenology is, in a broad sense, a philosophy or *theory of the unique*; it is interested in what is essentially not replaceable. We need to be reminded that in our desire to find out what is effective systematic intervention (from an experimental research point of view), we tend to forget that the change we aim for may have different significance for different persons.

What first of all characterizes phenomenological research is that it always begins in the lifeworld. This is the world of the natural attitude of everyday life which Husserl described as the original, pre-reflective, pre-theoretical attitude. In bringing to reflective awareness the nature of the events experienced in our natural attitude, we are able to transform or remake ourselves in the true sense of *Bildung* (education). Hermeneutic phenomenological research edifies the personal insight (Rorty, 1979), contributing to one's thoughtfulness and one's ability to act toward others, children or adults, with tact or tactfulness. In this sense, human science research is itself a kind of *Bildung* or *paideia*; it is the curriculum of being and becoming. We might say that hermeneutic phenomenology is a philosophy of the personal, the individual, which we pursue against the background of an understanding of the evasive character of the *logos* of *other*, the *whole*, the *communal*, or the *social*. Much of educational research tends to pulverize life into minute abstracted fragments and particles that are of little use to practitioners. So it is perhaps not surprising that a human science that tries to avoid this fragmentation would be gaining more attention. Its particular appeal is that it tries to understand the phenomena of education by maintaining a view of pedagogy as an expression of the whole, and a view of the experiential situation as the topos of real pedagogic acting.

The approach described in this text takes seriously a notion that is very self-evident and yet seldom acknowledged: hermeneutic phenomenological research is fundamentally a writing activity. Research and writing are aspects of one process. In a later chapter the pedagogical significance of the reflective nature of writing is explored and articulated. Hermeneutics and phenomenology are human science approaches which are rooted in philosophy; they are philosophies, reflective disciplines. Therefore, it is important for the human science researcher in education to know something of the philosophic traditions. This does not mean, however, that one must become a professional philosopher in an academic sense. It means that one should know enough to be able to articulate the epistemological or theoretical implications of doing phenomenology and hermeneutics—not losing sight of the fact that one is interested in the pedagogic praxis of this research; more accurately, it means that human science research practised by an educator is a pedagogic human science.

The end of human science research for educators is a critical pedagogical competence: knowing how to act tactfully in pedagogic situations on the basis of a carefully edified thoughtfulness. To that end hermeneutic phenomenological research reintegrates part and whole, the contingent and the essential, value and desire. It encourages a certain attentive awareness to the details and seemingly trivial dimensions of our everyday educational lives. It makes us thoughtfully aware of the consequential in the inconsequential, the significant in the taken-for-granted. Phenomenological descriptions, if done well, are compelling and insightful. The eloquence of the texts may contrast sharply with the toil, messiness, and difficulties involved in the research/writing process. "And this took that long to write, you say?" "After seven drafts!?"

It all seems somewhat absurd until we begin to discern the silence in the writing—the cultivation of one's being, from which the words begin to proliferate in haltingly issued groupings, then finally in a carefully written work, much less completed than interrupted, a blushing response to a call to say something worth saying, to actually *say* something, while being thoughtfully aware of the ease with which such speaking can reduce itself to academic chatter.

What Is a Hermeneutic Phenomenological Human Science?

What is hermeneutic phenomenology? There is a difference between comprehending the project of phenomenology intellectually and understanding it "from the inside." We tend to get a certain satisfaction out of grasping at a conceptual or "theoretical" level the basic ideas of phenomenology, even though a real understanding of phenomenology can only be accomplished by "actively doing it." As a first orientation, the philosophical idea of phenomenology will be sketched around a few introductory remarks, and then a fuller more active description of the nature of hermeneutic phenomenological research and writing will be attempted.

Phenomenological research is the study of lived experience.

To say the same thing differently: phenomenology is the study of the lifeworld—the world as we immediately experience it pre-reflectively rather than as we conceptualize, categorize, or reflect on it (Husserl, 1970b; Schutz and Luckmann, 1973). Phenomenology aims at gaining a deeper understanding of the nature or meaning of our everyday experiences. Phenomenology asks, "What is this or that kind of experience like?" It differs from almost every other science in that it attempts to gain insightful descriptions of the way we experience the world pre-reflectively, without taxonomizing, classifying, or abstracting it. So phenomenology does not offer us the possibility of effective theory with which we can now explain and/or control the world, but rather it offers us the possibility of plausible insights that bring us in more direct contact with the world. This project is both new and old. It is new in the sense that modern thinking and scholarship is so caught up in theoretical and technological thought that the program of a phenomenological human science may strike an individual as a breakthrough and a liberation. It is old in the sense that, over the ages, human beings have invented artistic, philosophic, communal, mimetic and poetic languages that have sought to (re)unite them with the ground of their lived experience.

Phenomenological research is the explication of phenomena as they present themselves to consciousness.

Anything that presents itself to consciousness is potentially of interest to phenomenology, whether the object is real or imagined, empirically measurable or subjectively felt. Consciousness is the only access human beings have to the world. Or rather, it is by virtue of being conscious that we are already related to the world. Thus all we can ever know must present itself to consciousness. Whatever falls outside of consciousness therefore falls outside the bounds of our possible lived experience. Consciousness is always transitive. To be conscious is to be aware, in some sense, of some aspect of the world. And thus phenomenology is keenly interested in the significant world of the human being. It is important to realize as well that consciousness itself cannot be described directly (such description would reduce human science to the study of consciousness or ideas, the fallacy of idealism). Similarly, the world itself, without reference to an experiencing person or consciousness, cannot be described directly either (such approach would overlook that the real things of the world are always meaningfully constituted by conscious human beings, the fallacy of realism). So, in cases when consciousness itself is the object of consciousness (when I reflect on my own thinking process) then consciousness is not the same as the act in which it appears. This also demonstrates that true introspection is impossible. A person cannot reflect on lived experience while living through the experience. For example, if one tries to reflect on one's anger while being angry, one finds that the anger has already changed or dissipated. Thus, phenomenological reflection is not *introspective* but *retrospective*. Reflection on lived experience is always recollective; it is reflection on experience that is already passed or lived through.

Phenomenological research is the study of essences.

Phenomenology asks for the very nature of a phenomenon, for that which makes a some-"thing" what it *is*—and without which it could not be what it is (Husserl, 1982; Merleau-Ponty, 1962). The essence of a phenomenon is a universal which can be described through a study of the structure that governs the instances or particular manifestations of the essence of that phenomenon. In other words, phenomenology is the systematic attempt to uncover and describe the structures, the internal meaning structures, of lived experience. A universal or essence may only be intuited or grasped through a study of the particulars or instances as they are encountered in lived experience. (By *intuition* we do not mean the kind of "problematic" intuition which becomes questionable when someone claims "intuitively" to have known that Mr. Jones was a crook.) From a phenomenological point of view, we are less interested in the factual status of particular instances: whether something actually happened, how often it tends to happen, or how the occurrence of an experience is related to the prevalence of other conditions or events. For example, phenomenology does not ask, "How do these children learn this particular material?" but it asks, "What is the nature or essence of the experience of learning (so that I can now better understand what this particular learning experience is like for these children)?" The essence or nature of an experience has been adequately described in language if the description reawakens or shows us the lived quality and significance of the experience in a fuller or deeper manner.

Phenomenological research is the description of the experiential meanings we live as we live them.

Phenomenological human science is the study of lived or existential meanings; it attempts to describe and interpret these meanings to a certain degree of depth and richness. In this focus upon meaning, phenomenology differs from some other social or human sciences which may focus not on meanings but on statistical relationships among variables, on the predominance of social opinions, or on the occurrence or frequency of certain behaviors, etc. And phenomenology differs from other disciplines in that it does not aim to explicate meanings specific to particular cultures (ethnography), to certain social groups (sociology), to historical periods (history), to mental types (psychology), or to an individual's personal life history (biography). Rather, phenomenology attempts to explicate the meanings as we live them in our everyday existence, our lifeworld.

Phenomenological research is the human scientific study of phenomena.

The term "science" derives from *scientia* which means to know. Phenomenology claims to be scientific in a broad sense, since it is a systematic, explicit, self-critical, and intersubjective study of its subject matter, our lived experience. It is *systematic* in that it uses specially practised modes of questioning, reflecting, focusing, intuiting, etc. Phenomenological human science research is *explicit* in that it attempts to articulate, through the content and form of text, the structures of meaning embedded in lived experience (rather than leaving the meanings implicit as for example in poetry or literary texts). Phenomenology is *self-critical* in the sense that it continually examines its own goals and methods in an attempt to come to terms with the strengths and shortcomings of its approach and achievements. It is *intersubjective* in that the human science researcher needs the other (for example, the reader) in order to develop a dialogic relation with the phenomenon, and thus validate the phenomenon as described. Phenomenology is a *human* science (rather than a natural science) since the subject matter of phenomenological research is always the structures of meaning of the lived *human* world (in contrast, natural objects do not have experiences which are consciously and meaningfully lived through by these objects).

Phenomenological research is the attentive practice of thoughtfulness.

Indeed, if there is one word that most aptly characterizes phenomenology itself, then this word is "thoughtfulness." In the works of the great phenomenologists, thoughtfulness is described as a minding, a heeding, a caring attunement (Heidegger, 1962)—a heedful, mindful wondering about the project of life, of living, of what it means to live a life. For us this phenomenological interest of doing research materializes itself in our everyday practical concerns as parents, teachers, teacher educators, psychologists, child care specialists, or school administrators. As educators we must act responsibly and responsively in all our relations with children, with youth, or with those to whom we stand in a pedagogical relationship. So for us the theoretical practice of phenomenological research stands in the service of the mundane practice of pedagogy: it is a ministering of thoughtfulness. Phenomenological pedagogical research edifies the same attentive thoughtfulness that serves the practical tactfulness of pedagogy itself.

Phenomenological research is a search for what it means to be human.

As we research the possible meaning structures of our lived experiences, we come to a fuller grasp of what it means to be in the world as a man, a woman, a child, taking into account the sociocultural and the historical traditions that have given meaning to our ways of being in the world. For example, to understand what it means to be a woman in our present age is also to understand the pressures of the meaning structures that have come to restrict, widen, or question the nature and ground of womanhood. Hermeneutic phenomenological research is a search for the fullness of living, for the ways a woman possibly can experience the world as a woman, for what it is to be a woman. The same is true, of course, for men. In phenomenological research description carries a moral force. If to be a father means to take active responsibility for a child's growth, then it is possible to say of actual cases that this or that is no way to be a father! So phenomenological research has, as its ultimate aim, the fulfillment of our human nature: to become more fully who we are.

Phenomenological research is a poetizing activity.

Thus, phenomenology is in some ways very unlike any other research. Most research we meet in education is of the type whereby results can be severed from the means by which the results are obtained. Phenomenological research is unlike other research in that the link with the results cannot be broken, as Marcel (1950) explained, without loss of all reality to the results. And that is why, when you listen to a presentation of a phenomenological nature, you will listen in vain for the punch-line, the latest information, or the big news. As in poetry, it is inappropriate to ask for a conclusion or a summary of a phenomenological study. To summarize a poem in order to present the result would destroy the result because the poem itself is the result. The poem is the thing. So phenomenology, not unlike poetry, is a poetizing project; it tries an incantative, evocative speaking, a primal telling, wherein we aim to involve the voice in an original singing of the world (Merleau-Ponty, 1973). But poetizing is not "merely" a type of poetry, a making of verses. Poetizing is thinking on original experience and is thus speaking in a more primal sense. Language that authentically speaks the world rather than abstractly speaking *of* it is a language that reverberates the world, as Merleau-Ponty says, a language that sings the world. We must engage language in a primal incantation or poetizing which hearkens back to the silence from which the words emanate. What we must do is discover what lies at the ontological core of our being. So that *in* the words, or perhaps better, *in spite of* the words , we find "memories" that paradoxically we never thought or felt before.

What Does it Mean to Be Rational?

The label "human science" derives from a translation of the German *Geisteswissenschaften*. This term has three components: Geist/wissen/schaffen. The word *Geist* is translated into English often as "mind" or "spirit." But this is not a satisfactory translation since the term *Geist* refers to an aspect of our humanness that includes a quality of inwardness, of spiritual refinement. The English term "mind" in contrast has cognitive overtones and more pragmatic connotations. The word *Geist* has complex and rich meanings which can be gleaned from expressions such as *Zeitgeist* which means the "spirit of the age"; *der Heilige Geist* which translates as the "Holy Spirit"; *geistig* which means witty in a refined or more intellectual sort of way; and *geistig* can also refer to the emotional or moral atmosphere that may reign in a home, in a school, or in such a lived space. Bollnow (1974) pointed out that in the human sciences knowledge is not a matter of the formal intellect alone. But knowledge as understanding is *geistig*—a matter of the depth of the soul, spirit, embodied knowing and being. Thus, the term *Geisteswissenschaften* is usually translated as "human sciences" in order to avoid a narrow cognitive interpretation of the word *Geist*.

There is an objective aspect to the term *Geist* that becomes self-evident when we consider how the meaningful experience of the world has a shared and historical character. Human beings express their experience of the world through art, science, law, medicine, architecture, etc., and especially through language. But in this language they also discover a world already meaningfully constituted. We should not think of "objective *Geist*" as some absolute notion or quality (in a Hegelian sense), rather objective *Geist* is itself a dynamic human life phenomenon: it tells us who we are but it is also ongoingly formed by us in a self-forming process. So what is meant and implied by the term *Geist* in the context of a human science approach to pedagogy as pursued in this text? It means that the human being is seen and studied as a "person," in the full sense of that word, a person who is a flesh and blood sense-maker. The human being is a person who signifies—gives and derives meaning to and from the "things" of the world. In other words the "things" of the world are meaningfully experienced, and on that basis these "things" are then approached and dealt with.

The next semantic elements of the phrase *Geisteswissenschaften* are *wissen* which means "knowing or knowledge," and *schaffen* which means "creating, producing, working." *Wissenschaft* is usually translated as "science." Here again there is a problem of straightforward translation. When a German person says *"Wissenschaften"* then he or she does not have the same image, the same activity in mind, that a North American person would who says "science." In Germany *Wissenschaft* is usually more broadly understood to include the arts and the humanities. So, the German word *Wissenschaft* cannot properly be translated into English, since in North America the word "science" immediately is associated with the attitude of the methodology of the natural (physical and behavioral) sciences. Thus, to speak of the "human sciences" is actually a misnomer if one is not aware of the broadened set of connotations that the word "sciences" should evoke in this coupling.

A distinguishing feature of a human science approach to pedagogy is how the notions of theory and research are to be related to the practice of living. In contrast to the more positivistic and behavioral empirical sciences, human science does not see theory as something that stands *before* practice in order to "inform" it. Rather theory enlightens practice. Practice (or life) always comes first and theory comes later as a result of reflection. "The integrity of praxis does not depend on theory," said Schleiermacher, "but praxis can become more aware of itself by means of theory" (1964, p. 40). And he points out, "In and of itself theory does not control praxis, the theory of any science of education comes always later. Theory can only make room for itself once praxis has settled" (p. 41). If it is phenomenologically plausible that in practical situations theory always arrives late, too late to inform praxis in a technical or instrumental way, then in the daily practice of living we are forever at a loss for theory. Yet in another less technical sense we usually are not really so helpless because theory has already prepared our bodies or being to act, so to speak. This preparation was referred to above as a process of *Bildung*.

Does that mean that the human sciences are less rational or less rigorous than the behavioral or experimental sciences? The answer depends on the criteria of rationality that one applies to the human sciences. If the criteria are the same as those that govern the natural sciences then the human sciences may seem rather undisciplined. But those criteria do not have the same meaning, of course, otherwise there would be no essential difference between the human and the natural sciences. The point is that the constraints of meaning on the criteria or standards of science define the horizons and pose the limits on what we can study and how we can rationalize the research as being scientific. The meaning of human science notions such as "truth, method, understanding, objectivity, subjectivity, valid discourse," and the meaning of "description, analysis, interpretation, writing, text," etc., are always to be understood within a certain rational perspective. The notion of "understanding" (*Verstehen*) tends to be interpreted much more narrowly in the behavioral sciences than in the human sciences—an issue which is sometimes debated in terms of the difference between rational understanding and empathic understanding (e.g., Wilson, 1970). Human science philosophers have argued that notions of "truth and understanding" in the human sciences require a broadening of the notion of rationality (e.g., Gadamer, 1975; Ricoeur, 1981). Against this argument, the critics of the human sciences in education have suggested that the discourse of human science is often just too fuzzy, too ambiguous, inadequately based on observational and measurable data, not replicable, poorly generalizable to definite populations, irrational, unscientific, subjectivistic, and so on.

Without doubt there is a certain body of so-called phenomenological, hermeneutic, or ethnographic human science work in education that may not pass any test of rational standards—they fail not only the standards of the natural science research perspective but also the standards set by the human sciences. There are also practitioners of human science research in education who disdainfully disclaim any need for criteria or standards; they claim that theirs is not a "rational" science, that to be rationalistic is to be intellectualistic, positivistic, scientistic, and insensitive to intuitive and more experiential dimensions of truth and understanding. What the latter do not tend to see, however, is that to reject the standard of rationality would mean that one assumes that there is no basis upon which human beings can come to common understandings; it tends to assume as well that there is no standard in the human sciences to which one needs to orient oneself in a self-reflective and disciplined manner.

In this text I will not deny the need for a rational foundation, but I will work towards a broadened notion of rationality. Consequently, our human science orientation to education redefines the meaning of concepts such as "objectivity" and "subjectivity," and it does not make unbridgeable distinctions between fact and value, the empirical and the normative.

Human science is rationalistic in that it operates on the assumption that human life may be made intelligible, accessible to human *logos* or reason, in a broad or full embodied sense. To be a rationalist is to believe in the power of thinking, insight and dialogue. It is to believe in the possibility of understanding the world by maintaining a thoughtful and conversational relation with the world. Rationality expresses a faith that we can share this world, that we can make things understandable to each other, that experience can be made intelligible. But a human science perspective also assumes that lived human experience is always more complex than the result of any singular description, and that there is always an element of the ineffable to life. However, to recognize that life is fundamentally or ultimately mysterious does not need to make one a scholarly mystic.

So, to believe in the power of thinking is also to acknowledge that it is the complexity and mystery of life that calls for thinking in the first place. Human life needs knowledge, reflection, and thought to make itself knowable to itself, including its complex and ultimately mysterious nature. It is a naive rationalism that believes that the phenomena of life can be made intellectually crystal clear or theoretically perfectly transparent. That is why a human science that tries to do justice to the full range of human experience cannot operate with a concept of rationality that is restricted to a formal intellectualist interpretation of human reason. Likewise, the language of thinking cannot be censured to permit only a form of discourse that tries to capture human experience in deadening abstract concepts, and in logical systems that flatten rather than deepen our understanding of human life. Much of social science produces forms of knowledge which fixate life by riveting it to the terms and grammar of forms of scientific theorizing that congeal the living meaning out of human living—until life itself has become unrecognizable to itself. It is important to make this point, precisely because human science is often accused of yielding texts that are vague, imprecise, inexact, nonrigorous, or ambiguous. When scholars such as Merleau-Ponty, Heidegger, Levinas, or Derrida employ seemingly evasive or even poetic writing styles and ways of saying things that seem elusive, it may be that such styles and means of expression are the concomitants of a more richly embodied notion of human rationality. On the downside, however, there is a danger as well: the danger that an individual of insufficient talent and inadequate scholarly experience may try to hide his or her lack of insight behind an obfuscating, flowery, or self-indulgent discourse.

Furthermore, we should acknowledge that human science operates with its own criteria for precision, exactness, and rigor. In the quantitative sciences precision and exactness are usually seen to be indications of refinement of measurement and perfection of research design. In contrast, human science strives for precision and exactness by aiming for interpretive descriptions that exact fullness and completeness of detail, and that explore to a degree of perfection the fundamental nature of the notion being addressed in the text. The term "rigor" originally meant "stiffness," "hardness." Rigorous scientific research is often seen to be methodologically hard-nosed, strict, and uncompromised by "subjective" and qualitative distinctions. "Hard data" refers to knowledge that is captured best in quantitative units or observ-

able measures. In contrast, human science research is rigorous when it
is "strong" or "hard" in a moral and spirited sense. A strong and rigorous
human science text distinguishes itself by its courage and resolve to
stand up for the uniqueness and significance of the notion to which it
has dedicated itself. And what does it mean to stand up for something
if one is not prepared to stand out? This means also that a rigorous
human science is prepared to be "soft," "soulful," "subtle," and "sensitive" in its effort to bring the range of meanings of life's phenomena to
our reflective awareness.

The basic things about our lifeworld (such as the experience of lived
time, lived space, lived body, and lived human relation) are preverbal
and therefore hard to describe. For this, subtlety and sensitivity are
needed: "It is as painstaking as the works of Balzac, Proust, Valéry or
Cézanne—by reason of the same kind of attentiveness and wonder, the
same demand for awareness, the same will to seize the meaning of the
world or of history as that meaning comes into being" (Merleau-Ponty,
1962, p. xxi). This gives phenomenological human science its fundamental fascination. To *do* hermeneutic phenomenology is to attempt
to accomplish the impossible: to construct a full interpretive description
of some aspect of the lifeworld, and yet to remain aware that lived life
is always more complex than any explication of meaning can reveal. The
phenomenological reduction teaches us that complete reduction is
impossible, that full or final descriptions are unattainable. But rather
than therefore giving up on human science altogether, we need to
pursue its project with extra vigour.

Hermeneutic phenomenological human science is interested in the
human world *as we find it* in all its variegated aspects. Unlike research
approaches in other social sciences which may make use of experimental
or artificially created test situations, human science wishes to meet
human beings—men, women, children—*there* where they are naturally
engaged in their worlds. In other words, phenomenological research
finds its point of departure in the *situation*, which for purpose of analysis,
description, and interpretation functions as an exemplary nodal point
of meanings that are embedded in this situation. Sometimes a researcher or theorist is likened to a traveller from mythical times who
sails off to strange and exotic places to eventually return to the common
people in order to tell them fascinating stories about the way the world
"really" is (Jager, 1975). For this reason there is the sense of awe
associated with the white-coated natural scientist who travels in

mysterious worlds of micro-physics, macro-physics, astro-physics or the astonishing world of computer technology, etc. In contrast, the human scientist does not go anywhere. He or she stays right there in the world we share with our fellow-human beings. And yet it would be wrong to say that the human scientist has no compelling "stories" to tell. Aren't the most captivating stories exactly those which help us to understand better what is most common, most taken-for-granted, and what concerns us most ordinarily and directly?

Phenomenology appeals to our immediate common experience in order to conduct a structural analysis of what is most common, most familiar, most self-evident to us. The aim is to construct an animating, evocative description (text) of human actions, behaviors, intentions, and experiences as we meet them in the lifeworld. To this purpose the human scientist likes to make use of the works of poets, authors, artists, cinematographers—because it is in this material that the human being can be found as *situated person*, and it is in this work that the variety and possibility of human experience may be found in condensed and transcended form. The Dutch phenomenological psychologist Buytendijk (1962) remarks that one can perhaps gain greater psychological insights from a great novelist such as Dostoevsky than from the typical scholarly theories reported in psychological social science books and journals. The author, the poet, the artist transforms (fictionalizes, poetizes, re-shapes) ordinary human experience in infinite variety. But this does not mean that human science is to be confused with poetry, story, or art; or that poetry, story, or art could be seen as forms of human science. Although literary narrative and human science narrative both find their fascination in situated life, in the situated human being, they locate their narratives in different starting points; they aspire to different epistemological ends. One difference is that phenomenology aims at *making explicit* and *seeking universal meaning* where poetry and literature remain implicit and particular. This may be the reason why many poets, authors, or artists do not want to have anything to do with those commentators who try to draw universal lessons from a certain poem, book, or painting. At any rate, the difference is partly that phenomenology operates with a different sense of directness. Linschoten (1953) pinpoints the geographical location of phenomenological human science when he says, "human science starts there where poetry has reached its end point."

Phenomenological research and writing is a project in which the normal scientific requirements or standards of objectivity and subjectivity need to be re-conceived. In the human sciences, objectivity and subjectivity are not mutually exclusive categories. Both find their meaning and significance in the oriented (i.e., personal) relation that the researcher establishes with the "object" of his or her inquiry (Bollnow, 1974). Thus, "objectivity" means that the researcher is *oriented* to the object, that which stands in front of him or her. Objectivity means that the researcher remains *true to the object*. The researcher becomes in a sense a guardian and a defender of the true nature of the object. He or she wants to show it, describe it, interpret it while remaining faithful to it—aware that one is easily misled, side-tracked, or enchanted by extraneous elements. "Subjectivity" means that one needs to be as perceptive, insightful, and discerning as one can be in order to show or disclose the object in its full richness and in its greatest depth. Subjectivity means that we are *strong* in our orientation to the object of study *in a unique and personal way*—while avoiding the danger of becoming arbitrary, self-indulgent, or of getting captivated and carried away by our unreflected preconceptions. Those entering the field of human science research may need to realize that the very meanings of "knowledge," "science," "theory," and "research" are based upon different assumptions. In this text we do not maintain the view held by traditional experimental or behavioral science where research is that inductive investigative process that produces empirical generalizations which are then formulated or built into theories. Neither is theorizing equated with a process of deductive or speculative reasoning done by philosophers or theoretical scientists. Rather, research and theorizing are often seen to be interchangeable concepts for that process of reflecting on lived experience that is involved in the various human science activities. Sometimes the emphasis would be on *doing research* when, for example, we are involved in the so-called data gathering practices of interviewing or hermeneutic analysis of texts; on other occasions we speak more pointedly of *theorizing* when the main aim is to bring to speech (by talking or writing) our reflective understanding of something.

In the natural or physical sciences we have a sense how new and improved theories often allow for more sophisticated technological advances. Computer technology is a good example of a triumph of theoretical progress. In the social or behavioral sciences similar expectations for progress with the advancement of knowledge exist. But what does progress mean in phenomenological human science research? It does *not* necessarily imply that sound human science will lead to increasingly effective management or control of human behavior. In fact, just the opposite may be the case. Human science operates on the principle of the recognition of the existence of *freedom* in human life. And self-consciously free human beings who have acquired a deepened understanding of the meaning of certain human experiences or phenomena may in fact be less susceptible to the effective management or control of others.

And yet, phenomenological human science, too, sponsors a certain concept of progress. It is the progress of humanizing human life and humanizing human institutions to help human beings to become increasingly thoughtful and thus better prepared to act tactfully in situations. In other words, sound human science research of the kind advocated in this text, helps those who partake in it to produce *action sensitive knowledge*. But, although this knowledge can be written and presented in textual form, ultimately it must animate and live in the human being who dialogues with the text. In chapter 7 we show how human science research as writing must indeed produce *oriented, strong, rich,* and *deep* texts—texts which invite dialogue with those who interact with it. Straus (1966) has used the term "pathic" to describe the invitational character of the world. For example, cool water invites us to drink, the sandy beach invites the child to play, an easy chair invites our tired body to sink in it, etc. Similarly, a phenomenological human science text invites a dialogic response from us.

What a Human Science Cannot Do

Sometimes people interested in doing research approach phenomenological human science as if it merely offers a different tool-kit for dealing with the same kinds of problems and questions that really belong to different research methodologies. It may be important therefore to state what phenomenological human science is not, or what it does not do.

(1) *Phenomenology is not an empirical analytic science.* It does not describe actual states of affairs; in other words, it is not a science of empirical facts and scientific generalizations, asking who did what? when? where? how many? to what extent? under what conditions? and

so forth. This does not mean, of course, that from a phenomenological point of view we are not deeply interested in experience (which is an empirical interest too). Phenomenological knowledge is empirical, based on experience, but it is not *inductively* empirically derived. It means that phenomenology goes beyond an interest in "mere" particularity. For example, case studies and ethnographies very appropriately focus on a certain situation, a group, a culture, or an institutional location to study it for what goes on *there*, how *these* individuals or members of *this* group perceive things, and how they might differ in time and place from other such groups or situations. There may be a phenomenological quality to such studies in that they ask people to talk about their experiences, but the end of case studies and ethnographies is to describe accurately an existing state of affairs or a certain present or past culture. And this state of affairs or culture might change quite drastically over time, and from place to place. Thus, it would be a misnomer to speak of "The Phenomenology of West Side High School," "The Phenomenology of Vancouver's China Town," "The Phenomenology of the Toronto Children's Hospital," and so forth. For this reason too, survey methods, statistical and other quantitative procedures are not the appropriate means of phenomenological human science research.

It is important as well to realize that phenomenology cannot be used to show or prove, for example, that one reading method is more *effective* than another reading method, or that certain instructional techniques produce higher achievement scores, and so forth. Phenomenology does not allow for empirical generalizations, the production of law-like statements, or the establishment of functional relationships. The only generalization allowed by phenomenology is this: Never generalize! Generalizations about human experiences are almost always of troublesome value. The phenomenologist would mischievously like to quote the novelist George Eliot who, in the novel *Middlemarch*, wrote that it is the "power of generalizing which gives men so much superiority in mistake over the dumb animals" (1871/1988). The tendency to generalize may prevent us from developing understandings that remain focused on the uniqueness of human experience.

(2) *Phenomenology is not mere speculative inquiry in the sense of unworldly reflection.* Phenomenological research always takes its point of departure from lived experience or empirical data. Some "meditative" philosophies may have affinities with a certain human science

reflectiveness, but phenomenology has an interest that goes beyond "sheer" universality. Phenomenological human science is a western research method which should not be confused either with certain "mystical" or eastern meditative techniques of achieving insights about the "meaning of life." One important difference is that western human science aims at acquiring understandings about concrete lived experiences by means of language, whereas eastern methods may practise other non-script-oriented reflective techniques.

(3) *Phenomenology is neither mere particularity, nor sheer universality.* The phenomenological attitude is more complex even than a mixture of empiricism and idealism, says Merleau-Ponty (1964a). The object of a phenomenological interest is "neither eternal and without roots in the present nor a mere event destined to be replaced by another event tomorrow, and consequently deprived of any intrinsic value (p. 92)." Thus, phenomenology consists in mediating in a personal way the antinomy of particularity (being interested in concreteness, difference and what is unique) and universality (being interested in the essential, in difference that makes a difference).

(4) *Phenomenology does not problem solve.* Problem questions seek solutions, "correct" knowledge, effective procedures, winning strategies, calculative techniques, "methods" which get results! A research study that pursues a certain problem is completed when the problem is solved (Marcel, 1950). *Phenomenological questions are meaning questions.* They ask for the meaning and significance of certain phenomena. Meaning questions cannot be "solved" and thus done away with (Marcel, 1949). Meaning questions can be better or more deeply understood, so that, on the basis of this understanding I may be able to act more thoughtfully and more tactfully in certain situations. But in some sense meaning questions can never be closed down, they will always remain the subject matter of the conversational relations of lived life, and they will need to be appropriated, in a personal way, by anyone who hopes to benefit from such insight.

Let us give an example that might illustrate the above arguments. Much social and human science research deals with "talk." There is much talk in life. Talk is the concrete stuff of human discourse—we can tape it, transcribe it, codify it, analyze it for its content and for certain frequencies of terms or ideas, and so forth. In fact, much of research, of course, focuses on talk or uses written or oral talk as its basic data source. But what is talk anyway? I am reminded of my mother who said once, upon the eve of leaving us to go home to her country of residence, "we haven't really talked." Of course, I knew exactly what she meant; and yet, I might have reacted by saying "come on, Mom, we've talked our heads off in the last few weeks." There had certainly been lots of chatter during the times we were together, shared meals, went for outings, and visited friends. Yet she was right, my mother and I had not really had a "true" talk while she had stayed with my family. That afternoon, we went for a walk along the river and we had our "talk" after all.

But what is the issue or question here? In order to understand this situation, do we need to formulate it as a "problem"? Is there a problem here that requires the application of certain knowledge for its solution? What is needed to be able to make a distinction between "real talk" and "mere chatter"? If we were to conceptualize a behavioral research study we might investigate the incidence of family reunions where no "real" talk takes place. We might hypothesize that certain factors are responsible for this (such as the presence of children, lack of shared time, number of years of estrangement). But would we get any closer to understanding in what sense a "real" talk differs from just any kind of talk? So a phenomenologically oriented human scientist would treat this topic more likely as a question that requires clarification of its lived meaning. A phenomenologist might want to study concrete examples of real talk, the quality of the relation between people, the nature of the space which is somehow "good" for having a talk (such as a walk along the river). A phenomenologist would not likely send around questionnaires, or place individuals in experimental situations to see under what controlled conditions real talk happens; and he or she would not simply start to "philosophize" about the nature of real talk either. A phenomenologist would treat the topic of "talk," not as a problem to be solved, but as a question of meaning to be inquired into.

Description or Interpretation?

Sartre's famous analysis of "The Look" (1956, pp. 252-302) is a well-known example of a careful description of a lived experience. What is it like to spy on someone? And what is it like to be seen looking at someone in this manner? Sartre describes how the act of looking at someone through a keyhole (motivated by jealousy, curiosity, or vice) is experienced in "a pure mode of losing myself in the world, of causing myself to be drunk in by things as ink is by a blotter." However, when all of a sudden I hear footsteps and realize that somebody is looking at me, an essential change occurs in my mode of awareness. Where moments before my mode of being was governed by unreflective consciousness, now "I *see* myself because *somebody* sees me. I experience myself as an object for the other." Sartre continues to describe the existential structure of this lived situation in great detail and with precise sensitivity. Another example of Sartre's phenomenological approach is his description of the experience of blushing.

> To "feel oneself blushing", to "feel oneself sweating", etc., are inaccurate expressions which the shy person uses to describe his state; what he really means is that he is vividly and constantly conscious of his body not as it is for him but as it is *for* the *Other* .... We often say that the shy man is "embarrassed by his own body". Actually this expression is incorrect; I cannot be embarrassed by my own body as I exist it. It is my body as it is for the Other which may embarrass me. (Sartre, 1956, p. 353)

Here we have, it could be said, a good example of descriptive existential phenomenology. Phenomenology is, on the one hand, description of the lived-through quality of lived experience, and on the other hand, description of meaning *of the expressions* of lived experience. The two types of descriptions seem somewhat different in the sense that the first one is an immediate description of the lifeworld as lived whereas the second one is an intermediate (or a mediated) description of the lifeworld as expressed in symbolic form. When description is thus mediated by expression (for example: by blushing, talk, action, a work of art, a text) then description seems to contain a stronger element of interpretation. Actually it has been argued that all description is ultimately interpretation. "The meaning of phenomenological description as a method lies in interpretation .... The phenomenology ... is a hermeneutic in the primordial signification of this word, where it designates this business of interpreting," says Heidegger (1962, p. 37).

Yet, it is possible to make a distinction in human science research between phenomenology (as pure description of lived experience) and hermeneutics (as interpretation of experience via some "text" or via some symbolic form). For example, philosophers such as Silverman (1984) make a distinction between descriptive phenomenology and interpretive or hermeneutic phenomenology. And strict followers of Husserl's transcendental method would insist that phenomenological research is pure description and that interpretation (hermeneutics) falls outside the bounds of phenomenological research. Some human scientists who follow this strict program of Husserl (e.g., Amedeo Giorgi, 1985) maintain that the object of phenomenological description is fully achieved "solely" through a direct grasping (intuiting) of the essential structure of phenomena as they appear in consciousness. From such a point of view, the notion of hermeneutics or interpretation already implies the acknowledgment of a distortion, of an incomplete intuiting.

Gadamer (1986) makes a distinction between two senses of interpretation: in its original meaning, he says, interpretation is a *pointing to* something; and interpretation is *pointing out* the meaning of something (p. 68). The first kind of interpreting "is not a reading in of some meaning, but clearly a revealing of what the thing itself already points to. . . .We attempt to interpret that which at the same time conceals itself" (p. 68).

Thus, this sense of interpreting is closely allied to Husserl's and Heidegger's notion of phenomenological description. The second kind of interpreting applies when we confront something that is already an interpretation, such as in the case of a work of art. As Gadamer says, "when we interpret the meaning of something we actually interpret an interpretation" (p. 68). Applied to the quality of a human science research text, we may say that phenomenological text is descriptive in the sense that it names something. And in this naming it points to something and it aims at letting something show itself. And phenomenological text is interpretive in the sense that it mediates. Etymologically "interpretation" means explaining in the sense of mediating between two parties (Klein, 1971, p. 383). It mediates between interpreted meanings and the thing toward which the interpretations point. Obviously there are many issues associated with these distinctions. In this text we will simply use the term "description" to include both the interpretive (hermeneutic) as well as the descriptive (phenomenological) element. And sometimes the term "phenomenology" is used when the descriptive function is emphasized, "hermeneutics" when the emphasis is on interpretation. Often the terms are employed interchangeably.

Beginning human science researchers sometimes have difficulty distinguishing between phenomenological (interpretive) descriptions and other types of descriptions that we may meet in the social and human sciences. What makes a phenomenological description different from other kinds of descriptions? It is helpful to be reminded that phenomenological descriptions aim at elucidating lived experience, as described in earlier paragraphs. The point is, of course, that the meaning of lived experience is usually hidden or veiled. We may say then that phenomenological descriptions can fail in several respects (which does not mean to say that those descriptions might not have merit in other respects).

(1) A description may fail to aim at lived experience, and instead have the character of conceptualization, journalistic accounts, personal opinions, or descriptions of some other state of affairs. Sometimes the experiential interest of phenomenological inquiry is confused with journalistic, biographic, or other types of writing.

(2) A description may properly aim at lived experience but somehow fail to elucidate the lived meaning of that experience. In this case the description simply fails to accomplish its own end.

(3) A description may elucidate, but what is elucidated is not lived experience; instead a description may succeed in conceptual clarification or theoretical explication of meaning.

A good phenomenological description is an adequate elucidation of some aspect of the lifeworld—it resonates with our sense of lived life. In one of his lectures Buytendijk once referred to the "phenomenological nod" as a way of indicating that a good phenomenological description is something that we can nod to, recognizing it as an experience that we have had or could have had. In other words, *a good phenomenological description is collected by lived experience and recollects lived experience—is validated by lived experience and it validates lived experience.* This is sometimes termed the "validating circle of inquiry." In order to become adept at this validating process one has to learn to insert oneself in the tradition of scholarship in such a way that one can become a participating member of the tradition.

Research—Procedures, Techniques, and Methods

We need to make a distinction between research *method* and research methodology, and between research *method* and research *technique* and *procedure*. On the one hand, "methodology" refers to the philosophic framework, the fundamental assumptions and characteristics of a human science perspective. It includes the general orientation to life, the view of knowledge, and the sense of what it means to be human which is associated with or implied by a certain research method. We might say that the methodology is the theory behind the method, including the study of what method one should follow and why. The Greek *hodos* means "way." And methodology means the *logos* (study) of the *method* (way). So methodology means "pursuit of knowledge." And a certain *mode* of inquiry is implied in the notion "method."

On the other hand, the word "techniques" refers to the virtually inexhaustible variety of theoretical and practical procedures that one can invent or adopt in order to work out a certain research method. Similarly, the term "procedure" refers to various rules and routines associated with the practice of research. For example, to select a sample of subjects for a study, or to pilot a survey questionnaire one employs certain *procedures* that are standard across the social sciences. Interviewing may be considered to be a general research procedure when no special techniques are involved, such as using special diagnostic or investigative instruments to structure the interview. So there are general psychological and journalistic procedures for making sure that the interview will yield information that will be useful for preparing a research report. *Procedures* allow us to proceed, to go forward, and to get something accomplished. For example, one may follow certain procedures for selecting subjects and assuring their anonymity.

Techniques sometimes are like procedures except that there is an element of expertise (*tekhne* meaning "art," "craft") associated with techniques—connotations of expertise in a professional or technical sense, as in the development and the conduct of a statistical design for interpreting quantitative data. Implied in the idea of technique is the concept of a larger technology from which certain techniques are derived. *Technology* refers to the scientific study of the arts, such as in "computer technology," "publishing technology," and so on.

In contrast, the notion of *method* is charged with methodological considerations and implications of a particular philosophical or epistemological perspective. For example, "the interview" for an ethnographer may mean something quite different than for a therapist, or for an investigative journalist. In each case the concept of interview is charged with the reality assumptions, truth criteria and the general goals of the disciplined methodology within which the interview functions. So when we speak of "interviewing" or "analyzing transcripts" in this text, then we mean special forms of interviewing and analyzing which may look procedurally common to other social or human science practices but which are methodologically quite different (see the section on

Interviewing, pp. 66-68). To the extent that certain research "procedures" and "techniques" may need to be invented to suit a particular study, these procedures and techniques need to be conceived within the general orientation that characterizes the present methodology. One should not confuse phenomenological-hermeneutical analysis of texts as a mere variation of well-known techniques of content analysis, or as identical to analytic-coding, taxonomic, and data-organizing practices common to ethnography or grounded theory method. For one thing, phenomenological method differs from content analysis in that content analysis specifies beforehand what it wants to know from a text. Content analysis posits its criteria beforehand by identifying certain words or phrases that reveal, for example, the extent to which a text displays gender bias. The method of content analysis implies that it already knows what the meaning is of the subject that it examines: for example, the meaning of "gender," "femininity," or "sexuality." In contrast, phenomenological human science is discovery oriented. It wants to find out what a certain phenomenon means and how it is experienced.

The methodology of phenomenology is such that it posits an approach toward research that aims at being presuppositionless; in other words, this is a methodology that tries to ward off any tendency toward constructing a predetermined set of fixed procedures, techniques and concepts that would rule-govern the research project. And yet, it is not entirely wrong to say that phenomenology and hermeneutics as described here definitely have a certain *methodos*—a way. Significantly, Heidegger talked about phenomenological reflection as following certain paths, "woodpaths," towards a "clearing" where something could be shown, revealed, or clarified in its essential nature. However, the paths (methods) cannot be determined by fixed signposts. They need to be discovered or invented as a response to the question at hand.

Perhaps the best answer to the question of what is involved in a hermeneutic phenomenological human science research method is "scholarship!" A human science researcher is a scholar: a sensitive observer of the subtleties of everyday life, and an avid reader of relevant texts in the human science tradition of the humanities, history, philosophy, anthropology, and the social sciences as they pertain to his or her domain of interest—in our case the practical and theoretical demands of pedagogy, of living with children. So in a serious sense there is not really a "method" understood as a set of investigative procedures that one can master relatively quickly. Indeed it has been said that *the*

method of phenomenology and hermeneutics is that there is no method!
(Gadamer, 1975; Rorty, 1979). And yet, phenomenology wants to claim
that it can have it both ways. While it is true that the method of
phenomenology is that there is no method, yet there is tradition, a body
of knowledge and insights, a history of lives of thinkers and authors,
which, taken as an example, constitutes both a source and a
methodological ground for present human science research practices.
Thus the broad field of phenomenological scholarship can be considered as a set of guides and recommendations for a principled form of
inquiry that neither simply rejects or ignores tradition, nor slavishly
follows or kneels in front of it.

It is hoped then that this text will be helpful in describing some
methodological themes and methodical features of human science research, which will enable the reader to select or invent appropriate
research methods, techniques, and procedures for a particular problem
or question. The six methodological themes introduced in the remainder of this chapter offer the kind of practical approaches that may
be helpful in doing hermeneutic phenomenological human science
research. The six sections included in the following pages are
elaborated in the six chapters 2 through 7. It speaks for itself that the
separation into six methods is somewhat artificial. Different distinctions could have been made, and in the practice of human science
research the various methodical activities cannot really be performed
in isolation. Discussions of method and methodology are meant not to
prescribe a mechanistic set of procedures, but to animate inventiveness
and stimulate insight.

Methodical Structure of Human Science Research

How can human science research be pursued? Reduced to its
elemental methodical structure, hermeneutic phenomenological research may be seen as a dynamic interplay among six research activities:

(1) turning to a phenomenon which seriously interests us and commits us to the world;

(2) investigating experience as we live it rather than as we conceptualize it;

(3) reflecting on the essential themes which characterize the
phenomenon;

(4) describing the phenomenon through the art of writing and
rewriting;

(5) maintaining a strong and oriented pedagogical relation to the phenomenon;

(6) balancing the research context by considering parts and whole.

First, I shall briefly introduce the six methodological themes in the remainder of this chapter. Next, each methodological theme is explored in more detail in the following six chapters.

Turning to the nature of lived experience

Every project of phenomenological inquiry is driven by a commitment of turning to an abiding concern. "To think is to confine yourself to a single thought that one day stands still like a star in the world's sky," said Heidegger (1971, p. 4). This commitment of never wavering from thinking a single thought more deeply is the practice of thoughtfulness, of a fullness of thinking. To be full of thought means not that we have a whole lot on our mind, but rather that we recognize our lot of minding the Whole—that which renders fullness or wholeness to life. So phenomenological research is a being-given-over to some quest, a true task, a deep questioning of something that restores an original sense of what it means to be a thinker, a researcher, a theorist. A corollary is that phenomenological research does not start or proceed in a disembodied fashion. It is always a project of someone: a real person, who, in the context of particular individual, social, and historical life circumstances, sets out to make sense of a certain aspect of human existence. But while this recognition does not negate the plausibility of the insights gained from a specific piece of phenomenological work, it does reveal the scope and nature of the phenomenological project itself. A phenomenological description is always *one* interpretation, and no single interpretation of human experience will ever exhaust the possibility of yet another complementary, or even potentially *richer* or *deeper* description.

Investigating experience as we live it

Phenomenological research aims at establishing a renewed contact with original experience. Merleau-Ponty (1962) showed that turning to the phenomena of lived experience means re-learning to look at the world by re-awakening the basic experience of the world (p. viii). This turning to some abiding concern of lived experience has been called a turning "to the things themselves," *Zu den Sachen* (Husserl, 1911/80, p.

116). It is becoming full of the world, full of lived experience. "Being experienced" is a wisdom of the practice of living which results from having lived life deeply. In doing phenomenological research this practical wisdom is sought in the understanding of the nature of lived experience itself. On the one hand it means that phenomenological research requires of the researcher that he or she stands in the fullness of life, in the midst of the world of living relations and shared situations. On the other hand it means that the researcher actively explores the category of lived experience in all its modalities and aspects.

Reflecting on essential themes

The understanding of some phenomenon, some lived experience, is not fulfilled in a reflective grasp of the facticity of this or that particular experience. Rather, a true reflection on lived experience is a thoughtful, reflective grasping of what it is that renders this or that particular experience its special significance. Therefore, phenomenological research, unlike any other kind of research, makes a distinction between appearance and essence, between the things of our experience and that which grounds the things of our experience. In other words, phenomenological research consists of reflectively bringing into nearness that which tends to be obscure, that which tends to evade the intelligibility of our natural attitude of everyday life. About any experience or activity, whether it be mothering, fathering, teaching, testing, reading, running, leading, lending, drawing, driving, or the experience of time, space, things, the body, others, we can reflectively ask what is it that constitutes the nature of this lived experience?

The art of writing and rewriting

So, we ask, what is it like to do phenomenological research? The question is not, "What is phenomenological research?" or "How do we write up our research findings?" For, indeed, to *do* research in a phenomenological sense is already and immediately and always a *bringing to speech* of something. And this thoughtfully bringing to speech is most commonly a writing activity. Is phenomenological writing thought brought to speech? Or is it language that lets itself be spoken and used as thought? Experientially, language and thinking are difficult to separate. When I speak I discover what it is that I wished to say, says Merleau-Ponty (1973, p. 142). And Gadamer (1975, pp. 366-397) notes how thinking and speaking, rationality and language, derive their contemporary meanings from the same root: *logos*. And in turn *logos* has retained the meaning of conversation, inquiry, questioning: of questioningly letting that which is being talked about be seen. So phenomenology is the application of *logos* (language and thoughtfulness) to a phenomenon (an aspect of lived experience), to what shows itself precisely as it shows itself. Or, to borrow Heidegger's (1962) phrase, phenomenology is "to let that which shows itself be seen from itself in the very way in which it shows itself from itself" (p. 58).

Maintaining a strong and oriented relation

Contrary to what some think, phenomenological human science is a form of qualitative research that is extraordinarily demanding of its practitioners. Unless the researcher remains strong in his or her orientation to the fundamental question or notion, there will be many temptations to get side-tracked or to wander aimlessly and indulge in wishy-washy speculations, to settle for preconceived opinions and conceptions, to become enchanted with narcissistic reflections or self-indulgent preoccupations, or to fall back onto taxonomic concepts or abstracting theories. To establish a strong relation with a certain question, phenomenon, or notion, the researcher cannot afford to adopt an attitude of so-called scientific disinterestedness. To be oriented to an object means that we are animated by the object in a full and human sense. To be strong in our orientation means that we will not settle for superficialities and falsities.

Balancing the research context by considering parts and whole

Qualitative research (*qualis* means "whatness") asks the *ti estin* question: What is it? What is this phenomenon in its whatness? But as one engages in the *ti estin* question, there is the danger that one loses sight of the end of phenomenological research: to construct a text which in its dialogical structure and argumentative organization aims at a certain effect. In other words, one can get so involved in chasing the *ti estin* that one gets stuck in the underbrush and fails to arrive at the clearings that give the text its revealing power. It also means that one needs to constantly measure the overall design of the study/text against the significance that the parts must play in the total textual structure. It is easy to get so buried in writing that one no longer knows where to go, what to do next, and how to get out of the hole that one has dug. At several points it is necessary to step back and look at the total, at the contextual givens and how each of the parts needs to contribute toward the total. Is the study properly grounded in a laying open of the question? Are the current forms of knowledge examined for what they may contribute to the question? Has it been shown how some of these knowledge forms (theories, concepts) are glosses that overlay our understanding of the phenomenon?

These above methods form the methodological structure of human science inquiry as pursued in this text. Now the question is, how can the procedural dimensions of the dynamic interplay of the above six methodological themes be further clarified? Although a certain order is implied in the methodological presentation this does not mean that one must proceed by executing and completing each "step." In fact, the organization of methodological themes in separate methodological chapters contributes to a certain artificiality and awkwardness of presentation. In the actual research process one may work at various aspects intermittently or simultaneously.

So, the next six chapters discuss and illustrate, in more detailed manner, what is involved in the six methods. But it needs to be emphasized again that one should not consult this text as a mechanistic "how to" primer on human science methods. The temptation to do this is very real since the following chapters have the appearance of a sequence of procedural steps in doing human science research. The technocratic mind believes that any problem or question can be solved or answered by some technique or method. However, one ought to discover soon that whatever "practical" suggestions are offered here, these suggestions always rely on a more tacitly understood grasp of the spirit of this kind of inquiry. There is no definitive set of research procedures offered here that one can follow blindly. Although spelling out the various aspects of the research process may help a reader, the critical moments of inquiry are ultimately elusive to systematic explication. Such moments may depend more on the interpretive sensitivity, inventive thoughtfulness, scholarly tact, and writing talent of the human science researcher.

CHAPTER 2

Turning to the Nature of Lived Experience

The Nature of Lived Experience

What is "lived experience?" This is an important question because phenomenological human science begins in lived experience and eventually turns back to it. Dilthey (1985) has suggested that in its most basic form lived experience involves our immediate, pre-reflective consciousness of life: a reflexive or self-given awareness which is, as awareness, unaware of itself.

> A lived experience does not confront me as something perceived or represented; it is not given to me, but the reality of lived experience is there-for-me because I have a reflexive awareness of it, because I possess it immediately as belonging to me in some sense. Only in thought does it become objective. (p. 223)

An analogy may be helpful here. When as a new teacher you stand in front of a class for the very first time you may find it hard for a while to forget that all these kids or teenagers are "looking at you." Some teachers have this same experience every time the new school year begins with a new class or classes. This "feeling looked at" may make it difficult to behave naturally and to speak freely. The same is true when one is being interviewed on television or when a person partakes in a panel discussion. All of a sudden all the eyes are on me and these eyes rob me of my taken-for-granted relation to my voice and my body. They force me to be aware of my experience while I am experiencing it. The result is awkwardness. However, as soon as I get involved in the debate and "forget" the presence of the audience, as it were, then I become involved again *immediately* and *naturally* in the activity. Only by later reflecting on it can I try to apprehend what the discussion was like.

Various thinkers have noted that lived experience first of all has a temporal structure: it can never be grasped in its immediate manifestation but only reflectively as past presence. Moreover, our appropriation of the meaning of lived experience is always of something past that can never be grasped in its full richness and depth since lived experience implicates the totality of life. The interpretive examination of lived experience has this methodical feature of relating the particular to the universal, part to whole, episode to totality.

Merleau-Ponty (1968) has given a more ontological expression to the notion of lived experience as immediate awareness which he calls "sensibility":

> The sensible is precisely that medium in which there can be being without it having to be posited; the sensible appearance of the sensible, the silent persuasion of the sensible is Being's unique way of manifesting itself without becoming positivity, without ceasing to be ambiguous and transcendent . . . . The sensible is that: this possibility to be evident in silence, to be understood implicitly. (p. 214)

Lived experience is the starting point and end point of phenomenological research. The aim of phenomenology is to transform lived experience into a textual expression of its essence—in such a way that the effect of the text is at once a reflexive re-living and a reflective appropriation of something meaningful: a notion by which a reader is powerfully animated in his or her own lived experience.

Dilthey (1985) suggested that lived experience is to the soul what breath is to the body: "Just as our body needs to breathe, our soul requires the fulfillment and expansion of its existence in the reverberations of emotional life" (p. 59). Lived experience is the breathing of meaning. In the flow of life, consciousness breathes meaning in a to and fro movement: a constant heaving between the inner and the outer, made concrete, for example, in my reflexive consciousness of hope for a child and the child as the object of hope. There is a determinate reality-appreciation in the flow of living and experiencing life's breath. Thus, a lived experience has a certain essence, a "quality" that we recognize in retrospect.

Gadamer (1975) observed that the word "experience" has a condensing and intensifying meaning: "If something is called or considered an experience its meaning rounds it into the unity of a significant whole" (p. 60). What makes the experience unique so that I can reflect on it and talk about it is the particular "structural nexus" (Dilthey, 1985), the motif, that gives this experience its particular quality (central idea or dominant theme). "Lived experiences are related to each other like motifs in the andante of a symphony," said Dilthey (1985, p. 227). He talked of "structure" or "structural nexus" (p. 228) as something that belongs to a particular lived experience (something like a pattern or unit of meaning), which becomes part of a system of contextually related experiences, explicated from it through a process of reflection on its meaning.

My son and I go for a bike ride. Since the bike ride has no purpose outside itself—we are not going anywhere special—it is this quality of space, mood and shared world that I now somehow associate with this thing of "going for a bike ride" with Mark. Each bike ride has some of the fullness of the regular bike rides we began taking during our summer stay in the countryside outside Victoria. What I do remember in the bike rides is not primarily the "cat walks," the "bunny hops," and the "front wheelies" we practised—even though "doing tricks" may have been the part that preoccupied Mark most at the time. Rather, the front wheelies are a way of recalling the conversational space which the road side created for Mark and his father. "Did you do bike tricks when you were my age?" "What kind of bike did you have?" "Did you have older friends?—I mean big kids like Michael Decore?" (Michael is a "cool" 12-year-old—the neighbourhood's champion skateboarder who "greets" Mark and teaches him how to do "tick tacks," "acid drops," "360's," and the like.) Our conversations keep pace as we pedal down the meandering country road, huff and puff up steep hills, or save space for a passing car.

Lived experiences gather hermeneutic significance as we (reflectively) gather them by giving memory to them. Through meditations, conversations, day dreams, inspirations and other interpretive acts we assign meaning to the phenomena of lived life. For example, "going for a bike ride" with my son makes a certain kind of talking, a certain togetherness possible that is quite different from the more personal talk we may have at bed time, which differs in turn from the atmosphere of the kitchen chatter in the morning during breakfast. Or do I enjoy the bike ride because it allows a certain tone in our relations: a closeness of feeling and yet a distance of intimacy, a physical involvement and yet an energy of separateness, a participation in the outside and yet a private preserve on the inside? "Going for a bike ride" with my seven-year-old son is a lived experience, that is to say, a determinate meaningful aspect of my life. There is a unity to this experience that makes it into something unique, and that allows me, upon reflection, to call it "going for a bike ride with my son."

But preceding or even apart from the reflective act, there reigns an implicit, non-thematic, non-reflective type of consciousness in our daily life, which consists in a simple presence to what I am doing. This consciousness is called "biking consciousness," "talking consciousness," "fathering consciousness," "teaching consciousness," and so forth. It is not (yet) a consciousness *of* biking, *of* talking, *of* teaching, *of* fathering—but a self-consciousness, a consciousness in these acts. In other words, to live life means being fatherly, motherly, teacherly, lovingly, actively, emotionally in the world—it is a non-thematic being conscious in the world. In contrast, reflective consciousness is continually fed by this non-reflective dimension of life, which it thematizes. And as Merleau-Ponty (1962) points out, phenomenology is that kind of human science research that must seize this life and give reflective expression to it.

The eventual aim of phenomenological human science is concentrated upon "re-achieving a direct and primitive contact with the world"—the world as immediately experienced, said Merleau-Ponty (1962, p. vii). And this involves a textual practice: reflective writing. This textual activity is what we call "human science research." It is the phenomenological and hermeneutical study of human existence: phenomenology because it is the descriptive study of lived experience (phenomena) in the attempt to enrich lived experience by mining its meaning; hermeneutics because it is the interpretive study of the expressions and objectifications (texts) of lived experience in the attempt to determine the meaning embodied in them.

Under the influence of post-modernism, deconstructionism, and other language-oriented human science approaches, the epistemology of experience and perception has been moved over somewhat to make space for an epistemology of language and text. Briefly, the main thrust of this shift of epistemologies is the realization that lived experience is soaked through with language. We are able to recall and reflect on experiences thanks to language. Human experience is only possible because we have language. Language is so fundamentally part of our humanness that Heidegger (1971) proposed that language, thinking and being are one. Lived experience itself seems to have a linguistic structure. Experience and (un)consciousness are structured like a language, and therefore one could speak of all experience, all human interactions, as some kind of text, according to Ricoeur (1981). If this metaphor is taken literally, all phenomenological description is text interpretation or hermeneutics. The idea of text introduces the notion of multiple, or even conflicting, interpretations. If all the world is like a text then everyone becomes a reader (and an author). And the question arises whose reading, whose interpretation, is the correct one.

In one sense the notion of textuality becomes a fruitful metaphoric device for analyzing meaning. If all experience is like text then we need to examine how these texts are socially constructed. Interpretation that aims at explicating the various meanings embedded in a text may then take the form of socially analyzing or deconstructing the text and thus exploding its meanings. We must not forget, however, that human actions and experiences are precisely that: actions and experiences. To reduce the whole world to text and to treat all experience textually is to be forgetful of the metaphoric origin of one's methodology.

Orienting to the Phenomenon

"Phenomenology is the study of essences," said Merleau-Ponty (1962, p. vii). But the word "essence" should not be mystified. By essence we do not mean some kind of mysterious entity or discovery, nor some ultimate core or residue of meaning. Rather, the term "essence" may be understood as a linguistic construction, a description of a phenomenon. A good description that constitutes the essence of something is construed so that the structure of a lived experience is revealed to us in such a fashion that we are now able to grasp the nature and significance of this experience in a hitherto unseen way. When a phenomenologist asks for the essence of a phenomenon—a lived experience—then the phenomenological inquiry is not unlike an artistic endeavor, a creative attempt to somehow capture a certain phenomenon of life in a linguistic description that is both holistic and analytical, evocative and precise, unique and universal, powerful and sensitive. So an appropriate topic for phenomenological inquiry is determined by the questioning of the essential nature of a lived experience: a certain way of being in the world.

A phenomenological concern always has this twofold character: a preoccupation with both the concreteness (the ontic) as well as the essential nature (the ontological) of a lived experience. Phenomenology is not concerned primarily with the nomological or factual aspects of some state of affairs; rather, it always asks, what is the nature of the phenomenon as meaningfully experienced? For example, a phenomenological interest in the reading experience of children would be unlikely to involve experimentation with some hypothetical variable(s) or testable skills by comparing the reading experiences of children from this group, class, or school with that group, class, or school. Instead, phenomenology asks, what is the reading experience itself like for children? What is it like for a young child to read?

Similarly, phenomenology is less concerned with the facticity of the psychological, sociological, or cultural peculiarities or differences of the meaning structures of human experience. It is important, therefore, for the researcher to focus carefully on the question of what possible human experience is to be made topical for phenomenological investigation. This starting point of phenomenological research is largely a matter of identifying what it is that deeply interests you or me and of identifying this interest as a true phenomenon, i.e., as some experience that human beings live through. The nature and number of possible human experiences are as varied and infinite as human life itself.

As the examples above suggest, to orient oneself to a phenomenon always implies a particular interest, station or vantage point in life. My orientation to the lifeworld is that of the educator: I orient to life as parent and as teacher. This definite sense of orientation does not imply that I am not also a husband, a friend, or someone who likes to read, and so forth. In this text I will use my pedagogic interest in the lifeworld as parent and as teacher as "example" for discussing the human science methods of phenomenology and hermeneutics. After all, these pedagogic interests cannot be separated from my interest in human science. It is because I am interested in children and in the question of how children grow up and learn that I orient myself pedagogically to children in a phenomenological hermeneutic mode.

So when one orients to a phenomenon one is approaching this experience with a certain interest. In these pages this oriented interest is pedagogic. Someone else may be oriented as a nurse, a psychologist, or a medical doctor.

When I am interested in the pedagogic lives that adults live with children, I may ask myself: Is it mothering or fathering I am interested in? And how is teaching like or unlike parenting in the sense that teachers function *in loco parentis*? I want to use the words "parent" and "teacher" to point at the lived experiences in which I am really interested. I ask: But what kind of care-giving to children is parenting? Are foster parents "parents" in this sense? And what about adoptive parents or other caretakers of children performing such a function? Should I allow for the possibility that not all (biological) parents act like real parents? I am really asking: Is there something essential to the experience of parenting? This kind of questioning focuses on the nature of the experience being investigated: the questioning of the identity of the phenomenon. As a father and as a teacher, I have ample opportunity to have an eye for the experiences parents and teachers have. And yet, as I reflect on these experiences, it ironically becomes less clear of what the experience consists. I help my three-year-old with his breakfast or supper; we playfully create a world of blocks and toys. We go for a toboggan ride. I worry about a nasty tumble he takes on the icy snow. I tell my children a story before bedtime. I tuck them in, and then I am called back again for an extra goodnight kiss. Or perhaps we are having a little chat about being afraid in the dark. Later, Mom and Dad discuss the wisdom of early music lessons and what to make of Michael's reaction to one of his friends. Is this parenting? Of course it is! But how so? In what sense are these experiences examples of parenting? Do parents play with their children differently than the way any person may happen to play with a child? Would not a trained teacher tell or read a story to my child better than I possibly could? Is there a difference between the way parents talk with and about their children and the way a teacher or others may talk with or about these children?

Things turn very fuzzy just when they seemed to become so clear. To do a phenomenological study of any topic, therefore, it is not enough to simply recall experiences I or others may have had with respect to a particular phenomenon. Instead, I must recall the experience in such a way that the essential aspects, the meaning structures of this experience as lived through, are brought back, as it were, and in such a way that we recognize this description *as a possible experience*, which means *as a possible interpretation* of that experience. This then is the task of phenomenological research and writing: *to construct a possible interpretation of the nature of a certain human experience.* In order to make a beginning, the phenomenologist must ask: What human experience do I feel called upon to make topical for my investigation?

Formulating the Phenomenological Question

It is not until I have identified my interest in the nature of a selected human experience that a true phenomenological questioning is possible. To do phenomenological research is *to question* something phenomenologically and, also, to be addressed by the question of what something is "really" like. What is the nature of this lived experience? The question that is at the center of the professional and personal life of an educator concerns the meaning of pedagogy. To someone who is a father and a teacher the question of the meaning of being a father and being a teacher is posed daily. It is posed in an existential sort of way by my own children who daily give me reason to reflect on the nature and adequacy of my fatherly behavior. And it is posed in a more explicit and intellectual way by my students—themselves teachers. They are keenly observant of the possible discrepancies between professed or theoretic explications of pedagogy and the way that this theorizing is exemplified or made true in lived life. It is in the academic and lived domain of all these tensions that the question of the meaning of parenting and of teaching presents itself. Many fathers and mothers have doubtlessly felt the force of the incredible transformation that a person may experience with the birth of a child. Living with children radically alters one's sense of life. In the professional life of teachers children enter our world somewhat differently; but even in teaching there is for many the unsettling experience of meeting one's first class at the beginning of the new school term.

What does it mean to be a teacher? It seems somewhat silly to ask this question. The literature of research on teaching implicitly or explicitly seems to have dealt with this question ad nauseam. But the fact that there is such abundance of theoretical material on teaching makes it even more puzzling that we can still embarrass educators with this question. What is teaching? What does it mean to be a teacher? What is it about your relation to these children that makes you a teacher? What does this child mean to you and what do you mean to this child? What is it about teaching that makes it possible for it to be what it is in its essence (is-ness)?

An important reminder for all phenomenological research, in all its stages, is to be constantly mindful of one's original question and thus to be steadfastly oriented to the lived experience that makes it possible to ask the "what it is like" question in the first place. So we ask, what is it about parenting and about teaching that renders those experiences their pedagogic significance? When we ask what the essence is of parenting then we seem to ask what is the pedagogic ground of parenting. Similarly, the question of the essence of teaching is concerned with the pedagogy of teaching.

Both teaching and parenting involve the adult in a pedagogical relation with children. Therefore, we will use the term "pedagogy" when we mean to subsume or refer to both parenting or teaching. When the question turns more specific, then the more specific modes of being a teacher, or father, or mother will be addressed. So, for the purpose of our example, we will settle on this formulation: "What is the pedagogy of parenting? And what is the pedagogy of teaching?" And, of course, we must not assume that the experiences of parenting and teaching are identical, or that mothering and fathering are the same. So what is it like to be a teacher? A mother? A father? Although this is not meant to be a phenomenological primer about pedagogy, we will use the questions of the meaning of teaching and the meaning of parenting (mothering, fathering) as occasions to exemplify the nature of human science method.

The essence of the question, said Gadamer (1975), is the opening up, and keeping open, of possibilities (p. 266). But we can only do this if we can keep ourselves open in such a way that in this abiding concern of our questioning we find ourselves deeply interested (inter-esse, to be or stand in the midst of something) in that which makes the question possible in the first place. To truly question something is to interrogate something from the heart of our existence, from the center of our being. Even minor phenomenological research projects require that we not simply raise a question and possibly soon drop it again, but rather that we "live" this question, that we "become" this question. Is this not the meaning of research: to question something by going back again and again to the things themselves until that which is put to question begins to reveal something of its essential nature? I can only genuinely ask the question of the nature of pedagogy if I am indeed animated by this question in the very life I live with children.

Moreover, every form of research and theorizing is shot through with values. Theorizing about some aspect of our pedagogic living with children or young people is already the showing of a form of life. We cannot ask questions about the lives of children without this activity in some way being related to the very lives of those whom we make the topic of our research. But how can a phenomenological question that makes us wonder and write about a certain phenomenon be treated in a phenomenological description? In most forms of research, the question that animates the research is stated unequivocally. In experimental research the question is formulated as a null hypothesis. The cleaner and less ambiguous the research question, the less ambiguous the interpretation of the research findings. In much social and human science research, it is assumed that a productive research question is formulated in such a clear-cut and prosaic manner that any competent and "disinterested" social or behavioral scientist can deal with the question. That is why so much research can be contracted out or delegated to assistants, research teams or agencies.

The matter lies quite differently with phenomenological research. A phenomenological question must not only be made clear, understood, but also "lived" by the researcher. A phenomenological researcher cannot just write down his or her question at the beginning of the study. There it is! Question mark at the end! No, in his or her phenomenological description the researcher/writer must "pull" the reader into the question in such a way that the reader cannot help but wonder about the nature of the phenomenon in the way that the human scientist does. One might say that a phenomenological questioning teaches the reader to wonder, to question deeply the very thing that is being questioned by the question. Sometimes this involves avoiding posing the question outright because such straightforward approach would lead the reader to misinterpret or underestimate its probing nature. Instead, one might, at the hand of a concrete story, draw the reader into a questioning mood with respect to the topic being addressed. Consider, for example, Heidegger's essay on language (1971, pp. 189-210). Heidegger asks, what is language? But he never reduces the question to such prosaic formulation. At other times one may have to discuss reflectively how a question is difficult to ask for we may have forgotten what lies at the core of the question (see the section entitled "Tracing Etymological Sources," pp. 58-60).

So, we adopt a phenomenological perspective in order to help us to bring to light that which presents itself as pedagogy in our lives with children. It is that kind of thinking which guides us back from theoretical abstractions to the reality of lived experiences—the lived experience of the child's world, the lived experience of schools, curricula, etc. Phenomenology asks the simple question, what is it like to have a certain experience, for example, an educational experience? An innocent question indeed. We may know that we have a certain experience, that we feel alone, afraid, in love, bored, amused, but we are quickly at wit's end when we are pressed to describe what such feeling consists of. Yet, in the field of curriculum we confidently talk about "selecting, planning or organizing learning experiences." This confidence begs a question— the question whether we know what it is like when a child "has an experience" or when the child "comes to understand something." Husserl's phrase "back to the things themselves" means that the phenomenological attitude is mindful of the ease with which we tend to rely on a reconstructed logic in our professional endeavors. We read theories into everything. And once a theoretical scheme has been brought to life we tend to search for the principles (*nomos*) that seem to organize the life to which the theory was brought. In our efforts to make sense of our lived experiences with theories and hypothesizing frameworks we are forgetting that it is living human beings who bring schemata and frameworks into being and not the reverse.

Some argue that phenomenology has no practical value because "you cannot do anything with phenomenological knowledge." From the point of view of instrumental reason it may be quite true to say that we cannot do anything with phenomenological knowledge. But to paraphrase Heidegger, the more important question is not: Can we do something with phenomenology? Rather, we should wonder: Can phenomenology, if we concern ourselves deeply with it, do something with us?

The phenomenological attitude towards the concerns of our daily occupation compels us to constantly raise the question: what is it like to be an educator? What is it like to be a teacher? And in order to ask the question what it is that makes it possible for us to think and talk about pedagogy in the first place, we ask, what is it about that form of life (being an educator) which makes a pedagogic existence different from other pursuits? As adults we meet children socially in many situations where pedagogy is not permitted or encouraged to enter. A person's interest in a child may be primarily for reasons of coaching a sporting event, selling music discs, or running a video arcade. But to say this challenges the question of what difference there is between hockey coach, sales person, Boy-Scout leader, math teacher, or school principal. No doubt there are commonalities between a coach and pedagogue. Both may be teachers of children. So there are essential and inessential differences between those who teach children. The teacher as pedagogue, however, shows a difference that makes a pedagogic difference. So we need to ask how the essence of pedagogy can be made intelligible. And now the simple and innocent phenomenological question "What is it like?" assumes a deeper dimension. Because now we are led to address the question: What kind of answer would meet the phenomenological requirement of intelligibility? How can we come to a deep understanding of that which makes it possible to say that between this teacher and this child there exists a pedagogic relation? What kind of speaking would satisfy such understanding? In phenomenology what kind of speaking counts as an answer?

One way of dealing with this question is to theorize about knowledge; to epistemologize our answer by theorizing, for example, about the distinctions between different types of knowledge. But if we wish to remain responsive to the commitment of phenomenology, then we should try to resist the temptation to develop positivistic schemata, paradigms, models, or other categorical abstractions of knowledge. Instead, we should refer questions of knowledge back to the lifeworld where knowledge speaks through our lived experiences. We, therefore, wish to ask: How can we pursue the question of what constitutes (phenomenological) knowledge in such a way that our way of addressing this question may become an example of what the question in its questioning seeks to bring to clarity? In other words, how can we show the what-ness of the pedagogic experience, at once in an iconic and in a recollective sense? From a phenomenological point of view we keep reminding ourselves that the question of knowledge always refers us back to our world, to our lives, to who we are, and to what makes us write, read, and talk together as educators: it is what stands iconically behind the words, the speaking and the language.

Explicating Assumptions and Pre-understandings

The problem of phenomenological inquiry is not always that we know too little about the phenomenon we wish to investigate, but that we know too much. Or, more accurately, the problem is that our "common sense" pre-understandings, our suppositions, assumptions, and the existing bodies of scientific knowledge, predispose us to interpret the nature of the phenomenon before we have even come to grips with the significance of the phenomenological question. Another way of stating this predicament is that scientific knowledge as well as everyday knowledge believes that it has already had much to say about a phenomenon, such as what the phenomenon of parenting is, or what parents do or should do, before it has actually come to an understanding of what it means to be a parent in the first place. How do we best suspend or bracket these beliefs? Husserl, who was at first a mathematician, used the term "bracketing" to describe how one must take hold of the phenomenon and then place outside of it one's knowledge about the phenomenon (1970b, pp. 33-42). But how does one put out of play everything one knows about an experience that one has selected for study? If we simply try to forget or ignore what we already "know," we may find that the presuppositions persistently creep back into our reflections. It is better to make explicit our understandings, beliefs, biases, assumptions, presuppositions, and theories. We try to come to terms with our assumptions, not in order to forget them again, but rather to hold them deliberately at bay and even to turn this knowledge against itself, as it were, thereby exposing its shallow or concealing character.

For example, I explore the literature by specialists of parenting, I note how the large majority of books do not address the question of the meaning of parenting. Instead, they tend to give advice to mothers and fathers of children of all ages. I notice too that parenting is often considered a "how to do" skill that can be taught: popular books are entitled *Parent Effectiveness Training, How to Deal with your Hyperactive Child, What to do with Your Growing Adolescent, Tough Love*, and so forth. No matter how practically compelling the contents of these books may be, they do not necessarily bring us any closer to understanding the nature of parenting itself.

In the research literature four metaphors have dominated the study of parenting: (1) At the time when child psychologists thought that the new-born had only primitive sensory functions, parents were advised to provide good physical care for their babies, but the baby's room was a sterile and empty place fitted only with crib and baby bottles. Good parents were seen to be people who took good care of the physical needs of their children. Even "mother" love was translated into something physical (witness the wire versus the cloth mother monkey experiments in Harlow's well-known studies of the importance of touch). And yet it was studies such as the ones by Harlow (1965) and Bowlby (1978) that led to the rediscovery of the importance of breast-feeding for both nutritional and bonding reasons. Even today many lay people believe that babies, for a few weeks or months at least, are incapable of significant perceptual awareness of their environment. So the essence of parenting at one time was seen to consist primarily of providing physical care. (2) This metaphor of the body shifted toward the mind as it was replaced with the notion that parenting essentially consists of a set of attitudes, a minding, a certain disposition we adopt toward our children. For example, mothers were told that maternal love and appropriate affections are critical in normal healthy development. (3) Next, in a move back to the body, but now purged of its banal functions, emerged the metaphor of parenting as stimulation: a spurring and goading of a passive-reactive child by means of behavioral techniques and stimulating environments. To be a good parent meant, for example, to reinforce positive behaviors by means of behavioral rewarding techniques. (4) The most recent metaphor is borrowed from linguistics. It defines the essence of parenting as interlocution or dialogue. Psychologists have discovered, with the aid of slow playback split-video recordings, the incredible variety and subtlety of infant interaction and communication with the mother. This research has led to new theories of the importance of physical face-to-face or eye contact that infants have with those who take care of them.

But what does this say about the nature of parenting? It would appear that the foundational element in research thinking on the essence of parenting largely consists of trading metaphor for metaphor in the attempt to find the common denominator. The research efforts initially focus on exploiting the productive elements of a certain conception of the essence of parenting. In time—for whatever ideological reasons or socio-historical circumstances—this conception gets to be seen as merely one of its various aspects. In other words, what was once considered essential now is merely an aspect or a view, while the deep meaning of these aspects remains out of reach. Psychologists who are engaged in research on parenting seem to be aware of these ambiguities. After reviewing the results of decades of research on parenting, Schaffer (1977) concludes that, in spite of all these research efforts, the question of the nature of parenting is still an unsolved problem. "Something essential is missing," he says. And he continues, in a sobering sort of way: "Ask any mother what she considers to be the essence of mothering and she will have no hesitation in replying: love. And yet, curiously," says Schaffer, "mother love has not yet become researchable" (p. 79). Schaffer may be right, but even those who feel that the essence of parenting lies in the "unreachable" neighborhood of love cannot escape a certain epistemological nihilism. In a scientific sense, we may not know (yet) what love is. No matter. Maternal and paternal love have been described as nothing more than a culturally sponsored phenomenon. At best, mother love is simply socially learned behavior, and at worst, some modern feminists say it is an historical conspiracy of man to snare woman in an artificial bondage to her children and spouse.

It would seem that it is such epistemological nihilism which forces us to always see the relative, historical, constructed, and social character of all truth at the expense of its deep hermeneutic facticity. But more disconcerting from a phenomenological point of view is the reminder that love too is only a metaphor for parenting. The word is more telling about the way we account for certain (affectionate) interactions than about the deep meanings of those interactions. Nietzsche once observed that all language, and therefore all truth and error, is metaphoric in origin (Nietzsche, 1873/1954, p. 46). Virtually every word we utter ultimately derives from some image, thereby betraying its metaphoric genesis. Our most prized certainties, our best proven ideas, our most neglected commonplaces must admit to their metaphoric genealogy. But does this metaphoric origin of speech render all truth regarding parenting arbitrary? Are truth and error indistinguishable? Does this mean that there is no way that we can know anything essential about parenting? Does this mean that there is no ground, no primordiality, that engenders and sponsors the notion of pedagogy? If this were so, then all we would ever be able to do is to uncover the latest metaphor about parenting and unmask its perspectivist nature. And perhaps, in some philosophical sense, this lack of ground is our predicament. But metaphor is not simply the bottomless ground, the empty core, the final destination of language. By way of metaphor, language can take us beyond the content of the metaphor toward the original region where language speaks through silence. This path of the metaphor is the speaking of thinking, of poetizing. Virginia Woolf once described how words not only find their semantic limit in metaphor; metaphor is also language's way of making it possible for the poet to transcend this limit:

> By the bold and running use of metaphor, the poet will amplify and give us not the thing itself, but the reverberation and reflection which, taken into his mind, the thing has made; close enough to the original to illustrate it, remote enough to heighten, enlarge, and make splendid. (1932, p. 32)

What does it mean, then, to have an understanding of the essence of parenting? Perhaps the primordiality of the pedagogy of parenting is much less something we can discover, construct, or identify by naming or conceptualizing it. Rather, the very idea of the primordial signifies that the pedagogy of parenting is something that must be brought back, recalled, or recollected from original experience. The pedagogy of parenting in this sense is, as Marcel (1950) would have said, not a problem in need of a solution but a mystery in need of evocative comprehension. To evoke the mystery of the pedagogy of parenting is, therefore, much less to attempt to unravel a problem than to try to recapture something: to re-achieve a direct contact with the world of living with children by awakening the soul to its primordial reality.

But, by terming pedagogy or parenting essentially a "mystery," are we therefore assigning less substance, less reality to it? Not at all. The mystery of parenting is knowable. We know it, one might say, in the way we cannot deny the reality of our feelings, intuition, conscience, will, mood. Parenting is not simply an entity, not a certain form of behavior, not even a feeling or an emotion like "love" or "care." And yet we sense this presence that we call mothering or fathering in our pedagogic lives with children. And this is because pedagogy announces itself not *as* entity, behavior, feeling, or emotion but *through* them. Parenting is utter mystery, yet knowable. The project of a phenomenology of parenting is, therefore, not to translate (reduce) the primordial relation of parenting into clearly defined concepts so as to dispel its mystery, but rather the object is to bring the mystery more fully into our presence (Marcel, 1950). Such a project has to make use of language in such a way as to make present to us what is inherently pre-linguistic and therefore essentially not transposable into a set of precisely delineated propositional statements.

But before completing this section, we must comment further on the assumptions of parenting as love or care. Psychologists have argued that it is not quantity but quality of parental care that matters for child development. This argument should be reassuring because ever-growing numbers of young children spend the "better" part of their waking hours in day-care institutions while their parents are at work. And yet, despite the stimulating educational nature of good day-care environments, it is not clear whether day-care workers can or should provide "parenting experiences" to those entrusted to their care. Can day-care workers provide parental care to children? What does parental love mean for the child if some other person (foster parent, teacher, or day-care worker) stands in for the "true" parent as expressed in the term *in loco parentis*? Is the biological parent automatically the (only) true parent?

CHAPTER 3

Investigating Experience as We Live It

The Nature of Data (datum: thing given or granted)

The lifeworld, the world of lived experience, is both the source and the object of phenomenological research. To make a study of the lived experience of parenting or teaching, one needs to orient oneself in a strong way to the question of the meaning of parenting or teaching. Nothing about the notion of pedagogy (parenting or teaching) should be considered "given" or "granted"; only that the meaning of pedagogy needs to be *found* in the experience of pedagogy, because the lived experience of pedagogy is all that remains if presuppositions are suspended. And so we need to search everywhere in the lifeworld for lived-experience material that, upon reflective examination, might yield something of its fundamental nature.

It should be clear already that the notion of "data" is ambiguous within the human science perspective. In this chapter we discuss various approaches to "gathering" or "collecting" lived-experience material of different forms. In some respect it is quite misleading to talk of "data" in this context, particularly since the concept of "data" has quantitative overtones associated with behavioral and more positivistic social science approaches. And to speak of "gathering" and "collecting" human science data, as if one is speaking of "objective information," may admittedly be an attempt to borrow the respect that the so-called "hard" sciences have enjoyed. And yet it is not entirely wrong to say that the methods of conversational interviewing, close observation, etc., involve the collecting or gathering of data. When someone has related a valuable experience to me then I have indeed gained something, even though the "thing" *gained* is not a quantifiable entity.

There is a further sense in which the notion of "data" has some relevance to phenomenology. Originally, "datum" means something "given" or "granted." And there is indeed a sense in which our experience is "given" to us in everyday life. And yet, we need to realize, of course, that experiential accounts or lived-experience descriptions—whether caught in oral or in written discourse—are never identical to lived experience itself. All recollections of experiences, reflections on experiences, descriptions of experiences, taped interviews about experiences, or transcribed conversations about experiences are already *transformations* of those experiences. Even life captured directly on magnetic or light-sensitive tape is already transformed at the moment it is captured. Without this dramatic elusive element of lived meaning to our reflective attention phenomenology might not be necessary. So, the upshot is that we need to find access to life's living dimensions while realizing that the meanings we bring to the surface from the depths of life's oceans have already lost the natural quiver of their undisturbed existence.

Using Personal Experience as a Starting Point

The ego-logical starting point for phenomenological research is a natural consequence of the above remarks. My own life experiences are immediately accessible to me in a way that no one else's are. However, the phenomenologist does not want to trouble the reader with purely private, autobiographical facticities of one's life. The revealing of private sentiments or private happenings are matters to be shared among friends perhaps, or between lovers, or in the gossip columns of life. In drawing up personal descriptions of lived experiences, the phenomenologist knows that one's own experiences are also the possible experiences of others.

To conduct a personal description of a lived experience, I try to describe my experience as much as possible in experiential terms, focusing on a particular situation or event. I try, as Merleau-Ponty says, to give a direct description of my experience as it is, without offering causal explanations or interpretive generalizations of my experience (1962, p. vii).

I will try to give a personal, experiential account of the beginning of my fatherhood:

How did "having children" enter my life? I remember several occasions when friends of ours would speak of the deep satisfaction of having young children of their own. How it changed their way of looking at life and at the world. I always thought I understood what they were saying (now I know that I did not). I countered that I felt no lack, no need for a family, and argued eloquently I believe, how the children I taught at school gave me similar satisfactions without having to "possess" some of my own. I felt a strong, almost physical dislike for the idea of fatherhood, and privately considered my friends to be quite foolish. Talking to young parents is like talking to religious converts, I said to Judith, my wife. As we would return home, we would talk about how we considered ourselves lucky to be able to enjoy each other, our quiet, our books, and our freedom to do what we liked and to go where we pleased. Very occasionally Judith would speak of her doubt about our resolve not to have children. I always resisted the discussion convincingly. I was thirty-something and felt young.

One day we visited Judith's cousin, who had just given birth to her third child. I recall the chaos of the home—food smells, crackers, junk, stains, toys, and blankets. Altogether I felt somewhat repulsed at the greasiness of the child scene—such contrast to our home or my classroom. One moment stands out clearly. My wife had taken the newborn baby in her arms and then I felt strangely moved—she and this new baby, so lovely—it seemed right, good. The next time the topic of having children came up (I might have brought it up myself), I still resisted, but weakly. I doubted my ability to be an enthusiastic father. Again I told Judith, but more feebly this time, that I distrusted the world we live in; it seemed so foolish, so egotistic to bring children into this madness. Secretly, I could hardly wait for our first child to be born. Yet at times I felt afraid. What if I could not love this child Judith was bearing? Feeling guilty, I only admitted my uncertainties to myself while talking supportively to my wife.

Of course, the above lived-experience description is not a phenomenological description. Lived-experience descriptions are data, or material on which to work. Note as well that in writing this recollection of my hesitant beginnings of fatherhood I refrained from trying to "explain" why I was reluctant and doubtful about becoming a father. It does not matter whether my reluctance might have been caused by facts of my childhood, my concept of self, my marriage, some influence of my job, or whatever hidden or subconscious factors on which one might want to speculate. Reluctant fatherhood was my initial reaction to the thought of having children of my own. The sharp contrast of the initial reluctance with the profoundly moving experience of birth, meeting and living with one's child is the psychological ground for my phenomenological interest in the question of the meaning of parenthood. And so this is just one possible experience of the early stage of parenting that one might encounter.

But in what way does this lived-experience description help to open up the question of the meaning of pedagogy? of being a parent? What I may glean from my reluctant transition into parenthood is that this transition was experientially speaking a true transformation: a transformative experience from man into father. With a self-evidence that is experientially undeniable I have now an immediate grasp of the fundamental difference that being a father makes to the man I was. And yet the nature of meaning of this difference is difficult to explicate. For that we need a phenomenological human science.

Here is another personal lived-experience description, this time a recollection from my life as a school teacher.

> The other day I thought of Jonathan again. Jonathan may have seemed an unremarkable child. At least that is what the comments of the various teachers reflected in their entries in Jonathan's cumulative-record. He was the kind of child you do not notice very much, even though he sat right up front in my grade five class. Physically Jonathan already looked like a small middle-aged person. He was somewhat pudgy, walked with a waddle, and behaved rather awkwardly in gym class. However, Jonathan sported a cheery disposition and a funnily mature way of talking which was emphasized by a British-Jewish accent. In almost all subjects Jonathan performed at a low average level. His math skills were definitely problematic. But I had been struck with Jonathan's uncanny feel for poetic thought and language. Strange that a child who appeared so mediocre in achievement in virtually all school subjects could write such fine and carefully crafted poems! In fact, other teachers in Jonathan's elementary school had been surprised when they heard of the hidden skill of this boy who was no favorite amongst his peers either.

> But grade five had become a year of unimagined productivity for Jonathan. He felt so special! With some encouragement and coaching Jonathan wrote poems on many significant events of his young life. He even published in a regional literary magazine. His parents were somewhat ambivalent about Jonathan's newly discovered talent. They would have been more pleased if he would have been able to acquire

higher passing marks in math. Jonathan was doing his best, but could never quite satisfy their ambitions for him. And when Jonathan went on to grade six and then to Junior High School the parents were no doubt relieved that his affair of enchantment with poetic language abruptly halted. It was in grade nine that I unexpectedly ran into Jonathan. I was visiting his school for the day. "Well, Jonathan," I said to him, "so nice to see you again. I have often wondered what has become of my poet." Jonathan admitted shyly that for the last four years his activities as a poet had come to an end. And that was that! He shrugged and smiled apologetically. "Too busy, you know!" Besides, writing poetry wasn't really his forte anymore. I think that I gave him a pondering glance and then we shook hands and parted. But a week later the mail delivered me an envelope. "From Jonathan!" Stuck inside were three poems. They sang an unmistaken promise. They did this, despite their somewhat unoriginal title: "Odes To A Teacher." I was overcome. "A poet after all," I thought.

The other day I thought of Jonathan again. It was not for any particular reason. Nor was it occasioned by some clear clue that I would associate with his memory. Jonathan just popped into my mind as other kids sometimes do from those early days as a school teacher. Jonathan should now be in his early thirties. And I wonder whether he still likes poetry. I wonder what has become of him.

As I now reflect on my own lived-experience description and I try to detect the overall thematic quality of this description (see the chapter, "Hermeneutic Phenomenological Reflection," pp. 77-109), I become aware of the special meaning that children may occupy in the life of a teacher. And I realize as well that it is pedagogically important for the child's growth and learning that the child knows that he or she means something "special" for his or her teacher. The experience of being a teacher manifests itself in having children on one's mind and wondering what one may expect to become of them.

It is to the extent that *my* experiences could be *our* experiences that the phenomenologist wants to be reflectively aware of certain experiential meanings. To be aware of the structure of one's own experience of a phenomenon may provide the researcher with clues for orienting oneself to the phenomenon and thus to all the other stages of phenomenological research. In actual phenomenological descriptions one often notices that the author uses the "I" form or the "we" form. This is done not only to enhance the evocative value of a truth experience expressed in this way, but also to show that the author recognizes both that one's own experiences are the possible experiences of others and also that the experiences of others are the possible experiences of oneself. Phenomenology always addresses any phenomenon as a *possible human experience*. It is in this sense that phenomenological descriptions have a universal (intersubjective) character.

Tracing Etymological Sources

The first thing that often strikes us about any phenomenon is that the words we use to refer to the phenomenon have lost some of their original meaning. Words that once could reverberate with lived meaning and reveal a living world now have become lame, limp, mute, emptied, and forgetful of their past power. What can still be conveyed by words such as "earth" or "water," "happiness" or "hope" (Gusdorf, 1965)? How flat words like "parent" or "teacher," "home" or "school," "knowledge" or "care" have become. Note, for example, how nowadays the word "caring" is being overused by social work, medical, legal, educational, and counseling professionals. And this occurs at a time when we no longer seem to know what it means to really care. We speak of medicare, day-care, legal care, health care, after school care, and so on. We hope to meet caring doctors and caring teachers for our children. But do we still know how to connect these social service professionals with the original meanings of "care" as sorrow? From an etymological point of view, and in its current usages, the term "care" possesses the dual meaning of worries, trouble, anxiety, lament on the one side, and charitableness, love, attentiveness, benefice on the other side. So in caring for another person I can relieve the other of "care" in the sense of trouble, worries, or anxiety. As a person whose first language is Dutch I am reminded that the Dutch term for caring, *zorgen*, seems to place a greater emphasis than the English on the more serious and troubling side of caring. For example, childcare is *kinderzorg* and a *zorgenkind* is a child who gives us special worry and who needs special care. Both worry and attentiveness are communicated in the term. To care for a child is to provide for and to attend to a child in such a way that we should not be suprised that we will be burdened by worries and deeply rooted concern. In caring for a child I want to relieve the child of "care" in the sense of untimely or inappropriate worries, troubles, anxieties. But as parent or teacher I must be conscious as well that in such caring the child may come to be more dependent and dominated by the adult than is pedagogically desirable in the process of childrearing and teaching. Thus, the task of the adult is to tactfully "care for" the child in such a way that the adult does not take the place of the child but rather that he or she prepares such place wherein and whereby the child is empowered to be and to become. As a parent or teacher I am not unduly relieving the child of "care" beyond what the child's obvious state of dependency and immaturity would require. Rather I am helping the child to develop self-understanding, self-responsibility, and material resourcefulness and spiritual freedom. Of course, retrieving or recalling the essence of caring is not a matter of simple etymological analysis or explication of the usage of the word. Rather, it is the reconstruction of a way of life: a willingness to live the language of our lives more deeply, to become more truly who we are when we refer to ourselves, for example, as teachers or parents.

Being attentive to the etymological origins of words may sometimes put us in touch with an original form of life where the terms still had living ties to the lived experiences from which they originally sprang. It can be shown, for example, that the words "parent," "child," "baby," "womb," and "birth" are all closely related to the verb "to bear" as in the experience of pregnancy, childbirth, as well as in the very experience of parenting as providing spaces that bear children, spaces in which children live and exist as children. The etymology of the word "parenting" refers both to *giving birth* and *bringing forth*; it has connotations of *origin* or *source*. To parent (*parere*) is to originate, to be the source, the origin from which something springs. How is this sense of source maintained in the experience of parenting? I may feel pride at the recognition of having brought this child into the world, but at the same time I know a deeper recognition: that it was not I who helped produce this child but rather something other and "larger" than me that made it possible for me to have this child in the first place. And so my experience of pride, as new father or mother, is tempered by the strange sense that I much less produced this child than that it came to me as a gift. My pride is then really a pride of being worthy of this gift that comes as if it were I who brought the child into being. And here is the theme of the effect which, in a deep sense, the child has on the mother and the father. The child is not simply received as a gift for which we make room in our lives. As Marcel expressed it, the truth is much more, that the gift is a call to which we have to make a response (1978). Parents bring forth children, but the child must be born in the dual sense of bearing and birth, bringing and awakening to the world. The English word "child" can be traced to the Gothic *kilthe,* meaning womb. Similarly, words akin to the term "baby" are translatable as the borne one, the one who is carried in the womb. An old word for child is still preserved in the Lowland Scots "bairn," cognate with Anglo-Saxon "bearn," meaning bearing and born. In my native Dutch language the word for womb is *baarmoeder,* literally "mother who bears," mother who holds, carries the child. So both childbearing and giving birth are aspects of the same verb "to bear."

In these persistent etymological references to bearing and safekeeping of the child, we may find clues to the meaning of parenting and of teaching as *in loco parentis.* In providing bearing for their children, parents give and teach the very young something without which growing up or even the living of a life becomes quite impossible. Parents who bear, give bearing to children, make available space and ground for being. They teach their children that the world can be experienced as home, a place for safe dwelling, a habitat in which human beings can "be," where we can be ourselves, where we can have habits: ways of being and doing things. So to bear children is, in a broad sense, to provide place and space for them to live, to be. The child is carried, borne inside the womb at first, then it is born into the world where it remains, for a while at least, most helpless, dependent, in need of nurture, warmth, caresses, holding fast, and safe outside the womb. Conversely, it is in the fact of the worldly experience of separateness, lostness, without a bearing, without the security of safe ground that the primordial nature of parenting can be intuited.

Searching Idiomatic Phrases

It is sometimes surprising how didactic language itself is if we allow ourselves to be attentive to even the most common of expressions associated with the phenomenon we wish to pursue. The reason is that idiomatic phrases largely proceed phenomenologically: they are born out of lived experience. For example, we say, "every child needs a home." In the concept of home or dwelling, there is a strong sense of watching over something, preserving a space in which the human being can feel sheltered, protected, and what is thus preserved in the idea of a house with its wall and fences is a safekeeping, holding, or bearing of something that needs to be watched over. This caring modality of parenting, this nurturing, sheltering, and providing protective ground for the child is not something theoretical that needs to be proven or tested as our response to the child's experiences of fear and being afraid. Rather, it is something primordial which defies literal language and precise definition.

Ordinary language is in some sense a huge reservoir in which the incredible variety of richness of human experience is deposited. The problem often is that these deposits have silted, crusted, or fossilized in such a way that the original contact with our primordial experiences is broken. For example, of the reading experience we say of someone that she is "lost in a book." But what does this expression reveal? Is the reader truly lost? While absorbed in a book a reader may lose her sense of time, place, body, etc. Who has not had the experience of showing up late for supper, an appointment, or missing a bus stop because of being lost in a book? But in another sense, the reader who is lost in a story is not lost at all. We may be temporarily "absorbed" in a different world from that of the one who made the remark, but the reader lacks nothing, misses nothing, needs nothing; that is why the reading experience is so absorbing. The person who is much more nearly lost is the person who made the remark. Indeed, when someone says of his companion that she is lost in a book, then *he* is the one who experiences a loss, namely the attentive presence of his companion. The expression "she is absorbed in a book" can show us more clues of the nature of the reading experience. It raises the question of the meaning of the sense of spatiality that belongs to the text. What is the nature of reading space? And how is the experience of this space related to the experience of the space where we see the reader sitting while submerged in the book? What is it about a space that makes it a good place to read? And what is the nature of the time experience and the experience of one's body in those different dimensions? Similarly, with respect to the phenomenon of parenting, what other expression might provide helpful occasions for phenomenological reflection on the lived experiences from which the expressions derive their meaning? This search of etymological sources can be an important (but often neglected) aspect of phenomenological "data collecting."

We say "like mother, like daughter" or "like father, like son." What could be the experiential significance of this phrase? The word mother is associated with a variety of expressions: "mother earth," "mother language," "mother tongue," etc. We speak of "fatherland," "fore-fathers," etc. And the word "parenting" is often used to connote "creating," "originating," "begetting," "to be the source of something."

The point is not that one blindly collects a multitude of linguistic items associated in some way with the phenomenon, but that one reflectively holds on to the verbal manifestations that appear to possess interpretive significance for the actual phenomenological description. For idiomatic language (as well as the language of writers and poets) is an inexhaustible source for phenomenological analysis.

Obtaining Experiential Descriptions from Others

In phenomenological research the emphasis is always on the meaning of lived experience. The point of phenomenological research is to "borrow" other people's experiences and their reflections on their experiences in order to better be able to come to an understanding of the deeper meaning or significance of an aspect of human experience, in the context of the whole of human experience. So in the phenomenological investigation of the experience of parenting, we wish to understand what being a parent is like for this or that person as an aspect of his or her life and, therefore, by extension, as an aspect of the possibilities of our being human.

But why do we need to collect the "data" of *other* people's experiences? *We gather other people's experiences because they allow us to become more experienced ourselves.* We are interested in the particular experiences of this child, this adolescent, or this adult since they allow us to become "in-formed," shaped or enriched by this experience so as to be able to render the full significance of its meaning. Traditionally, techniques used to obtain "data" from "subjects" are by way of interviewing, eliciting written responses, participant observation, and so forth. Phenomenological research may proceed along similar lines, but with some important qualifications. From a phenomenological point of view we are not primarily interested in the subjective experiences of our so-called subjects or informants, for the sake of being able to report on how something is seen from their particular view, perspective, or vantage point. Of course, we may want to know what mothering or fathering is like from the viewpoint of the single parent, or the bereaved parent, or from the perspective of working-class parents or more well-to-do parents who employ nannies or babysitters, and so forth. However, the deeper goal, which is always the thrust of phenomenological research, remains oriented to asking the question of what is the nature of this phenomenon (parenting) as an essentially human experience. To bring the difference between phenomenology and other so-called qualitative research approaches (such as ethnography, ethnomethodology, symbolic interactionism, conceptual analysis, biography, etc.) better into focus, we should recognize the force of the essential phenomenological question. No matter how any particular parent (or group of parents) relates to a child, we always want to know: How is this parenting? Is this what it is like to parent? Is this what it means to be a mother or father? Similarly, when we teach reading to young people, we ask: How is this reading? And teaching? Is this what it means to read? Is this what the reading experience is like?

For the sake of discussing the various methodological aspects of phenomenological human science research, a distinction is made in this chapter and in the next chapter between "gathering" experiential material and "analyzing" this material. However, as with all aspects of the research process, these two acts are not really separable and they should be seen as part of the same process. For example, depending on the nature of the project and the stage of the inquiry process, the conversational interview method may serve either to mainly *gather* lived-experience material (stories, anecdotes, recollections of experiences, etc.) or serve as an occasion to *reflect* with the partner (interviewee) of the conversational relation on the topic at hand. In the latter case the conversational interview turns increasingly into a hermeneutic interview as the researcher can go back and again to the interviewee in order to dialogue with the interviewee about the ongoing record of the interview transcripts. The hermeneutic interview tends to turn the interviewees into participants or collaborators of the research project. Of course, the *gathering of* and *reflecting on* lived-experience material by means of conversational interviewing may be two different stages in a single research project. It may be helpful to keep these two different functions of the interview in mind.

Protocol Writing (lived-experience descriptions)

The "data" of human science research are human experiences. It seems natural, therefore, that if we wish to investigate the nature of a certain experience or phenomenon, the most straightforward way to go about our research is to ask selected individuals to write their experiences down. The term "protocol" derives from the Greek, referring quite appropriately to the original draft (the first sheet of a papyrus roll bearing the original date of manufacture). Protocol writing is the generating of original texts on which the researcher can work. Before we embark on this route, however, we need to prepare ourselves and consider several potential difficulties. The first obvious consideration is the task of writing itself. Most people find writing difficult. They will talk with much more ease and eloquence and with much less reserve than they will write their thoughts on paper. And unless a person has a fair amount of experience or education they may not be able to produce much text on paper for us. Especially with young children this is a handicap. Often educational researchers like to ask children to write about their experiences or to keep a log or diary, and they end up being somewhat disappointed with the material they were able to generate from children in this way. Writing forces the person into a reflective attitude—in contrast to face-to-face conversation in which people are much more immediately involved. This reflective attitude together with the linguistic demands of the writing process place certain constraints on the free obtaining of lived-experience descriptions.

Before we ask others to furnish us with a lived-experience description about a phenomenon that we wish to examine, we might do well to try such descriptions ourselves first, so that we have a more precise sense of what we are attempting to obtain. For purpose of exercise it is best to start with a personal description rather than a description which involves a more complex social event. For example, we may start with a body or space experience such as the experience of "being sick in bed," "going for a swim," or "a favourite childhood play-space." Sometimes the research question is concerned with the human significance of an object, such as "the child's toy," "the playground," or "the secret place." But even here we need to be aware that the human science question always is concerned with the *experience* of the toy, the *experience* of the playground, the *experience* of the secret place in the life of the child (e.g., see Langeveld, 1983a, 1983b). Here are some suggestions for producing a lived-experience description:

(1) You need to describe the experience as you live(d) through it. Avoid as much as possible causal explanations, generalizations, or abstract interpretations. For example, it does not help to state what *caused* your illness, *why* you like swimming so much, or why you feel that children *tend to* like to play outdoors more than indoors.

(2) Describe the experience from the inside, as it were; almost like a state of mind: the feelings, the mood, the emotions, etc.

(3) Focus on a particular example or incident of the object of experience: describe specific events, an adventure, a happening, a particular experience.

(4) Try to focus on an example of the experience which stands out for its vividness, or as it was the first time.

(5) Attend to how the body feels, how things smell(ed), how they sound(ed), etc.

(6) Avoid trying to beautify your account with fancy phrases or flowery terminology.

It is important to realize that it is not of great concern whether a certain experience actually happened in exactly that way. We are less concerned with the factual accuracy of an account than with the plausibility of an account—whether it is true to our living sense of it. Once we know what a lived-experience description looks like, we can go about obtaining such descriptions of individuals who have the experiences that we wish to study. To gain access to other people's experiences, we request them to write about a personal experience. We ask: *Please write a direct account of a personal experience as you lived through it.*

We may want to give additional suggestions depending on the object of study. Here is an example of a lived-experience description, provided by a mother, of the daily experience of mothering:

> Lately I have been wondering if I expect too much of my son. He gets all mixed up in his homework, is overtired, can't think straight, and spends hours doing one straightforward assignment when he should just be relaxing and enjoying family life like all the other kids in his class; he has misread the instructions and has to do the whole thing again; he has a thousand ideas for a report on gorillas, but can't seem to get it together to write even the opening sentence. So yesterday I looked at Robbie's cumulative-file at school. I felt guilty in a way, resorting to that, especially since those numbers have so little to say about a person. And my love and hopes for him are unconditional of course, they don't depend on his achievement or IQ scores. But the numbers weren't supposed to tell me whether Rob is special or not — they were supposed to tell me what to do: whether it is alright for me to tease, prod and cajole him about his homework, and say, "Hey, you lazy schmuck, get some of this work finished in school instead of fooling around," or maybe, "Of course you can't think straight when you're so tired. You'll have to get home earlier and do this homework before supper."

From the example above we can learn many things. We will consider analyzing or interpreting written protocols in the next chapter. At this point it may be worthwhile to be reminded that all writing tends to instill into the writer a certain reflectivity. This may be a problem when we ask individuals to write down an experience *as he or she lived through it*. And so, the researcher needs to be attuned to the tendency of subjects to include explanations and interpretations with their descriptions of lived experiences.

Interviewing (the personal life story)

In the various strands and disciplines in the social and human sciences the interview may serve very different purposes: to study ways of doing and seeing things peculiar to certain cultures or cultural groups (ethnography); to study the way individuals see themselves and others in certain situations (psychological perception); to study the way people feel about certain issues (social opinion); etc. These different functions of interview method in qualitative research are not to be confused with the function of conversational interviewing as we discuss it in this text.

In hermeneutic phenomenological human science the interview serves very specific purposes: (1) it may be used as a means for exploring and gathering experiential narrative material that may serve as a resource for developing a richer and deeper understanding of a human phenomenon, and (2) the interview may be used as a vehicle to develop a conversational relation with a partner (interviewee) about the meaning of an experience. This second function will be discussed in the next section.

In both uses of the conversational interview it is important to realize that the interview process needs to be disciplined by the fundamental question that prompted the need for the interview in the first place. Too often a beginning researcher enthusiastically goes about "interviewing subjects" using the so-called "unstructured or open-ended interview method" without first carefully considering what interest the interview is to serve. One needs to guard against the temptation to let method rule the question, rather than the research question determining what kind of method is most appropriate for its immanent direction.

Sometimes it happens that a researcher is confused about his or her real interest or research question, and then the interview is somehow expected to bring about that clarity. Usually this is idle hope. Either one may end up with material that consists of lots of short (too short) responses to long-winded or leading questions by the researcher, or the researcher may gain an unmanageable quantity of tapes or transcripts. Interview material that is skimpy and that lacks sufficient concreteness in the form of stories, anecdotes, examples of experiences, etc., may be quite useless, tempting the researcher to indulge in over-interpretations, speculations, or an over-reliance on personal opinions and personal experiences. In contrast, an over-abundance of poorly managed interviews may lead either to total despair and confusion (what do I do now? what method can I use for analyzing all these hundreds of transcript pages?), or to a chaotic quest for meaning (there's so much here! what do I include? exclude?). The important lesson is that one does not want to get in this kind of predicament in the first place. Thus, before embarking on a busy interview schedule one needs to be oriented to one's question or notion in such a strong manner that one does not get easily carried away with interviews that go everywhere and nowhere.

So another way of collecting accounts of personal experiences is to have taped (or otherwise recorded) conversations with people who might tell us *personal life stories* (anecdotes, stories, experiences, incidents, etc.). As it was noted above, sometimes it is easier to talk than to write about a personal experience, because writing forces the person into a more reflective attitude, which may make it more difficult to stay close to an experience as it is immediately lived. As we interview others about their experience of a certain phenomenon, it is imperative to stay close to experience as lived. As we ask what an experience is like, it may be helpful to be very concrete. Ask the person to think of a specific instance, situation, person, or event. Then explore the whole experience to the fullest. Naturally, it is impossible to offer ready-made questions. For example, if we were to interview women about the process of becoming mothers, we may wish to begin at the very beginning, examining the way that children entered their lives.

"How did the idea of having children first arise?"
"How did you *decide* on having children?"
"Was it a real planning kind of decision?"
"Did you always assume that you would have children some day?"
"How did you talk about it with your husband?"
"Who said what?"
"How did you feel about that?"
"You say that you caught yourself looking at children differently?"

"In what way?"

"Can you give an example?"

"What was it like to discover that you were pregnant?"

"How did you become aware of it?"

"What did it feel like?"

"What was it like to meet or tell others?"

"How did you announce it to your spouse, etc.?"

Often it is not necessary to ask so many questions. Patience or silence may be a more tactful way of prompting the other to gather recollections and proceed with a story. And if there seems to be a block, then it is often enough to repeat the last sentence or thought in a questioning sort of tone and thus trigger the other to continue. "So you say that people began to look at your stomach instead of your face . . .?" And whenever it seems that the person being interviewed begins to generalize about the experience, you can insert a question that turns the discourse back to the level of concrete experience: "Can you give an example?" "What was it like?" etc.

Observing (the experiential anecdote)

A third way of collecting experiential material from others is the more indirect method of *close observation*. For example, with young children, it is often difficult to generate written descriptions or to engage in conversational interviewing. So to gain access to the experience of young children, it may be important to play with them, talk with them, puppeteer, paint, draw, follow them into their play spaces and into the things they do while you remain attentively aware of the way it is for children. Naturally it is not only in situations with young children that close observation may be the preferred approach. "Close observation," in the way that this term is used here, generates different forms of experiential material than we tend to get with the written or the interview approach. Perhaps the most interesting type of material is the "anecdote" which is discussed below and in subsequent chapters.

"Close observation" is exactly what the phrase suggests. In contrast to the more experimental or behavioral observational research techniques, close observation tries to break through the distance often created by observational methods. Rather than observing subjects through one-way windows, or by means of observational schemata and checklists that function symbolically not unlike one-way mirrors, the human science researcher tries to enter the lifeworld of the persons whose experiences are relevant study material for his or her research project. The best way to enter a person's lifeworld is to participate in it. However, as soon as this is said we should be cautious of a too simplistic interpretation of close observation as a variation of participant observation. Close observation involves an attitude of assuming a relation that is as close as possible while retaining a hermeneutic alertness to situations that allows us to constantly step back and reflect on the meaning of those situations. It is similar to the attitude of the author who is always on the look-out for stories to tell, incidents to remember. The method of close observation requires that one be a participant and an observer at the same time, that one maintain a certain orientation of reflectivity while guarding against the more manipulative and artificial attitude that a reflective attitude tends to insert in a social situation and relation.

The researcher who is involved in closely observing situations for their lived meaning is a gatherer of anecdotes. (And, of course, personal experience and the interview are also sources for anecdotes.) What is important in collecting anecdotes is that one develops a keen sense of the *point* or *cogency* that the anecdote carries within itself. Without this *point* an anecdote is merely loose sand in a hand that disperses upon gathering it. In collecting written descriptions and conversational interviews (transcripts) one looks for the emerging themes *after* one has gathered the material; in collecting anecdotes one has to recognize what parts of the "text" of daily living are significant for one's study *while* it is happening. Sometimes the best anecdotes are *re*-collected as one tries to make sense of things that somehow seem interesting now, in hindsight. Such recollections occasionally makes it difficult to remember what precisely was being said or what exactly happened that made a situation stand out. And yet it is important to try to recover those living phrases and incidents that give the anecdote a *cogent* power or *point*. Therefore it may be necessary to go back to retrieve the relevant "trivia" that help to construct the anecdote.

In gathering anecdotes, one needs to be quite rigorous and construct accounts that are trimmed of all extraneous, possibly interesting but irrelevant aspects of the stories. An anecdote is a certain kind of narrative with a point, and it is this point that needs honing (see the chapter, "Hermeneutic Phenomenological Writing," pp. 111-133).

Experiential Descriptions in Literature

Literature, poetry, or other story forms serve as a fountain of experiences to which the phenomenologist may turn to increase practical insights. The phenomenological value of a novel, for example, is determined by what may be called the perceptiveness and the intuitive sensitivity of the author. Phenomena such as love, grief, illness, faith, success, fear, death, hope, struggle, or loss are the stuff of which novels are made. The titles of some celebrated works, such as *Crime and Punishment* (Dostoevsky), *Nausea* (Sartre), *The Trial* (Kafka), *Remembrance of Things Past* (Proust), announce fundamental life experiences which are available to our interpretive reading. In reading Sartre's *Nausea*, we cannot help but feel invaded by the same mood which inhabits Roquentin. And so as readers we find the experience of everyday life irresistibly shifted to the world of the novel where such fundamental life experiences are lived through vicariously. As we identify ourselves with the protagonist of a story, *we* live his or her feelings and actions without having to act ourselves. Thus we may be able to experience life situations, events, and emotions that we would normally not have. Through a good novel, then, we are given the chance of living through an experience that provides us with the opportunity of gaining insight into certain aspects of the human condition. Put in more general terms, the significance of story for human science is that:

(1) story provides us with *possible human experiences*;

(2) story enables us to experience life situations, feelings, emotions, and events *that we would not normally experience*;

(3) story allows us to broaden the horizons of our normal existential landscape by creating *possible worlds*;

(4) story tends to appeal to us and involve us *in a personal way*;

(5) story is an artistic device that lets us turn back to *life as lived*, whether fictional or real;

(6) story evokes the quality of vividness in *detailing unique and particular aspects of a life* that could be my life or your life;

(7) and yet, great novels or stories *transcend the particularity of their plots* and protagonists, etc., which makes them subject to thematic analysis and criticism.

Poetry too is a literary form that transforms lived experience into poetic language, the poetic language of verse. Poetry allows the expression of the most intense feelings in the most intense form. For this reason we encounter the frequent use of lines from poetic texts in hermeneutic or phenomenological writing. A poet can sometimes give linguistic expression to some aspect of human experience that cannot be paraphrased without losing a sense of the vivid truthfulness that the lines of the poem are somehow able to communicate.

Biography as a Resource for Experiential Material

Biographies, autobiographies, personal life histories are all potential sources for experiential material. It is important to note, however, that the intent of biographic interests is usually the private, personal and unique events of individual lives: bio-graphy literally means "description of a life." We usually read (auto)biographies because we are interested in the unique life history of a famous person, a favorite musician, or a public figure of some sort. Often that interest does not extend beyond a desire to simply want to know more about the life of this person, when one is an ardent admirer or fan of a certain politician, musician, composer, scholar, painter, author or poet. Sometimes we are interested in someone's biography because we hope to cull clues about certain aspects of the meaning of this person's work that fascinates us. We hope that getting to know details about a poet's childhood, upbringing, friendships, and other life circumstances may help us to better interpret his or her poems. We may wonder: How did this person get that way? And what private thoughts may this biography or diary reveal about his or her inner life? How can we better understand the life decisions and choices this person made? Moreover, biographies provide us with details concerning specific dates, places, and events of people's lives, and these details may reveal patterns that are of interest to someone who wants to (re)construct an historical or genealogical account of the development of certain forms or trends of poetry, music, political phenomena, or scholarly subjects. Between close friends there is usually a certain amount of autobiographic sharing of one's life history. We like to be understood by our friend and by understanding more of each other's biographies we also feel closer united. This desire in the sharing of biographic details of our lives is felt even more strongly between lovers.

Educators always have had a special biographic interest in the educational lives of individuals. Educators want to gain insights in the lives of particular students in order to understand them or help them. It is important to know where a child "is coming from" (e.g., the home background, or what it is that the child brings to school) in order to understand more sensitively where a child "is" at present, and where he or she seems "to be going." And educators have a professional interest in (auto)biographies because from descriptions of lives of individuals they are able to learn about the nature of educational experiences and individual developments.

However, all the various interests cited above should not be confused with the interest a human science researcher may have in the experiential value of biographic material. It is not unusual for biographic texts to contain rich ore of lived-experience descriptions for phenomenological analysis or for converting into anecdote or story. So, while biography is oriented to individual or private meaning, phenomenology is oriented to existential meaning.

Let us look at an example of autobiographic writing from the book by Phyllis Chesler, *With Child: A Diary of Motherhood* (1979). The following excerpt may be shown to contain some fundamental themes of the nature of mothering (see section entitled "Gleaning Thematic Descriptions from Artistic Sources," pp. 96-97). The text is evocative, to a certain extent transcending the autobiographic style of diary writing.

> Last year I died. My life without you ended. Our life together — only nine months! — ended too: abruptly and forever, when you gave birth to me. Being born into motherhood is the sharpest pain I've ever known. I'm a newborn mother: your age exactly, one year old today.
>
> *I've dropped ten thousand years down an ancient well. My own life threatens to peel off: insignificant, recent. My stomach knots, my nails redden, to break my fall. Screaming. I write this book to chart my descent. To slow my descent. And to thank you for coming. Little ancestor, sweet baby! How you temper me, deepen me, like an ancient smithy working slowly. You — who need everything done for you — are the most powerful teacher I've ever known.*
>
> Last night, lying in a hot, white-foamed tub, I was suddenly pregnant with you again. I wept, aware that you no longer slept beneath my heart.
>
> It was you — Ariel — in there, in me. I didn't know that. Will I grow sad every year in winter, when you leave me to be born? This soft belly, rounded still, with your footprint. Proof of your origin, your passage through. Here, here is where you walked, without setting foot to earth. Your first moon, little astronaut. Because of you, I'll return to Earth, transformed: no longer a virgin, but a mother, married to a child.

Together we have engaged in alchemy.

Know, Ariel: We have always been separate. While I was pregnant. During labor. From the moment you were born. Always I had some sense of your utter separate reality.

And who could be closer than we two? (pp. 281, 282)

In a section below we will attempt to glean some themes from this fragment. But at this point it is worthwhile to note that this diary fragment is not primarily of value to us because we are biographically interested in the life of Chesler. In other words, we are not interested here in the number of children Chesler may now have, where and when she lived, or how many books she wrote in this stage of her life, etc. Rather, we are interested in Chesler's description precisely because it may be examined as an account of the possible experience of other women.

Diaries, Journals, and Logs as Sources of Lived Experiences

Another common interest in the human sciences are diaries, journals, and logs for purposes that are of educational, research, personal growth, religious, or therapeutic value. Keeping a regular diary may help a person to reflect on significant aspects of his or her past and present life. And journal writing may help in setting oneself life-goals to work or to strive for. A workshop in intensive journal writing is used for the purpose of "self-discovery" or for coming to terms with personal problems or issues in one's private life (e.g., Progoff, 1975). And teachers have found that practising diary writing with students may contribute to the learning process as the students are encouraged to continue reflecting on their learning experiences and to try discovering relationships that they might otherwise not see. Researchers, too, have found that keeping a journal, diary or log can be very helpful for keeping a record of insights gained, for discerning patterns of the work in progress, for reflecting on previous reflections, for making the activities of research themselves topics for study, and so forth.

For any of the above mentioned purposes of journal, diary, or log writing, it is likely that such sources may contain reflective accounts of human experiences that are of phenomenological value. For example, *The Confessions* of St. Augustine (1960) contains many journal entries that have contributed to a phenomenological understanding of time by such great phenomenologists as Husserl in his *The Phenomenology of*

Internal Time-Consciousness (1964), Heidegger in his *Being and Time* (1962), and Straus in his *Man, Time, and World* (1982).

Art as a Source of Lived Experience

Although phenomenologists often use literary sources (poetry, novels, stories, plays, etc.) as case material and as textual resources for phenomenological writing, non-discursive artistic material is also commonly used for phenomenological human science. Of course, each artistic medium (painting, sculpture, music, cinematography, etc.) has its own language of expression. Objects of art are visual, tactile, auditory, kinetic texts—texts consisting of not a verbal language but a language nevertheless, and a language with its own grammar. Because artists are involved in giving shape to their lived experience, the products of art are, in a sense, lived experiences transformed into transcended configurations. In a hermeneutic study on the relation between education and culture, Mollenhauer (1983, 1986) shows how a sensitive attending to the portrayal of the interaction between children and adults in historical paintings, medieval woodcuts, etc., yields insights into the emotional and pedagogic quality of the relation between parents and their children that historical studies of childhood have often overlooked. Other examples of the use of fine arts in phenomenological studies are found in Heidegger's use of Van Gogh's painting of "Shoes of the Peasant" in his reflections on truth (1977, pp. 144-187); in Merleau-Ponty's studies of language (1964b, pp. 39-83), etc.

Consulting Phenomenological Literature

We have seen that literature, biography and other artistic sources may provide us with powerful examples of vicarious lived experiences and insights normally out of range of the scope of our personal everyday experiences. Phenomenological literature is of a different kind.

(1) *Phenomenological literature may contain material which has already addressed in a descriptive or an interpretive manner the very topic or question which preoccupies us.* There is a wealth of phenomenologically or hermeneutically oriented journals and texts available to the researcher. Many research questions have in some way been addressed before and it is our responsibility to search for these materials. Naturally, it is not always possible to find sources on certain topics. A researcher who is studying the child's experience of playgrounds may not be able

to find already existing human science studies of this phenomenon. But there are various related studies available of the lived experience of space (e.g., Bollnow, 1960), of neighbourhood play-spaces (e.g., Hart, 1979), of toys (e.g., Langeveld, 1984), all of which may throw certain light on the question of the meaning of playgrounds for children. Or if one is interested in a topic, such as the meaning of "step-fathering," one may not be able to find any phenomenological or hermeneutic studies which have focused on this topic. Therefore one needs to look for related notions (such as "family" or "fathering") in phenomenological sources to find relevant material. Sometimes phenomenological or hermeneutic discussions on certain topics are buried in larger texts. For example, Marcel has written about fatherhood in his *Homo Viator: Introduction to a Metaphysics of Hope* (1978, pp. 98-124). Sometimes phenomenological or hermeneutic studies are available in different language sources to which one may be able to gain indirect access. For example, the Dutch scholar Langeveld wrote about fatherhood in the German language (1971, pp. 211-231). Indeed, both Marcel and Langeveld have written about the process of becoming a father as a kind of affirmation. Langeveld writes of the importance of commitment and active involvement of the father in the child's life, and Marcel writes about the essence of fatherhood as a "creative vow."

(2) *Thus the work of other phenomenologists turns into a source for us with which to dialogue.* In other words, we begin to partake in a tradition. As we develop a *conversational relation* with a certain notion that has captured our interest, we cannot ignore the insights of others who have already maintained a conversational relation with that same phenomenon. Naturally we should not assume that we must uncritically accept or integrate those insights into our frame. Fitting ourselves into a research tradition means that we contribute to this tradition: (a) in gaining a better grasp of the topics to which this tradition has dedicated itself, and (b) in articulating and in experimenting with new methodological approaches that further the human science tradition.

(3) *Selected phenomenological materials enable us to reflect more deeply on the way we tend to make interpretive sense of lived experience.* As we read and study other sources we notice the variety of ways in which human science scholars have developed methodological innovations and personal approaches to research questions and topics. From observing this variety of approaches we should not conclude that human

science research methods are merely idiosyncratic ways of working. On the contrary, it is against the backdrop of an embedded research methodology that we notice an innovative approach, a productive procedure, a certain style, a way with language, a rhetorical manner that characterizes the work of great scholars such as Merleau-Ponty, Heidegger, Marcel, Foucault (in philosophy), and scholars such as Langeveld, van den Berg, Buytendijk, Bollnow (in pedagogy and psychology). This does not mean that we should try to imitate *that* unique procedure, *that* personal style or *that* personal linguistic facility. But attentiveness to the "personal signature" that characterizes the work of human science researchers may help us to develop an approach that brings out our own strength, and not simply serve as unfortunate private indulgence.

(4) *Phenomenological sources allow us to see our limits and to transcend the limits of our interpretive sensibilities.* When we read Langeveld on the child's experience of space (1983a, 1983b), or Buytendijk on the significance of the first smile of the young child (1988), or Bollnow on the meaning of the pedagogical atmosphere between an adult and a child (1970), then we come face to face with texts that challenge and stretch our own descriptive or interpretive sensibilities. Here are thoughtful authors, scholars of pedagogy, who show us how pedagogical human science is done.   Clearly, a human science researcher may benefit from studying how other human science scholars have addressed and brought to text their understandings of selected pedagogical topics. In this way, a phenomenological study of a topic of our interest may suggest different ways of looking at a phenomenon, or reveal dimensions of meaning which we had hitherto not considered. The question is whether one should turn to such phenomenological human science sources in the initial or in the later phases of one's research study. If one examines existing human science texts at the very outset then it may be more difficult to suspend one's interpretive understanding of the phenomenon. It is sound practice to attempt to address the phenomenological meaning of a phenomenon on one's own first. However, sooner or later one must test one's insights against those who belong to the tradition of one's subject of study. And it is then that a researcher becomes aware of as yet unformulated or unsuspected specifications and dimensions of meaning.   In this way the work of others turns into a conversational partnership that reveals the limits and possibilities of one's own interpretive achievements.

CHAPTER 4

Hermeneutic Phenomenological Reflection

The purpose of phenomenological reflection is to try to grasp the essential meaning of something. Phenomenological reflection is both easy and difficult. It is easy because, as Husserl (1980) showed, to see the meaning or essence of a phenomenon is something everyone does constantly in everyday life. For example, when I see my son's teacher I do not just perceive a man or a woman. I see a person who differs from other men and women precisely in that respect which makes me talk of this person as "a teacher." In other words, I, as everybody else, have a notion of what a teacher is. But what is much more difficult is to come to a reflective determination and explication of what a teacher is. This determination and explication of meaning then is the more difficult task of phenomenological reflection. A more famous philosophical example concerns the experience of time. What could be more easily grasped than time? We regulate our lives by time. We carry the time around on our wrist. We divide the day into morning, afternoon, evening and night time. And we reflect on past time and anticipate the time to come. We even talk about the time going by, sometimes fast, and at other times more slowly. And yet when someone asks us "what is time anyway?" we are quickly at our wit's end to describe it. What is it that goes by fast or slowly when we say that the time is elapsing? So there is a difference between our pre-reflective lived understanding of the meaning of time and a our reflective grasp of the phenomenological structure of the lived meaning of time. To get at the latter is a difficult and often laborious task. The insight into the essence of a phenomenon involves a process of reflectively appropriating, of clarifying, and of making explicit the structure of meaning of the lived experience.

Ultimately the project of phenomenological reflection and explication is to effect a more direct contact with the experience as lived. I want to grasp the meaning of teaching, of mothering, of fathering, so that I can live my pedagogic life with children more fully. Therefore, when I reflect on the experience of teaching I do not reflect on it as a professional philosopher, or as a psychologist, as a sociologist, as an ethnographer, or even as a phenomenologist or critical theorist. Rather, *I reflect phenomenologically on experiences of teaching and parenting as a teacher or as a parent. In other words, I attempt to grasp the pedagogical essence of a certain experience.*

The meaning or essence of a phenomenon is never simple or one-dimensional. Meaning is multi-dimensional and multi-layered. That is why the meaning of pedagogy can never be grasped in a single definition. Human science meaning can only be communicated textually—by way of organized narrative or prose. And that is why the human science researcher is engaged in the reflective activity of textual labor. To do human science research is to be involved in the crafting of a text. In order to come to grips with the structure of meaning of the text it is helpful to think of the phenomenon described in the text as approachable in terms of meaning units, structures of meaning, or themes. Reflecting on lived experience then becomes reflectively analyzing the structural or thematic aspects of that experience.

Conducting Thematic Analysis

The notion of theme is used in various disciplines in the humanities, art, and literary criticism. In literature, "theme" refers to an element (motif, formula or device) which occurs frequently in the text. The term "theme" is often applied to some thesis, doctrine or message that a creative work has been designed to incorporate. "Theme analysis" refers then to the process of recovering the theme or themes that are embodied and dramatized in the evolving meanings and imagery of the work.

In human science research the notion of theme may best be understood by examining its methodological and philosophical character. Too often theme analysis is understood as an unambiguous and fairly mechanical application of some frequency count or coding of selected terms in transcripts or texts, or some other break-down of the content of protocol or documentary material. On the basis of these applications there are now computer programs available that claim to do the theme analysis for the researcher. Let us examine, therefore, what meaning the idea of theme has for phenomenological description and interpretation in the human sciences. As we are able to articulate the notion of theme we are also able to clarify further the nature of human science research. Making something of a text or of a lived experience by interpreting its meaning is more accurately a process of insightful invention, discovery or disclosure—grasping and formulating a thematic understanding is not a rule-bound process but a free act of "seeing" meaning. Ultimately the concept of theme is rather irrelevant and may be considered simply as a means to get at the notion we are addressing. Theme gives control and order to our research and writing.

Human science research is concerned with meaning—to be human is to be concerned with meaning, to desire meaning. When we have just seen a compelling movie, when we have recently finished an intriguing novel, when we have observed a behavior in a child that strikes us in a puzzling way, then we experience this "desire to make sense," "desire to make meaning." Desire is not just a psychological state; it is a state of being. Desire refers to a certain attentiveness and deep interest in an aspect of life. Originally the term "desire" meant "to expect from the stars." Without desire there is no real motivated question. As in the case of a love I desire, it makes me go back time and again to seek its meaning.

Phenomenological themes may be understood as the *structures of experience*. So when we analyze a phenomenon, we are trying to determine what the themes are, the experiential structures that make up that experience. It would be simplistic, however, to think of themes as conceptual formulations or categorical statements. After all, it is lived experience that we are attempting to describe, and lived experience cannot be captured in conceptual abstractions. Let us illustrate the determination of phenomenological meaning at the hand of an everyday life concern. It may help clarify the methodological significance of the idea of "theme" in reflecting on concrete situations: children, our lives with children, prompt us to ask increasingly reflective questions. The question, "Did I do that right?" forces us to come to terms with the *particular* (this child, this situation, this action) under the guidance of our understanding of the *universal* (what is the meaning of pedagogy—parenting, teaching—in this?).

A common incident in the lives of parents with children is the child's experience of "feeling left or abandoned" when the parent(s) needs to be away for a longer or shorter period. This feeling of being left is especially common with young children. What does a parent do with such situations? It depends on how the parent understands the child's experience of feeling left or abandoned. What follows are descriptions of several situations which will be treated as concrete occasions for examining the nature and role of meaningful themes in human science research and writing.

Situations

Jeff:

Six-year-old Jeff complains that his parents go out too often on holidays by themselves, leaving him and his sister with a nanny at home. "I don't like you leaving us," says Jeff. The parents explain that they are both hardworking professionals who need to get away every now and then from their busy lives of work and children. "Don't be selfish, Jeff," they say, "You are in good hands and we will only be gone for twelve days. If you behave yourselves, who knows, we may bring back a present for you." Certainly parents deserve a break from their normal duties and obligations. But as they fly away to their vacation destination they may wonder: "How do the children feel now?" "Is there anything wrong with leaving them?" "How do other parents handle this kind of situation?" "Surely the children will be all right." To be sure, all children are left sometimes. And children react differently in such situations.

Patty:

A father takes his little girl, Patty, to day-care where Patty spends between seven and eight hours a day. The father mentions that he has noticed how Patty, when she is being picked up to go home, is a very different child from the one described to him at the day-care. There Patty is well-behaved, malleable, obedient, apparently happy, and easy to handle for the day-care workers. However, as soon as the child gets in her father's or mother's car she starts to complain, becomes recalcitrant, does the opposite of what is expected of her, acts loving one moment and hostile the next. After an hour or so her mood evens out and she becomes more cooperative. The parents have different opinions about the meaning of Patty's behavior. One thinks that the child is so tired after spending all that energy at day-care that she becomes irritable in the late afternoon. "As soon as she has some food in her stomach she usually seems to lose her crankiness." The other parent thinks that Patty needs her mother or father to act out the accumulated frustrations from the day spent in the day-care institution. They may both be correct. The situation may be more complex as well—Patty's behavior may have something to do with the daily experience of being left in a place where you cannot be yourself since there is nobody for whom you really are a "self," a unique and very special person: the difference between a parent and a teacher (or day-care worker) is that for a parent this child is *the* most special person whereas a teacher needs to treat all children as special. It has often been said that every child needs at least one person by whom it is unconditionally loved—someone who is unconditionally there for the child. A teacher usually cannot be that person.

David:

To some people David may seem somewhat overly anxious about being left. When his parents go to a movie and leave the seven-year-old David and his five-year-old brother Tommy at home with a babysitter, he asks them: "Where are you going?" "When will you be back?" "Not later than 9:30?" "Will you phone if it is going to be later?" Then David gives his parents a nice hug and a kiss. "Have fun!" he says. But his body communicates a different message. And even when the parents walk out to their car David will open the door once more and shout: "Come straight back home, okay?" His parents assure him several times but otherwise they do not make much out of David's behavior. They know that this is the way David *is*, while his brother meanwhile hardly takes notice that his parents are leaving.

Julie:

When the father takes the kids to school in the morning, Tommy rushes off into the playground while Julie always gives a goodbye kiss and quickly quizzes, "Are you going to work at home this morning? Or do you go to the office?" Her father knows that Julie feels better when she knows where her parents are while she is at school. Julie likes it best when her father or mother are home—even when she herself is at school, or playing at the park or at a friend's house. What is Julie's problem? Does she have a problem? A psychologist might consider her behavior a manifestation of developmental insecurity or the result of too much dependence on her parents. But for anyone who knows Julie she is a normal sensitive child with a healthy sense of adventure and self-confidence. Most parents know how almost from birth onwards, children in their desire to become independent are practising to leave the parent and the safe home. Julie too strikes out on her own to play in the park a few blocks away or to visit friends in the neighbourhood. But it seems that the risk of leaving has to be taken on Julie's own terms. She wants to be in control. And, as Julie says, she does not "feel good" when she knows that her parents "are not within her reach." This is what a home means to a child: a safe center from where she can explore the world.

Hansel and Gretel:

Stories of children being left behind abound in the literature. *Hansel and Gretel* is often cited as the classic child's nightmare of the parents' ultimate betrayal: to leave their children in the wilderness to fend for themselves. Not the mother but the unfeeling stepmother and the dominated and weak father leave the children abandoned in the forest. Bettelheim (1975, pp. 159-166) sees in this fairy tale something positive: the symbolism of a reality requirement, the child's need to break his or her dependency on the parent. And of course it is true that children have to learn to face the world by themselves. But, for whatever other relevant insights he provides, what Bettelheim does not see is that it is not the parent who should abandon the child but the child who should leave the parent.

Danny:

Kim, a graduate student, herself a mother of a young child, visits regularly a local day-care centre where she plays with a mentally handicapped child in order to learn how better to understand the child's lifeworld. The child has become very fond of her. But one thing puzzles Kim: whenever she has to leave and whenever she says goodbye to Danny, he merely gestures or simply turns away. He never shows regret, he never asks her to stay or to come back. And Kim confesses that she has even felt a little hurt about this. Does Danny not care that she leaves him? One possible interpretation is that Danny's day-care, in which he spends about ten of his daily waking hours, is not experienced by him as a true home; one cannot feel "left" in a place where one is already left to begin with.

James James Morrison:

In Milne's poem *Disobedience* (1979, pp. 32-35) the child is afraid that the mother who leaves to "go down to the end of town" without him will never return. And this, so the poem goes, is what actually happens: "James James Morrison's mother hasn't been heard of since." Here we have a child's nightmare made real in what we must admit (with apologies to Milne) is really a capricious child's verse. Just as a child knows that he or she may lose his or her way when wandering too far from home so, the child fears, a parent can get lost or have an accident and never return from that big world out there.

Boy:

The Dutch novelist Anna Blaman (1963) once wrote a haunting short story of a boy who is left home to go to sleep upstairs in his bedroom while his parents go out for a walk. However, soon after the parents have left, the house gradually begins to lose its trusted atmosphere. Otherwise familiar sounds originating from inside and outside of the house seem to gather danger. The darkness of the bedroom and the hallway at the top of the stairs seem to conceal a sense of some perilous presence. As the boy desperately battles his fears he distinctly becomes aware of an approaching presence downstairs in the house. In a panic he gets out of bed and watches in a dizzying whirl from the top of the stairs how the front door of the house suddenly swings open. There is a scrambling move and the young boy tumbles down the stairs. In a stir he sees his parents enter the door: Safe at last! But when he comes to rest at the bottom of the stairs he is dead. A theme in Blaman's story is that a home may fundamentally change its safe and trusted character when the parents no longer fill its space with their presence. Feeling left can have far-reaching consequences in a child's life.

Girl:

In Francois Truffaut's cinematographic study of children's lives, *Small Change* (1976/81), there is a scene in which the parents, irritated with their eleven-year-old daughter's determination to take her "ugly" purse along to the Sunday brunch, tell her to leave the purse at home. Otherwise she will have to stay home, and the parents will leave without her. The little girl persists in her resolve to take the purse and the parents, annoyed, depart without her, leaving her alone in the apartment. But soon the girl is able to draw, from her balcony, the attention of all the neighbours living in the apartments around her. Before long everyone pulls together and a food basket, abundantly filled, is ingeniously hoisted with much fanfare through her third-story window. Sweet revenge speaks from the face of the little girl. Her Sunday morning brunch has turned a lot more exciting than a meal in the local restaurant would have been. "They all looked at me," she finally says to herself, "They all looked at me!" Of course, the message Truffaut wants to give his viewers is that this child, who was not really being "seen" by her own father and mother, now acted out of the need to be acknowledged in her own being while feeling part of the lives of others.

Buber:

In his "Autobiographical Fragments" Martin Buber (1970) recalls an incident from his earliest memory, going back to the time when he was four years old. The year previously his parents had divorced and his mother had left. But, says Buber, although no one ever talked about it with him, "the child himself expected to see his mother return soon." Then one day, when he was four, an older neighbour girl said something that now forms his earliest memory. They were standing on the balcony of the house of Buber's grandparents: "We both stood near the banister. I cannot remember whether I had spoken about my mother to my older playmate. At any rate, I can still hear how this older girl said to me: 'No, she will never come back.' I know that I kept silent but also that I no longer doubted the truth of her words. It stayed with me and each year it affixed itself more deeply to my heart. But already after about ten years I began to feel that it was something that did not only concern me but all people" (Buber, 1970, p. 88). As Buber reminisces about this incident he uses the word "misencounter" to describe the missed and inauthentic relationship that he now feels was at the core of his experience of his mother who had left him and the girl who uttered those fatal words. When Buber, much later in life (he was married and had a family), finally meets his mother he says, "I could not look into her still wonderfully beautiful eyes without hearing coming from somewhere this word *misencounter* as a word that was spoken to me." And he adds: "I suspect that all real encounters that I have experienced in the course of my life, find their origin in that moment on the balcony" (Buber, 1970, p. 88). Martin Buber grew up as a Jewish boy in the middle-class comfort of the care of his father, his grandmother and his grandfather, each of whom contributed significantly to his education and growth. It is pedagogically fascinating, however, that the central significance which his earliest memorable experience occupies, is his sense-making of his mother's leaving of him as a very young child.

Ruth:

For a child, a home may not be experienced as a home when the child feels left behind. Then a home is merely a house. And this is the way it for the young girl, Ruth, in Robinson's novel, *Housekeeping* (1980). What can "housekeeping" mean when the only parent, the mother, has abandoned the children in suicide? That is a question and a theme which the book raises. For Ruth life becomes one long endless waiting. When reflecting on her unusual sense of identity she muses: "it was when my mother left me waiting for her, and established in me the habit of waiting and expectation which makes any present moment most significant for what it does not contain" (Robinson, 1980, p. 214). Ruth considers other explanations that might account for her unsettled existential sense of life; but then she returns to the theme of being left: "Then there is the matter of my mother's abandonment of me. Again, this is the common experience. They walk ahead of us, and walk too fast, and forget us, they are so lost in thoughts of their own, and soon or late they disappear. The only mystery is that we expect it to be otherwise" (p. 215). A child who feels abandoned by the parent may never receive the meaning of inner rest—of being guarded by the existence of a center, a safe haven. And so *Housekeeping* turns into an endless wait, a lifelong longing for a mother, a home. Intuitively, most of us know this: that the small child's feeling of abandonment is deeply unsettling and consequential for the child's view of life.

Sophie's child:

In *Sophie's Choice* (Styron, 1980) there is this deep terror: a mother is forced by a soldier to choose which one of her two children to leave behind as she boards a train to safety from an uncertain fate in the Nazi concentration camp. What made Sophie's "choice" so terrible is that a parent knows the impossibility of such choice, which can only be experienced as betrayal by the child. So, the child's nightmare of being left behind is also the parent's terror of grief and guilt which can never be extinguished.

In everyday life the experience of feeling left is often less dramatic than some of the examples described above. But from the child's point of view even "normal" incidents, such as the parents leaving the child in someone else's care while going on a vacation, can acquire the significance of a big drama for the child. A mother recently told me how her five-year-old daughter had acted rather revengefully, or unusually spitefully, upon the mother's return from a ten-day trip abroad. "She didn't talk to me for about three days. Completely ignored me!" It silently occurred to me, with some surprise, that I had read about a similar reaction of a child in John Bowlby's now classic study (1978).

Seeking Meaning

As we examine the above situations taken from real life and from fictional experience, the way to bring the examples to reflective understanding is to fix them in some way. The situations were all gathered around the notion of the child's experience of "being left." But now we need to see how these examples may open up a deepened and more reflective understanding of the notion of "feeling left." In other words, we try to unearth something "telling," something "meaningful," something "thematic" in the various experiential accounts—we work at mining meaning from them. Even as the various situations were selected, different thematic meanings seemed to emerge. I read over the examples and wonder, what is going on here? What is this example an example of? What is the essence or *eidos* of the notion of "being left" and how can I capture this *eidos* by way of thematic reflection on the notion? As I examine the situations I try some thematic formulations:

Jeff—A child's experiences of being left is different from the adult's experience in leaving the child.

Patty—A child who has been left may not experience self in a full and unique manner.

David—Being left is the experience of vulnerability, insecurity, incompleteness.

Julie—Knowing where the parents are provides the child with a sense of control, the security of a home base, being able to reach.

Hansel and Gretel—A child wants to leave the parents (become independent of the parents) but the child does not want to be left behind by the parents.

Danny— A child can only feel left from the basis of a relation or situation of at homeness or belonging.

James James Morrison—A parent who leaves a child to do some business in the big wide world may be feared never to return.

Boy—When the parents leave a child at home, the home may change its trusted character or atmosphere.

Girl—A child who is not really "seen" by his or her parent is already in some sense "left".

Buber—The early memory of feeling left may have profound consequences for one's later vocation in life.

Ruth—An adult who was abandoned as a child may experience life as an endless waiting for something profoundly absent.

Sophie's child—Being left can be experienced as a form of betrayal.

There are many themes here. And they all seem to say something significant about the notion of "abandonment" or "feeling left." And yet, undoubtedly, the above group of themes is not exhaustive of the full meaning of the notion of "feeling left."

I have constructed a list of themes, but for the present my question again is: what is this notion of "theme" that seemed to have helped me to get a better fix on the significance of the situations? I need to put the idea of "theme" in its own thematic context. What is the experience of theme in the process of phenomenological reflection? Here I offer some theme-like statements about themes. They seem to answer the question: What is a theme? How does theme relate to the phenomenon that a researcher is interested in studying (like the notion of "feeling left")?

What Is a Theme?

(1) *Theme is the experience of focus, of meaning, of point.* As I read over an anecdote I ask, what is its meaning, its point?

(2) *Theme formulation is at best a simplification.* We come up with a theme formulation but immediately feel that it somehow falls short, that it is an inadequate summary of the notion.

(3) *Themes are not objects one encounters at certain points or moments in a text.* A theme is not a thing; themes are intransitive.

(4) *Theme is the form of capturing the phenomenon one tries to understand.* Theme describes an aspect of the structure of lived experience.

Articulating themes is not just a skill or a cognitive process that can be described and then learned or trained. But it may still be useful to ask: How do themes come about? The following statements may capture some of the phenomenological qualities of the experience of themes as emerging lived meanings in life:

(1) *Theme is the needfulness or desire to make sense.* As a parent I have the deep need to understand what is the pedagogic significance of the child's experience of feeling left or abandoned.

(2) *Theme is the sense we are able to make of something.* As I try to put into symbolic form (words) what something means to me then I produce theme-like statements.

(3) *Theme is the openness to something.* While I have the experience of fixing something with a theme, I can only do so by opening myself to the fullness, the promise of the notion embedded in lived experience.

(4) *Theme is the process of insightful invention, discovery, disclosure.* As I arrive at certain thematic insights it may seem that insight is a product of all of these: *invention* (my interpretive product), *discovery* (the interpretive product of my dialogue with the text of life), *disclosure of meaning* (the interpretive product "given" to me by the text of life itself).

Next we may wonder how theme relates to the notion that is being studied? In other words, what does the notion of theme have to do with the phenomenon of "feeling left or abandoned?"

(1) *Theme is the means to get at the notion.* The theme is my tool for getting at the meaning of the experience of "feeling left." There is a certain instrumentality, a *techne* to the employment of theme and theme formulation.

(2) *Theme gives shape to the shapeless.* A notion such as the experience of "feeling left" can find expression in an infinite variety of forms—theme fixes or expresses the ineffable *essence* of the notion in a temporary and exemplary form.

(3) *Theme describes the content of the notion.* A good theme formulation somehow seems to touch the core of the notion we are trying to understand.

(4) *Theme is always a reduction of a notion.* No thematic formulation can completely unlock the deep meaning, the full mystery, the enigmatic aspects of the experiential meaning of a notion.

The Pedagogy of Theme

Reflecting on the child's experience of feeling abandoned has become the occasion to reflect on the theme of theme. However, my interest in theme—my fundamental research orientation—is not primarily epistemological or methodological, but pedagogical. Similarly, my interest in the child's experience of feeling left finds its real motivation in my life as educator and parent with children. My child's behavior becomes the topic of my fatherly (pedagogic) reflection. Thus pedagogic reflection is a form of "self-reflectivity." Self-reflection is the manner by which pedagogy tries to come to terms with self (the parent, the educator) and other (the child). In other words, self-reflection is the way in which pedagogy reflects on itself while serving other. "Self" and "other" are fundamental categories of the pedagogic relation. In everyday life the antinomy of self-other may express itself in tensions such as those described in the situational anecdotes on being left. On the one hand, these are the tensions of the parents' needs and desires for their personal interests versus the child's needs for a parent who is unconditionally there. On the other hand, the child is sometimes left "for some good" such as on the first day of school. The experience of loneliness is something every child is to face—whether it be during the first sleep-over, at summer camp, at bedtime in a dream, through the vicarious experience of story, when the parents are out for an errand, and so forth. Some children will sometimes have the experience of feeling left, while others may experience the same moment as adventure, as boredom, etc.

In a deeper sense "self" and "other" are more fundamental categories that constitute the poles of the pedagogic relation and distinguish the pedagogic relation from any other sort of relation that may exist between an adult and a child. "Self" is the sense of pedagogy out of which a parent or teacher acts when he or she acts as a parent or teacher. Pedagogy is that essence, that transformation, that converts woman into mother, man into father (into teacher, into therapist, into grandparent, etc.). At this level belongs the thoughtfulness and the practical tact that knows how to appraise the pedagogic significance of being left for this or that child. Perhaps no child ever ought to have the experience of feeling left. But there is the fact that life is never perfect and we must all battle our personal fears. Some battles are victorious, some leave deep and permanent scars, and others end in irredeemable loss. In the lifestory of *Housekeeping,* Ruth calls her own life of expectation and waiting for her mother "a mystery" (Robinson, 1980). She knows her mother cannot, will never, return. Yet she lives in waiting, in hope. Why? Because the mystery is that in spite of some deep fears, we experience our parents as the solid ground, the home of our existence. A child whose mysterious expectation has been betrayed must learn to deal with a fundamental archetype of human existence: the experience of the vulnerable center, the broken whole, the neglected hearth, the absent Other. Like Ruth, such a child may forever be homeless. And we are not even touching upon the overwhelming tragedy of abandoned street children living in the major cities of the world.

My pedagogic understanding of the theme of "being left" as "the experience of homelessness, brokenness" is that insight that permits me to make sense of the text of life and to be practically responsive, as author, to the text of life. This means also that I cannot just treat the topic of the child's experience of "feeling left" as solely an academic or research issue. I am not *just* a researcher who observes life, I am also a parent and a teacher who stands pedagogically in life. Indeed, is it not odd that educational researchers often seem to need to overlook the children's interests (including their *own* children's interests) in order to pursue their research careers which are supposed to be in the interests of those very children? We may even wonder whether in the final analysis the ability to make sense of life's phenomena does not reside in the *strength* of that fundamental *orientation* that one assumes as theorist and researcher (see chapter 6, "Maintaining a Strong and Oriented Relation," pp . 135-160).

Uncovering Thematic Aspects

We saw above that phenomenological themes are not objects or generalizations; metaphorically speaking they are more like knots in the webs of our experiences, around which certain lived experiences are spun and thus lived through as meaningful wholes. Themes are the stars that make up the universes of meaning we live through. By the light of these themes we can navigate and explore such universes. Themes have phenomenological power when they allow us to proceed with phenomenological descriptions. For example, when we are interested in the phenomenology of reading a novel, we may soon notice some possible themes: (1) When we read a book, *we enter it*, as it were.

(2) Reading a novel means that *we begin to care* for the people who make up the novel. (3) While we read a story *we experience action without having to act.* (4) When we interrupt a book, *we exit the world created by the word*, etc. (See van Manen, 1985.)

These kinds of themes are only fasteners, foci, or threads around which the phenomenological description is facilitated. Let us take the example of parenting again. In what way are the themes of mothering different from the themes of fathering? Or is the experience of mothering and fathering in principle the same phenomenon? An obvious and immediate difference between mothering and fathering is the nature of the initial body-relationship between parent and child. A child is "given" to the mother in a different way than a child is "given" to the father. Is this initial relationship experientially different for the woman than for the man? Marcel (1978) and Langeveld (1987) have suggested that there are experiential consequences to the fact that it is the woman who bears and gives birth to the child (see the section entitled "Consulting Phenomenological Literature," pp. 74-76). A man has initially a less intimate or symbiotic relation to a child. Whereas a man has to acknowledge a child as his, a woman already has the child before she can accept or reject the newcomer. The experience of a new father seems to be such that, in order to become a father, he has to accept, to say "yes" to a child; whereas a woman, already a mother by virtue of bearing and giving birth to the child, can only say "no." A woman who is pregnant is literally embodied—inhabited—by the child, say Langeveld and Marcel, and so she experiences a knowledge of the child which is more symbiotic than the way a man initially knows his child.

The question is now: Is such experiential difference plausible? And if so, how do we capture this experiential difference in a thematic manner? We might say that the possible experience of becoming a father includes the theme of "accepting" or "affirming" the child as his. But how is this experience lived? As noted above, Langeveld (1987) and Marcel (1978) have provided descriptions of this theme. They probably experienced their own fatherhood in this manner. But does every man have to "decide" or "vow" to take up his responsibility as a father by making a "commitment" to a newly born? The experience itself appeared to me as a father much less rational, less deliberate. Does this mean that Langeveld and Marcel were wrong? Not necessarily. But it may mean that Langeveld's "decision" and Marcel's "vow" are forms of commitment that are more complex than these words allow us to comprehend and grasp. The commitment of becoming a father may be something that is much less "made" than encountered. The theme of "commitment" is experientially there when the man takes the child in his arms, and in the gesture of accepting and holding the child, the man finds himself face to face with "responsibility," with something utterly new. This encounter is often a profoundly moving experience— now he is the father of the child. But to *be* a father, he has to continue *acting* as father as well.

The point is that no conceptual formulation or single statement can possibly capture the full mystery of this experience. So a phenomenological theme is much less a singular statement (concept or category such as "decision," "vow" or "commitment") than a fuller description of the structure of a lived experience. As such, a so-called thematic phrase does not do justice to the fullness of the life of a phenomenon. A thematic phrase only serves to point at, to allude to, or to hint at, an aspect of the phenomenon.

Isolating Thematic Statements

It has been noted already that lived-experience descriptions can be found in a multitude of expressions or forms: in transcribed taped conversations; in interview materials; in daily accounts or stories; in supper-time talk; in formally written responses; in diaries; in passing comments; in reflections on other people's writings; in accounts of vicarious experiences of drama, film, poetry, or novels; in the play-acting of little children; in the talk that accompanies bedtime story-telling; in heart-to-heart conversations among friends; and so on. Naturally, some types of descriptions of lived experiences are more difficult to gather than others.

Any lived-experience description is an appropriate source for uncovering thematic aspects of the phenomenon it describes. But it is true that some descriptions are richer than others. It confirms our experience that in our conversations or dialogues we tend to learn more about life from some people than from others. Nevertheless, when a person shares with us a certain experience then there will always be something there for us to gather.

Generally we can take three approaches toward uncovering or isolating thematic aspects of a phenomenon in some text:

(1) the wholistic or sententious approach;

(2) the selective or highlighting approach;
(3) the detailed or line-by-line approach.

(1) In the wholistic reading approach we attend to the text as a whole and ask, *What sententious phrase may capture the fundamental meaning or main significance of the text as a whole?* We then try to express that meaning by formulating such a phrase.

(2) In the selective reading approach we listen to or read a text several times and ask, *What statement(s) or phrase(s) seem particularly essential or revealing about the phenomenon or experience being described?* These statements we then circle, underline, or highlight.

(3) In the detailed reading approach we look at every single sentence or sentence cluster and ask, *What does this sentence or sentence cluster reveal about the phenomenon or experience being described?*

As we thus study the lived-experience descriptions and discern the themes that begin to emerge, then we may note that certain experiential themes recur as commonality or possible commonalities in the various descriptions we have gathered. The task is to hold on to these themes by lifting appropriate phrases or by capturing in singular statements the main thrust of the meaning of the themes. For example, in the personal experience description by the mother of Robert (see the section entitled "Protocol Writing (lived-experience descriptions)," pp. 63-66), we note that the theme that seems to emerge is the one of "having hopes and expectations" about a child's (school) life and future. In experiential accounts from other mothers and fathers this theme recurs again and again.

Let us look again at Robert's mother's lived-experience description and practise the three approaches toward uncovering themes:

> Lately I have been wondering if I expect too much of my son. He gets all mixed up in his homework, is overtired, can't think straight, and spends hours doing one straightforward assignment when he should just be relaxing and enjoying family life like all the other kids in his class; he has misread the instructions and has to do the whole thing again; he has a thousand ideas for a report on gorillas, but can't seem to get it together to write even the opening sentence. So yesterday I looked at Robbie's cumulative-file at school. I felt guilty in a way, resorting to that, especially since those numbers have so little to say about a person. And my love and hopes for him are unconditional of course; they don't depend on his achievement or IQ scores. But the

numbers weren't supposed to tell me whether Rob is special or not — they were supposed to tell me what to do: whether it is alright for me to tease, prod and cajole him about his homework, and say, "Hey, you lazy schmuck, get some of this work finished in school instead of fooling around," or maybe, "Of course you can't think straight when you're so tired. You'll have to get home earlier and do this homework before supper."

The wholistic or sententious approach:

Expressing the fundamental or overall meaning of a text is a judgement call. Different readers might discern different fundamental meaning. And it does not make one interpretation necessarily more true than another. But there is much possibility here to err or to see meaning that is idiosyncratic. As we read over the text we see a mother who feels that her child has a problem with schoolwork and this places a cloud over her hopes for her child to do well. She does not want to be insensitive to the child, to his school experience, to his abilities or attitude. In other words, she wants to know what to say or do in dealing with her child, in a way that is helpful and yet thoughtful of the child's feelings. Perhaps this active sensitivity can appropriately be captured with the notion of tact. So we try the following sententious formulation:

"A parent needs to be able to know how to act tactfully toward a child in the child's best interest."

The selective or highlighting approach:

Are there any phrases that stand out? Can we select some sentences or part-sentences that seem to be thematic of the experience of parenting? We try the following:

"I have been wondering if I expect too much of my son."
To parent is to distinguish what is good and what is not good for a child.

"my love and hopes for him are unconditional of course"
The fundamental experience of parenting is hope.

"they were supposed to tell me what to do"
Parents constantly need to know what to do.

The detailed or line-by-line approach:

First we need to read each sentence or sentence cluster carefully.

[Sentence 1:] Lately I have been wondering if I expect too much of my son.

[Sentence 2:] He gets all mixed up in his homework, is overtired, can't think straight, and spends hours doing one straightforward assignment when he should just be relaxing and enjoying family life like all the other kids in his class; he has misread the instructions and has to do the whole thing again; he has a thousand ideas for a report on gorillas, but can't seem to get it together to write even the opening sentence.

[Sentences 3 & 4:] So yesterday I looked at Robbie's cumulative-file at school. I felt guilty in a way, resorting to that, especially since those numbers have so little to say about a person.

[Sentence 5:] And my love and hopes for him are unconditional of course; they don't depend on his achievement or IQ scores.

[Sentence 6] But the numbers weren't supposed to tell me whether Rob is special or not—they were supposed to tell me what to do:

[Sentence 7] whether it is alright for me to tease, prod and cajole him about his homework, and say, "Hey, you lazy schmuck, get some of this work finished in school instead of fooling around," or maybe, "Of course you can't think straight when you're so tired. You'll have to get home earlier and do this homework before supper."

Now we ask what each sentence or sentence cluster seems to reveal about the nature of parenting.

Sentence [1] shows how we have parental expectations as well as doubts about them.

Sentence [2] shows how particular situations, occurrences, or events give meaning to our expectations.

Sentences [3 & 4] show how we try to check our expectations by trying to look at a child differently.

Sentence [5] shows that underlying the specific expectations we may cherish, there lies a more fundamental sense of hope.

Sentence [6] shows that we want to understand a child because we want to know how to live with this child.

Sentence [7] shows how our understanding needs to orient our possibility for tactful acting toward the child.

Composing Linguistic Transformations

As we gain themes and thematic statements from our various sources, we may wish to capture the thematic statements in more phenomenologically sensitive paragraphs. Thus we write notes and paragraphs on the basis of our reading and other research activities. An interesting example of this process can be found in the second part of the posthumously published text by Maurice Merleau-Ponty, *The Visible and the Invisible* (1968). This text gives us insights into how a great phenomenologist prepared for his writing.

Composing linguistic transformations is not a mechanical procedure. Rather, it is a creative, hermeneutic process. By way of example, I might attempt such linguistic transformation of the themes of pedagogic expectations and hopes identified in the previous section entitled "Isolating Thematic Statements":

> We commonly say that to be a parent or a teacher is to have expectations and hope for a child. But "hope" is only a word, and a word soon becomes overworked, worn out, and forgetful of its original relation to our basic life experience. So we must examine how the living with children, at home or at school, is experienced such that we may call it "hope," "having hope for children." The act of hoping, of having hope for a child, is much more a way of being present to the child than a kind of doing. Hope for the parent or the teacher is a mode of being. In everyday living we entertain many particular expectations and desires: "I hope that my child will do well in school." "I hope that he can keep up with his homework." "I hope that my daughter will not give up her violin." These are the hopes which come and go with the passing of time. But children make it possible for men or women to transcend themselves and to say "I hope . . . I live with hope; I live life in such a modality that I experience children as hope." This experience of hope distinguishes a pedagogic life from a non-pedagogic one. It also makes clear that we can only hope for children we truly love, not in a romantic idealistic sense, but in the sense of pedagogic love. What hope gives us is the simple avouchment, "I will not give up on you. I know you can make a life for yourself." Thus hope refers to that which gives us patience, tolerance, and belief in the possibilities of our children. Hope is our experience of the child's possibilities and becoming. It is our experience of confidence that a child will show us how a life is to be lived, no matter how many disappointments may have tested us in our confidence. Is this not the experience of parenting as bearing? Thus hope gives us pedagogy itself. Or is it pedagogy which grants us hope? Like all great values, their ontological roots seem to merge.

Gleaning Thematic Descriptions from Artistic Sources

For the artist, as well as for the phenomenologist, the source of all work is the experiential lifeworld of human beings. Just as the poet or the novelist attempts to grasp the essence of some experience in literary form, so the phenomenologist attempts to grasp the essence of some experience in a phenomenological description. A genuine artistic expression is not just representational or imitational of some event in the world. Rather, it transcends the experiential world in an act of reflective existence. An artistic text differs from the text of everyday talking and acting in that it is always arrived at in a reflective mood. In other words, the artist recreates experiences by transcending them. These are some of the themes that may belong to the experience of mothering as gleaned from Phyllis Chesler's description (see the sections on locating experiential descriptions in literature, art, etc., in Chapter 3, pp. 70-76).

(1) The transformation from womanhood to motherhood is as dramatic as birth itself. ("when you gave birth to me")

(2) The birthday of the young child is experienced as the birthday of this transformation to motherhood. ("your age exactly")

(3) Becoming a mother puts a woman in touch with something primordial. ("an ancient well")

(4) The new child teaches the mother a more depthful understanding of life. ("you deepen me")

(5) The mother experiences the little child as a being who seems to have a mission or purpose of its own. ("little astronaut")

(6) Having given birth to a child is sometimes experienced as a longing for original oneness, a torn intimacy. ("no longer beneath my heart")

(7) Motherhood is experienced as if on new ground, connected to a newly born. ("married to a child")

(8) Yet, paradoxically, the child is also always experienced as a miracle. ("alchemy")

Notice that one of the differences between literary narrative or poetry on the one hand, and phenomenology on the other hand, is that literature or poetry (although based on life) leaves the themes implicit, and focuses on plot or particular incident, whereas phenomenology attempts to systematically develop a certain narrative that explicates themes while remaining true to the universal quality or essence of a certain type of experience.

Interpretation through Conversation

We have described the phenomenological orientation as a kind of conversational relation that the researcher develops with the notion he or she wishes to explore and understand. In fact, every conversation that we share in with an other person has this structure as well. A conversation is not just a personal relation between two or more people who are involved in the conversation. A conversation may start off as a mere chat, and in fact this is usually the way that conversations come into being. But then, when gradually a certain topic of mutual interest emerges, and the speakers become in a sense animated by the notion to which they are now both oriented, a true conversation comes into being. So a conversation is structured as a triad. There is a conversational relation between the speakers, and the speakers are involved in a conversational relation with the notion or phenomenon that keeps the personal relation of the conversation intact. Gadamer (1975) has described this process as having the dialogic structure of questioning-answering. Every time a view is expressed one can see the interpretation as an answer to a question that the object, the topic or notion, of the conversation asks of the persons who share the conversational relation. The conversation has a hermeneutic thrust: it is oriented to sense-making and interpreting of the notion that drives or stimulates the conversation. It is for this reason that the collaborative quality of the conversation lends itself especially well to the task of reflecting on the themes of the notion or phenomenon under study.

The art of the researcher in the *hermeneutic interview* is to keep the question (of the meaning of the phenomenon) open, to keep himself or herself and the interviewee oriented to the substance of the thing being questioned. "The art of questioning is that of being able to go on asking questions, i.e., the art of thinking," says Gadamer (1975, p. 330). The interviewee becomes the co-investigator of the study. It has been noticed by those conducting hermeneutic interviews that the volunteers or participants of the study often invest more than a passing interest in the research project in which they have willingly involved themselves. They begin to care about the subject and about the research question. And accordingly, the researcher develops a certain moral obligation to his or her participants that should prevent a sheer exploitative situation. It is in this sense that Socrates, in the *Meno*, likened the fundamental structure of the conversation to the relation of friendship (Plato, 1961, p. 358). It is talking together like friends. And that is also why, when the participants of the conversation try to out-argue each other, the conversation disintegrates.

So by setting up situations conducive to collaborative hermeneutic conversations, the researcher can mobilize participants to reflect on their experiences (once these have been gathered) in order to determine the deeper meanings or themes of these experiences. For this purpose a series of interviews may be scheduled or arranged with selected participants that allows reflection on the text (transcripts) of previous interviews in order to aim for as much interpretive insight as possible.

Once transcript themes have been identified by the researcher then these themes may become objects of reflection in follow-up hermeneutic conversations in which both the researcher and the interviewee collaborate. In other words, both the interviewer and the interviewee attempt to interpret the significance of the preliminary themes in the light of the original phenomenological question. Both the researcher and the interviewee weigh the appropriateness of each theme by asking: "Is this what the experience is really like?" And thus the interview turns indeed into an interpretive conversation wherein both partners self-reflectively orient themselves to the interpersonal or collective ground that brings the significance of the phenomenological question into view. For example, a researcher who studies the phenomenon of "birthing pain" will go back several times to the women with whom she conducts hermeneutic conversations about the experience. The women then read her next draft description of the phenomenological themes as a starting point for further sharing about the nature of the lived experience of birthing pain, and so forth.

Bollnow (1982) has described how good conversations tend to end: they finally lapse into silence. He does not mean, of course, that after such conversation is transcribed into print, further conversational interpretation is not possible. Often, the sense of truth experienced in a good conversation leads to a satisfaction that asks for further work. At the same time, when a conversation gradually diminishes into a series of more and more pauses, and finally to silence, something has been fulfilled. It is the same fulfillment that marks the triumph of an effective human science text: to be silenced by the stillness of reflection—

> reflection on what has been said and on what remains to be said, even merely with a feeling of gratitude for the profundity achieved in the conversation. And when the conversation finally does sink into silence, it is no empty silence, but a fulfilled silence. The truth, not only of the insight that has been acquired, but the truth of life, the state of being

in truth that has been achieved in the conversation, continues to make itself felt, indeed becomes deeper, in the course of this silence. (Bollnow, 1982, p. 46)

So the conversation aims at producing themes, insights, that the researcher eventually needs to create a text to which the themes, the fruits of the conversational relation, are able to minister.

Collaborative Analysis: The Research Seminar/Group

Collaborative discussions or hermeneutic conversations on the themes and thematic descriptions of phenomena may also be conducted by a research group or seminar—these too are helpful in generating deeper insights and understandings. For example, one participant researching a certain phenomenon will read a first (second, third, or fourth) draft of his or her paper. And on the basis of this description other participants share their views of the way the description does or does not resonate with their own experiences. Thus themes are examined, articulated, re-interpreted, omitted, added, or reformulated. Each collaborative paper usually benefits significantly in various draft stages from three or four of such shared seminar reflections.

There are many formal and informal ways that researchers or authors seek collaborative assistance in their writing. The research group or seminar circle is a formal way for convening and gathering the interpretive insights of others to a research text. But there are also less formal ways of testing one's work—such as sharing the text with advisers, consultants, reviewers, colleagues, or friends. Whether formal or informal, what one seeks in a conversational relation with others is a common orientation to the notion or the phenomenon that one is studying. Gadamer (1975) describes the method of a conversational relation as "the art of testing" (p. 330). And the art of testing consists in the art of questioning—meaning "to lay open, to place in the open" the subject matter of the conversation. And so the collaborative activity of discussing and testing a research text should not be a situation wherein the discussants of the text try to outwit the author or the other partners of the discussion group by polemical debate or argumentative confrontation. As indicated above, the structure of the conversational relation much more resembles the dialogic relation of what Socrates called the situation of "talking together like friends." Friends do not try to make the other weak; in contrast, friends aim to bring out strength.

Similarly, the participants of a human science dialogue try to strengthen what is weak in a human science text. They do this by trying to formulate the underlying themes or meanings that inhere in the text or that still inhere in the phenomenon, thus allowing the author to see the limits of his or her present vision and to transcend those limits (cf. McHugh, *et al.*, 1974).

Lifeworld Existentials as Guides to Reflection

All phenomenological human science research efforts are really explorations into the structure of the human lifeworld, the lived world as experienced in everyday situations and relations. Our lived experiences and the structures of meanings (themes) in terms of which these lived experiences can be described and interpreted constitute the immense complexity of the lifeworld. And, of course, we can even speak of the multiple and different lifeworlds that belong to different human existences and realities. And so we know that the lifeworld of the child has different experiential qualities from the lifeworld of the adult. Similarly there are the lifeworlds of the teacher, the parent, the researcher, the administrator, and so forth. And each of us may be seen to inhabit different lifeworlds at different times of the day, such as the lived world of work and the lived world of the home (Schutz and Luckmann, 1973).

As we remain at the most general level of the lifeworld we may find that this grounding level of human existence may also be studied in its fundamental thematic structure. For example, fundamental existential themes such as "life," "death," "being," "otherness," "meaning," and "mystery" have occurred in the phenomenological human science literature. In the following paragraphs we identify four such fundamental existential themes which probably pervade the lifeworlds of all human beings, regardless of their historical, cultural or social situatedness. In order not to confuse these fundamental lifeworld themes with the more particular themes of certain human phenomena, such as parenting or teaching that we want to study, we shall refer to these fundamental lifeworld themes as "existentials." There are four existentials that may prove especially helpful as guides for reflection in the research process: *lived space* (spatiality), *lived body* (corporeality), *lived time* (temporality), and *lived human relation* (relationality or communality).

The four fundamental existentials of spatiality, corporeality, temporality, and relationality may be seen to belong to the existential ground by way of which all human beings experience the world, although not all in the same modality of course. In the phenomenological literature these four categories have been considered as belonging to the fundamental structure of the lifeworld (see, for example, Merleau-Ponty, 1962). This is not difficult to understand, since about any experience we can always ask the fundamental questions that correspond to these four lifeworld existentials. Therefore, spatiality, corporeality, temporality, and relationality are productive categories for the process of phenomenological question posing, reflecting and writing.

Lived space (spatiality) is felt space. When we think of space we usually first speak of mathematical space, or the length, height and depth dimensions of space. We talk easily about distances between major cities (how many miles/kilometers, hours driving), about the spatial dimensions of the house or apartment in which we live, etc. But *lived* space is more difficult to put into words since the experience of lived space (as lived time, body) is largely pre-verbal; we do not ordinarily reflect on it. And yet we know that the space in which we find ourselves affects the way we feel. The huge spaces of a modern bank building may make us feel small, the wide-open space of a landscape may make us feel exposed but also possibly free, and just the opposite from the feeling we get in a crowded elevator. As we walk into a cathedral we may be overcome by a silent sense of the transcendental even if we ordinarily are not particularly religious or churchgoing. Walking alone in a foreign and busy city may render a sense of lostness, strangeness, vulnerability, and possibly excitement or stimulation. In general, we may say that we become the space we are in.

The home reserves a very special space experience which has something to do with the fundamental sense of our being. Home has been described as that secure inner sanctity where we can feel protected and by ourselves (Bollnow, 1960; Heidegger, 1971). Home is where we can *be* what *we are*. After having spent time somewhere we get up to "go home." We feel a special sorrow for the homeless because we sense that there is a deeper tragedy involved than merely not having a roof over one's head. In a general sense too, lived space is the existential theme that refers us to the world or landscape in which human beings move and find themselves at home. When we want to understand a person we ask about his or her world, profession, interests, background, place of birth and childhood, etc. Similarly, to understand "the nature of reading," "having a friendly talk," "giving birth to a child," it is helpful to inquire into the nature of the lived space that renders that particular experience its quality of meaning. For example, when we feel like reading a favorite novel we tend to look for a certain space that is good for reading: perhaps a nice overstuffed chair, a quiet corner somewhere, or a small table in a coffee shop where we feel shielded from traffic noise by the lull of quiet music and the muted talk of patrons. Phenomenologically it appears that the structure of the reading experience asks for a certain space experience. In other words, reading has its own modality of lived space and may be understood by exploring the various qualities and aspects of lived space. Similarly, the process of writing seems to require its own space; for writing this text I feel best at my own desk where I have my own things arranged around me.

Children probably experience space in a different modality than adults. For one thing, adults have learned the social character of space, conventional space. The same is true for lived time and body. There are cultural and social conventions associated with space that give the experience of space a certain qualitative dimension. We notice this, for example, in the space people feel that they need around themselves to feel comfortable or intimate. Bollnow (1960) discusses various aspects of lived space, such as lived distance, the road, etc. He notes how objective distance may not at all accord with the felt distance between two places. A place may be geographically close and yet feel further away because we have to cross a river or some high traffic roads. The roads themselves too have a certain quality. Highways and thoroughfares are not places where we can feel at rest—they are no place *to be*, they are means for travelling from one place to another. How different is the hiking path in the woods, or the trail through the ravine or the neighborhood where we like to walk! So it appears that lived space is a category for inquiring into the ways we experience the affairs of our day to day existence; in addition it helps us uncover more fundamental meaning dimensions of lived life.

Lived body (corporeality) refers to the phenomenological fact that we are always bodily in the world. When we meet another person in his or her landscape or world we meet that person first of all through his or her body. In our physical or bodily presence we both reveal something about ourselves and we always conceal something at the same time—not necessarily consciously or deliberately, but rather in spite of ourselves.

When the body is the object of someone else's gaze, it may lose its naturalness (Linschoten, 1953; Sartre, 1956) or instead it may happen that it grows enhanced in its modality of being. For example, under the critical gaze the body may turn awkward, the motions appear clumsy, while under the admiring gaze the body surpasses its usual grace and its normal abilities. Similarly, the person in love may incarnate his or her erotic mode of being in a subtle glow or radiant face or sometimes, under the eyes of the beloved, in a blushing response.

Lived time (temporality) is subjective time as opposed to clock time or objective time. Lived time is the time that appears to speed up when we enjoy ourselves, or slow down when we feel bored during an uninteresting lecture or or when we are anxious, as in the dentist's chair. Lived time is also our temporal way of being in the world—as a young person oriented to an open and beckoning future, or as an elderly person recollecting the past, etc. Here again, when we want to get to know a person we ask about his or her personal life history and where they feel they are going—what their project is in life. The temporal dimensions of past, present, and future constitute the horizons of a person's temporal landscape. Whatever I have encountered in my past now sticks to me as memories or as (near) forgotten experiences that somehow leave their traces on my being—the way I carry myself (hopeful or confident, defeated or worn-out), the gestures I have adopted and made my own (from my mother, father, teacher, friend), the words I speak and the language that ties me to my past (family, school, ethnicity), and so forth. And yet, it is true too that the past changes under the pressures and influences of the present. As I make something of myself I may reinterpret who I once was or who I now am. The past changes itself, because we live toward a future which we already see taking shape, or the shape of which we suspect as a yet secret mystery of experiences that lie in store for us (Linschoten, 1953, p. 245). Through hopes and expectations we have a perspective on life to come, or through desperation and lack of will to live we may have lost such perspective. Bollnow (1988) describes very aptly the mood of life of youth as one of expectation and a pervasive sense of "morningness" as when we start a promising day.

Lived other (relationality) is the lived relation we maintain with others in the interpersonal space that we share with them. As we meet the other, we approach the other in a corporeal way: through a handshake or by gaining an impression of the other in the way that he or she is physically present to us. Even if we learn about another person only indirectly (by letter, telephone, or book) we often already have formed a physical impression of the person which later may get confirmed, or negated when we find out, to our surprise, that the person looks very different from the way we expected. As we meet the other we are able to develop a conversational relation which allows us to transcend our *selves*. In a larger existential sense human beings have searched in this experience of the other, the communal, the social for a sense of purpose in life, meaningfulness, grounds for living, as in the religious experience of the absolute Other, God.

These four existentials of lived body, lived space, lived time, and lived relation to the other can be differentiated but not separated. They all form an intricate unity which we call the lifeworld—our lived world. But in a research study we can temporarily study the existentials in their differentiated aspects, while realizing that one existential always calls forth the other aspects. Consider very briefly how in reflecting on our pedagogic life with our children these four existentials allow us to perceive an immediate immense richness of meaning (even if not all parenting experience is necessarily positive, without grief or worry).

From the point of view of *lived body* I experience my children as utterly separate from me and yet as physically close. For many people there is a deep significance in the knowledge that parents and children are of one flesh. And in the physical holding and parental embrace we know our child in a profoundly symbiotic way. We also sense in the lived bodily encounter a primordial sense of security for the child. In my relation to my children I embody my fatherhood, such that I look with fatherly eyes at the mess they have made in the house, or the skin injury my child incurred while playing, or the feverish color of my child in his sickbed, etc. And this "seeing" prompts me to do something, to act the way a father should. In the parental experience of the child there is also the sense of *lived time* in the modality of hope which I cherish for my child's happiness and becoming. And we experience a sense of lived time in the child's desire to become someone himself or herself, to live for something and to create personal meaning in life. And the parent and the child both share a history which we call family time and which has its own horizons. Especially meaningful are the lived time experiences of the special days and times of the year when significant events are celebrated in the family and in the school or the community. And then there are of course the mealtimes, the evenings together, the outings and the weekends when time acquires qualities that turn eventually into positive or negative memories of childhood. The house is the location of our shared *lived space*, the home. In the home and in its immediate environment the child is offered the opportunity to explore the world from a safe haven. The space experience of the home may turn out to be supportive or neglectful, open or smothering, liberating or oppressive for the child. And in this immediate environment, too, the child experiences favorite play spaces, forbidden places, hiding places, secret spaces where the child can gather himself or herself, places for sharing such as the kitchen, and spaces such as the bedroom or under the covers of the bed where the child withdraws near the end of the day into the inner systole of sleep. Similarly the school is experienced as a special place where the child knows the atmosphere and quality of the classroom, the special desk, the hallway with its locker-spaces where the child meets friends, and so on. Finally, the parent-child relation as well as the teacher-child relation is experienced as a special *lived relation to the other* in the sense that this relation is highly personal and charged with interpersonal significance. In this lived relation the child experiences a fundamental sense of support and security that ultimately allows him or her to become a mature and independent person. And in this lived relation the child experiences the adult's confidence and trust without which it is difficult to make something of oneself.

Determining Incidental and Essential Themes

In setting ourselves the aim of attempting a more full-fledged phenomenological textual description, we need to determine the themes around which the phenomenological description will be woven.

In the previous sections we have explored the notion of theme and we have shown how the phenomenological meaning of phenomena may be claimed and articulated. For purpose of clarity we need to make the distinction again between incidental themes and essential themes. Not all meanings that we may encounter in reflecting on a certain phenomenon or lived experience are unique to that phenomenon or experience. And even the themes that would appear to be essential meanings are often historically and culturally determined or shaped.

The most difficult and controversial element of phenomenological human science may be to differentiate between essential themes and themes that are more incidentally related to the phenomenon under study. We might illustrate this point by distinguishing the pedagogy of parenting from the pedagogy of teaching. On the one hand, the phenomenon of pedagogy can be seen to take in what is common to the lived experience of parenting and teaching. And on the basis of the explorations that we have done to exemplify this human science approach we could determine an essential theme of this general notion of pedagogy. For this purpose we would ignore whatever differences there may exist between parenting and teaching and focus solely on that which gathers both teaching and parenting in our living with children.

In determining the universal or essential quality of a theme our concern is to discover aspects or qualities that make a phenomenon what it is and without which the phenomenon could not be what it is. To this end the phenomenologist uses the method of free imaginative variation in order to verify whether a theme belongs to a phenomenon essentially (rather than incidentally). The process of free imaginative variation can also be used to generate other essential themes.

In the process of apprehending essential themes or essential relationships one asks the question: Is this phenomenon still the same if we imaginatively change or delete this theme from the phenomenon? Does the phenomenon without this theme lose its fundamental meaning? For example, we presume that having offspring or children is essential to the notion of parenting. To test this theme we try to conceive of the experience of parenting such that the experience does *not* include children. This seems impossible. So we determine that "having a mothering or fathering relation to children" is an essential theme of parenting because it would be impossible to think of being a parent (without altering the meaning of parenting) and not having a fathering or mothering relation to a child. Of course, it is possible to have had children who have died and still think of oneself as a parent. In fact, Marcel (1978) gives an example of a mother whose son has died; but while she is fully aware of her son's death she still somehow waits for him to return home. This mother lives with the real presence of an absent child. So, to be a parent is to live in a mothering or fathering relation to a child. And we leave out of consideration the question of distinctions between biological parent, adoptive parent, step-parent, etc.

Now we might turn this question around and wonder whether "having had children" necessarily means that one has been a parent. And, here it may be conceivable that the answer is negative. One may have "had" children in different capacities. And we might sometimes say about biological parents that he or she had children but that this person never was a "real parent" to them. Thus, one may have been a parent in a superficial or mere biological sense, but not in a meaningful sense. It is not enough to just give birth to a child; in order to be a parent one has to *live as a parent* side by side this child as well.

The situational sketches of children's experiences of feeling left or abandoned by the parent (in the following chapter) may help to bring out the fuller significance of the meaning of the presence of the parent in children's lives. "Don't go away! Stay here. Be with me," says the child. A parent who does not understand the meaning of his or her own presence in the child's life threatens the child's possibility to be a child. A child who feels left or abandoned by the parent experiences the threat of a fundamental disruption of his or her childlike existence, the rupture of the child's relation of connectedness to the parents. In being truly present to a child I give myself to this child: a genuine giving of my parental commitment. In saying "yes" to a child at birth, the new parents affirm the meaning and value of this child in their lives. To really say "yes" to a child is to open one's life to this child, and to dwell together as a genuine "we." Without being able to elaborate much further on the essence of the child in the lives of parents, we may describe the parenting relation as one of togetherness, homeness, being there for the child, intimacy, closeness. It is the relation of family, of living together by growing familiar together.

The refusal to dwell together is indifference. Indifference is the failure to recognize the other human being in a genuine encounter or personal relation. Indifference is a failure or crisis of the "we." And so the child may experience the feeling of being left as indifference on the part of the parent. The child feels that he or she does not really make a difference in the lives of these adults who call themselves parents. So the parent who must temporarily leave the child needs to let the child know that absence can still be experienced as presence. The latter is possible only when the child experiences his or her relation to the parents as an unconditional and deeply personal relation. In the parents' absence such a child may feel alone but not fundamentally lonely. One needs to wonder, however, if in many contemporary families or modern living arrangements there is enough time and enough space left in the daily life of parents and children for such an unconditional bond to be experienced by the children.

We can see in the above example that "having a mothering or fathering relation to a child and being present in a child's life" is an essential theme of parenting. And we can see as well that the determination of such essential theme allows the phenomenologist to develop narrative elaborations of the lived meaning of parenting.

We might now turn to the phenomenon of teaching and ask if "having hope for children" is an essential theme of the experience of teaching. Can one imagine being a teacher without having hope for children? Is such person still a teacher or would the meaning of teaching lose its fundamental meaning if it were not sustained by hope? and so forth.

CHAPTER 5

Hermeneutic Phenomenological Writing

Attending to the Speaking of Language

In phenomenological human science, writing does not merely enter the research process as a final step or stage. As was indicated earlier, and as will be elaborated in this chapter, human science research *is* a form of writing. Creating a phenomenological text is the object of the research process. And, of course, this purpose stands in the service of the fundamental commitment that animates the research questions.

So, we always need to be mindful of the question: what does research and writing serve? In the case of the present project we want writing to serve pedagogy. Language is the only way by which we can bring pedagogic experience into a symbolic form that creates by its very discursive nature a conversational relation. Writing and reading are the ways in which we sustain a conversational relation: a discourse about our pedagogic lives with children. Much depends, therefore, on the quality of our language and writing (theorizing). One might even wonder whether the charge of pedagogy to address adequately its own nature is possibly too much to ask of ordinary conversational discourse. What form of writing is needed to do justice to the fullness of pedagogy and pedagogic experience?

The phenomenological method consists of the ability, or rather the art of being sensitive—sensitive to the subtle undertones of language, to the way language speaks when it allows the things themselves to speak. This means that an authentic speaker must be a true listener, able to attune to the deep tonalities of language that normally fall out of our accustomed range of hearing, able to listen to the way the things of the world speak to us. The world is no conglomeration of mere objects to be described in the language of physical science, says van den Berg (1972). The world is our home, our habitat, the materialization of our subjectivity. Whoever wants to become acquainted with the world of teachers, mothers, fathers, and children should listen to the language spoken by the things in their lifeworlds, to what things mean in this world.

Silence — the Limits and Power of Language

Phenomenologists like to say that nothing is so silent as that which is taken-for-granted or self-evident. Therefore, silence makes human science research and writing both possible and necessary. In everyday life we sense the power of silence when a person gives someone "the silent treatment"—as in the punishing silence of the parent, the defiant or revengeful silence of the child. There is the silence of withdrawal and secrecy as in a relation of insecurity or mistrust. And silence can also be experienced positively as in the trusting intimacy of friends or lovers who share an evening together in which few words are spoken.

Silence is not just the absence of speech or language. It is true that in our own groping for the right words we sense the limits of our personal language. And even in the most profound and eloquent poem it seems that the deep truth of the poem lies just beyond the words, on the other side of language. Speech rises out of silence and returns to silence, says Bollnow (1982). Not unlike the way that an architect must be constantly aware of the nature of space out of which and against which all building occurs, so the human scientist needs to be aware of the silence out of which and against which all text is constructed. There are various categories of silence operating in human science research generally and in hermeneutic phenomenology particularly.

First, there is *literal silence*, as in the absence of speaking. Sometimes it is better to remain silent than to speak or write. For example, in interview situations it is often more effective to remain silent when the conversation haltingly gropes forward. Out of this space of silence a more reflective response often may ensue than if we try to fill the awkwardness of the silence with comments or questions that amount to little more than chatter. Similarly, in writing, we often say that quality is more important than quantity. This means that in phenomenological human science the process of writing involves more than merely communicating information. The textual quality or form of our writing cannot quite be separated from the content of the text. Instead of committing the sin of "overwriting" it is sometimes more important to leave things unsaid. The text as a whole aims at a certain effect, and thus the silence of spaces is as important (speaks as loudly) as the words that we use to speak.

Second, there is something we might call *epistemological silence*. This is the kind of silence we are confronted with when we face the unspeakable. Various philosophers have referred to this kind of silence. For example, Polanyi (1958, 1969) has explained how there is a tacit form of knowing as in the common case where we sense "that we know more than we can tell" (1969, pp. 159-207). Beyond the range of our ordinary speaking and writing there is the rich domain of the unspeakable that constantly beckons us. Polanyi gives the example of witnesses who are unable to describe a person they saw, and yet are able to assist a police artist in the drawing up of a portrait by identifying what does and what does not resemble the person. We may have knowledge on one level and yet this knowledge is not available to our linguistic competency.

For our purpose it may be helpful to make several distinctions here:

(a) When we experience the unspeakable or ineffable in life, it may be that what remains beyond one person's linguistic competence may nevertheless be put into words by another person (Dienske, 1987)— perhaps by someone who has special skill in writing. Indeed we sometimes are surprised when someone is able to say what we wanted to say while we could not find the words. It is for this reason also that the research-writing process requires of us that we sometimes "borrow" the words of another since this other person is able, or has been able, to describe an experience in a manner (with a directness, a sensitivity, or an authenticity) that is beyond our ability. Sometimes this other person is a thoughtful poet, a philosopher, an author of fiction, or a person with a certain verbal talent. Sometimes this other person is a member of a group that has access to certain experiences which are unique for reasons that are cultural, generational, social, professional, or gender specific, such as children, the sick, the poor, prostitutes, athletes, women, gays, fathers, and so on.

(b) The experience of something that appears ineffable within the context of one type of discourse may be expressable by means of another form of discourse. For example, while behavioral science has great difficulty giving a satisfactory account of the experience of love, this subject is portrayed in a celebrated manner in the language of poetry, music and the fine arts. Of course, we need to acknowledge that the epistemological objectives of the discourse of behavioral science differ from those of aesthetic discourse. In other words, the very notion of truth has different meanings in the different linguistic communities (Gadamer, 1975). It is important for human science to recognize that the truth-experience made possible through the language of poetry, novels, paintings, music, and cinematography may be reflected upon phenomenologically, and thus imported into phenomenological writing.

(c) What appears unspeakable or ineffable one moment may be captured, however incomplete, in language the next moment. Indeed, this is also the common experience. As we orient ourselves to a certain notion we sometimes amaze ourselves about what we are able to put into words. And we wonder: Did I say that? In conversations with a friend or late at night at our desk, or in the car on our way home, we catch ourselves saying, writing, or thinking something with an eloquence that comes as a surprise. Much of real writing occurs in this way. The poet Rilke described how lived experience, memory, time, and reflection are all involved in the writing of a good poem:

> One must have memories . . . and still it is not yet enough to have memories. One must be able to forget them when they are many and one must have the great patience to wait until they come again. For it is not yet the memories themselves. Not till they have turned to blood within us, to glance and gesture, nameless and no longer to be distinguished from ourselves — not till then can it happen that in a most rare hour the first word of a verse arises in their midst and goes forth from them. (In Mood, 1975, p. 94)

Although it is obvious that human science discourse is not the same project as poetry, it is not entirely wrong to say that phenomenological research/writing also requires a high level of reflectivity, an attunement to lived experience, and a certain patience or time commitment.

Third, there is *ontological silence*, the silence of Being or Life itself. In ontological silence we meet the realization of our fundamental predicament of always returning to silence—even or perhaps especially after the most enlightening speech, reading, or conversation. It is indeed at those moments of greatest and most fulfilling insight or meaningful experience that we also experience the "dumb"-founding sense of a silence that fulfills and yet craves fulfillment. Bollnow (1982) describes this as the fulfilling silence of being in the presence of truth.

Anecdote as a Methodological Device

A common rhetorical device in phenomenological writing is the use of anecdote or story. "Story" means narrative, something depicted in narrative form. On the one hand, all human science has a narrative quality (rather than an abstracting quantitative character). And the story form has become a popular method for presenting aspects of qualitative or human science research. Here we wish to focus on a specific story form or narrative form: the anecdote. Anecdotes are a special kind of story. For example, when Langeveld (1984) wants to explain the significance of a thing in a child's life, he tells a story about a little girl who offers her baby brother a tiny feather: "The four-year old comes to her mother, who is busy with the newborn baby, and has a 'treasure' in her hand. It is a tiny feather of a sparrow. This is for little brother, because he is still so small . . . . Now that is a true gift!" says Langeveld (p. 218). And he uses the anecdote to make a distinction between a present and a gift. A present is something we give to someone as a wedding present or as fulfillment of an obligation or debt. The French have a saying that small presents maintain friendship. Langeveld shows that it is directly reversed with gifts: "A present can make friendship, but love and friendship make gifts, even the smallest ones, possible . . . . So the little girl's feather is small—so be it: Isn't the little brother small too? But how delicate and soft the feather is! It almost makes the beholder delicate and soft too!" (p. 218). And so Langeveld continues, whoever gives a present to someone, gives something from the store, often merely just a suggestion from the salesperson. But whoever gives a gift (and not just a mere present) gives himself or herself. He or she *is* the thing.

Here is another example: In his introduction to *Person and World*, van den Berg tells an anecdote of a native of the Malayan jungles (van den Berg and Linschoten, 1953). In order to learn what impression a large and modern city would make on an inhabitant of the jungle, one had placed this man unexpectedly and without much ado in the middle of the large city of Singapore. One walked with him through the busy streets in order to provide the native with ample opportunity to observe whatever a metropolis could offer. When at the end of the trip one asked him what had struck him most, he did not, as one might have expected, talk about the paved streets, the brick houses, concrete buildings, cars, streetcars and trains. Instead, he mentioned how to his

amazement one person could carry so many bananas. What he appeared to have seen was a street vendor who transported his bunches
of bananas on a push cart. "For the rest the native hardly had seen
anything," says van den Berg (1953, p. 5). A person who lives in the
jungle is engaged in a dialogue with the things of his world which allows
him to see things in a manner which we could not possibly share. The
native is engaged in a different conversation with things. Every new
object he sees appears in front of his eyes in a modality that permits a
certain role in that conversation. Any object that cannot adopt such
modality therefore cannot meaningfully enter the conversational relation. It does not speak to him and therefore cannot be seen, says van
den Berg. This is how van den Berg uses, among other things, the
anecdote as a device for making comprehensible the phenomenon of
conversational relation which every human being maintains with his or
her world. What van den Berg wants to show by way of anecdote and
phenomenological explication is that the human being not only stands
in a certain conversational relation to the world—the human being
really *is* this relation.

Anecdotes, in the sense that they occur in the phenomenological
writings of, for example, Sartre, Marcel, Merleau-Ponty are not to be
understood as *mere* illustrations to "butter up" or "make more easily
digestible" a difficult or boring text. Anecdote can be understood as a
methodological device in human science to make comprehensible some
notion that easily eludes us.

Webster's definition of anecdote is "a usually short narrative of an
interesting, amusing, or biographical incident." And the Oxford Dictionary defines anecdote as "secret, private, or hitherto unpublished
narratives or details of history." It speaks of the narrative of an incident
or event as "being in itself interesting or striking." The term derives
from the Greek meaning "things unpublished," "something not given
out." And indeed, Cicero (and later Renaissance scholars as well) used
to describe some of his unpublished manuscripts as anecdotes, "things
not given out." Anecdotes are social products. In everyday life the
anecdote usually begins its course as part of an oral tradition. Often, it
is originally a fragment of the biography of some famous or well-known
person. Thus, Samuel Johnson described anecdote as "a biographical
incident; a minute passage of private life." Biographers and historians
value anecdotes for their power to reveal the true character of persons

or of times which are hard to capture in any other manner (Fadiman, 1985, p. xxi).

But often anecdote was information meant for insiders, stuff that for discretionary reasons did not make the written record. Sometimes the anecdote was used to characterize a way of thinking or a style or figure which was really too difficult to approach in a more direct manner. This is one epistemologically interesting feature of anecdote, that if we cannot quite grasp the point or essence of a subject and we keep looking at it from the outside, as it were, then we may be satisfied with an anecdotal story or fragment (Verhoeven, 1987).

There is an amusing anecdote about Edmund Husserl whose voluminous writings on phenomenology contain painstaking refutations of every conceivable objection to his philosophical system. As a boy Edmund wanted to sharpen his knife. And he persisted in making the knife sharper and sharper until finally he had nothing left (de Boer, 1980, p. 10). The anecdote aptly demonstrates the perfectionist qualities in Husserl's character. Husserl was accustomed to reflect with his pen and paper. His phenomenological research was truly a textual labor. He would revise, rewrite, and edit endlessly his fundamental writings. And after his death was discovered an astonishing collection of about 40,000 pages written in stenographic script.

An interesting case of the significance of anecdotes in human science thinking concerns the doctrine or philosophy of Diogenes Laertius, also called The Cynic or The Dogman, or "a Socrates gone mad" (Herakleitos and Diogenes, 1979, p. 35). There are no authentic texts left from this thinker, who at any rate considered living more important than writing. What is available are just anecdotes. Legend has it that the youthful Alexander the Great one day went to visit the philosopher Diogenes about whom he had heard such strange stories. He came upon the philosopher while the latter was relaxing in the beautiful sunshine.

> Alexander: I am Alexander the Great.
> Diogenes: I am Diogenes, the dog.
> Alexander: The dog?
> Diogenes: I nuzzle the kind, bark at the greedy, and bite louts.
> Alexander: What can I do for you?
> Diogenes: Stand out of my light. (p. 30)

While Alexander wanted to show his benevolence and generosity to the thinker, the latter showed that he knew only too well the nature of worldly temptations. But rather than to theorize and to get entrapped into the addictive sphere of philosophical abstraction, Diogenes "showed" his argument in verbal gesture: "get out of my sun." By means of this pantomimic demonstration Diogenes shows more effectively than theoretical discourse might do how the philosopher frees himself from the politician. He was the first person who was free enough to be able to put the mighty Alexander in his place. Diogenes' answer not only ignored the desire of power, but also the overwhelming power of desire (Sloterdijk, 1983, p. 265). And so, this humble and wretched philosopher showed himself more powerful and autonomous than the feared ruler Alexander who went all the way to the borders of India to satisfy his need for power. Did Alexander recognize the sense of superiority of the moral life of the cynic? History has it that Alexander once said: "If I were not Alexander, I would be Diogenes" (Herakleitos and Diogenes, 1979, p. 36). Diogenes and Alexander the Great died on the same day, a fact to which people have attached superstitious significance.

So, Diogenes set out to teach his fellow citizens not by giving speeches or by writing books but by means of pantomimic exercise and by living example. A kind of street theatre, one might say. Sloterdijk (1983) has argued that the aureole of anecdotes that surrounds the figure of Diogenes are actually more clarifying of his teachings than any writings could have been. And yet the reason that Diogenes' philosophy has not been more influential may also find its cause in the fact that it is *only* anecdotes that have been preserved. Anecdotes have enjoyed low status in scholarly writings, since, in contrast to historical accounts or reports, they rest on dubious factual evidence. The shady reputation of anecdote may derive from the sixth-century Byzantine historian Procopius who called his posthumously published scandalous account of the Emperor Justinian *Anecdota* or *Historia Arcana* (Secret History).

In everyday life, too, anecdotes may get negative reactions. For example, we may hear someone say that a certain account should be distrusted since "it rests merely on anecdotal evidence." Evidence that is "only anecdotal" is not permitted to furnish a proper argument. Of course, it is entirely fallacious to generalize from a case on the basis of mere anecdotal evidence. But empirical generalization is not the aim of phenomenological research. The point that the critics of anecdotes miss is that the anecdote is to be valued for other than factual-empirical or factual-historical reasons.

An historical account describes a thing that has happened in the past, but an anecdote is rather like a poetic narrative which describes a universal truth. What Aristotle says about the poetic epic of his time applies to the anecdotal narrative of our time:

> the poet's function is to describe, not the thing that has happened, but a kind of thing that might happen, i.e., what is possible as being probable or necessary . . . poetry is something more philosophic and of graver import than history, since its statements are of the nature rather of universals, whereas those of history are singulars. (*Poetics*, 1451)

Anecdotes may have a variety of functions (see Verhoeven for some distinctions, 1987; also Fadiman, 1985), but the ones that are of significance to human science discourse may include the following characteristics:

(1) *Anecdotes form a concrete counterweight to abstract theoretical thought.* The object of phenomenological description is not to develop theoretical abstractions that remain severed from the concrete reality of lived experience. Rather phenomenology tries to penetrate the layers of meaning of the concrete by tilling and turning the soil of daily existence. Anecdote is one of the implements for laying bare the covered-over meanings.

(2) *Anecdotes express a certain disdain for the alienated and alienating discourse of scholars who have difficulty showing how life and theoretical propositions are connected.* Thus, anecdotes possess a certain pragmatic thrust. They force us to search out the relation between living and thinking, between situation and reflection. In this connection Fadiman (1985, p. xxi) notes how anecdote has acted as a levelling device, how it humanizes, democratizes, and acts as a counterweight to encomium.

(3) *Anecdotes may provide an account of certain teachings or doctrines which were never written down.* Socrates and Diogenes are examples of great thinkers about whom anecdotal life stories form both their biographies as well as the essence of their teachings. This historical phenomenon also shows the great potential and generally unacknowledged power of anecdote in human science discourse. Plato's *Dialogues* is a collection of anecdotes about Socrates, the philosopher. It differs markedly from the large body of philosophical writings that

have followed it down the ages. At the methodological level Plato's writings are round-about or indirect reflections about fundamental human experiences such as friendship (*Lysis*), love (*Phaedrus, Symposium*), teaching virtue (*Meno*), and so forth.

(4) *Anecdotes may be encountered as concrete demonstrations of wisdom, sensitive insight, and proverbial truth.* Classical figures considered their anecdotes as narrative condensations of generally acknowledged truths (Fadiman, 1985, p. xxi). For example, the anecdote of the cave in Plato's *Republic* is offered by Plato as allegory or possible story. Plato's accounts are offered not as factual truths in the empirical or historical sense but, in Plato's words, as "likely stories." By their anecdotal quality we come to see what is possible and what is not possible in the world in which we live (Cairns, 1971, p. xv).

(5) *Anecdotes of a certain event or incident may acquire the significance of exemplary character.* Because anecdote is concrete and taken from life (in a fictional or real sense) it may be offered as an example or as a recommendation for acting or seeing things in a certain way. In everyday life an anecdote may be told as a tactful response (a "message") to let the recipient of the anecdote sense or perceive a certain truth that is otherwise difficult to put into clear language.

What is often not seen is that anecdotal narrative as story form is an effective way of dealing with certain kinds of knowledge. "Narrative, to narrate," derives from the Latin *gnoscere, noscere* "to know." To narrate is to tell something in narrative or story form. The paradoxical thing about anecdotal narrative is that it tells something *particular* while really addressing the *general* or the *universal*. And vice versa, at the hand of anecdote fundamental insights or truths are tested for their value in the contingent world of everyday experience. And so one may say that the anecdote shares a fundamental epistemological or methodological feature with phenomenological human science which also operates in the tension between particularity and universality.

The Value of Anecdotal Narrative

D'Israeli termed anecdotes "minute notices of human nature and of human learning" (in Fadiman, 1985). Anecdotes can teach us. The use of story or of anecdotal material in phenomenological writing is not merely a literary embellishment. The stories themselves are examples or topics of practical theorizing. Anecdotal narratives (stories) are important for pedagogy in that they function as experiential case material on which pedagogic reflection is possible. Methodologically speaking, story is important because it allows the human science text to acquire a narrative quality that is ordinarily characteristic of story. A hybrid textual form is created, combining the power of philosophic or systematic discourse with the power of literary or poetic language. Anecdote particularizes the abstracting tendency of theoretical discourse: it makes it possible to involve us pre-reflectively in the lived quality of concrete experience while paradoxically inviting us into a reflective stance vis-à-vis the meanings embedded in the experience. The important feature of anecdotal as well as phenomenological discourse is that it simultaneously pulls us in but then prompts us to reflect.

The significance of anecdotal narrative in phenomenological research and writing (cf. Rosen, 1986) is situated in its power:

(1) *to compel*: a story recruits our willing attention;

(2) *to lead us to reflect*: a story tends to invite us to a reflective search for significance;

(3) *to involve us personally*: one tends to search actively for the story teller's meaning via one's own;

(4) *to transform*: we may be touched, shaken, moved by story; it teaches us;

· (5) *to measure one's interpretive sense*: one's response to a story is a measure of one's deepened ability to make interpretive sense.

To conclude, the lacing of anecdotal narrative into more formal textual discourse, if done well, will create a tension between the prereflective and reflective pulls of language.

Varying the Examples

In his lectures, the Dutch phenomenologist Buytendijk once termed phenomenology "the science of examples." With this phrase he was referring to the iconic quality of phenomenological knowledge. A phenomenological study does not describe the nature of a phenomenon in the same sense that, for instance, an ethnographer describes a certain culture. When an ethnographer describes the culture of a teen-centre or a day-care environment, then the description is expected to exhibit a certain degree of reality validity for the way this particular youth culture or that particular day-care setting is experienced by these young people or children. In contrast, phenomenological research as it has been approached in this text aims at elucidating those phenomenologically structural features of a phenomenon that help to make visible, as it were, that which constitutes the nature or essence of the phenomenon. In other words, every phenomenological description is in a sense only an example, an icon that points at the "thing" which we attempt to describe. A phenomenological description describes the original of which the description is only an example. To say it differently, a phenomenological description is an example composed of examples. If the description is phenomenologically powerful, then it acquires a certain transparency, so to speak; it permits us to "see" the deeper significance, or meaning structures, of the lived experience it describes. How is such transparency achieved? It is a function of the appropriateness of the themes that we have identified as well as a function of the thoughtfulness that we have managed to muster in creating exemplary descriptions by, for example, being sensitive to the evocative "tone" of language in which the descriptions are captured. A description is a powerful one if it reawakens our basic experience of the phenomenon it describes, and in such a manner that we experience the more foundational grounds of the experience. Varying the examples is the way in which we address the phenomenological themes of a phenomenon so that the "invariant" aspect(s) of the phenomenon itself comes into view.

Sometimes this method of varying the examples is used for showing how phenomena differ; for example, how pedagogic hope differs from other kinds of "hope." In this case we may vary the example by attending to the kind of meaning of "hope" that is implied in the language of teaching. In doing so, we may gain a momentary view of the phenomenological meaning of the experience of pedagogic hope. In the next few paragraphs let us illustrate these different aspects of hope by focusing for a moment on the modern "behavioral objectives" or "management by objectives" talk in terms of which educational theorists and administrators try to define teaching competence.

What are we to make of the language of teaching that is thus made available to teachers? Herein lies the irony of a profound contradiction: the language by way of which teachers are encouraged to interpret themselves and reflect on their living with children is thoroughly imbued by hope, and yet it is almost exclusively a language of doing—it lacks being. We do not know how to talk of our being with children as a being present with hope for these children. The language of objectives, aims, teacher expectations, intended learning outcomes, goals, or ends in view is a language of hope out of which hope itself has been systematically purged. The language of aims and objectives, therefore, is a language of hopeless hope. It is an impatient language that neither bears nor truly awakens. How does "having measurable objectives" differ from "having hope"? Teacher expectations and anticipations associated with certain aims and objectives differ from having hope for our children in that expectations and anticipations easily degenerate into desires, wants, certainties, predictions. As teachers we tend to close ourselves off from possibilities that lie outside the direct or indirect field of vision of the expectations. To hope is to believe in possibilities. Therefore hope strengthens and builds. On the other hand, the phenomenology of specific educational objectives or broad goals is to be involved with the future of the children we teach in such a way that we always see the past as present and the present as past. And inherent in such living with children is the danger of always treating the present as burden, as something that must be overcome. There is little dwelling in such living.

The point is not that the curricular language of educational aims, objectives, or instructional intentions is wrong. Seen in proper perspective this language is an administrative convenience. Teachers have always planned what should go on in a particular course, class, or lesson. The problem is that in an age in which the administrative and technological influences have penetrated into the very blood of our lifeworld, teachers and even parents seem to have forgotten a certain kind of understanding: what it means to bear children, to hope for children entrusted to their care. Recalling what thus seems to be forgotten is a kind of recollecting of what belongs to the being of parenting and of what belongs to the being of teaching as *in loco parentis*.

The nihilistic forgetfulness of the essence of our being as teachers curiously turns loose a certain self-destructiveness. This is evident in the problem lately referred to as teacher burn-out. Teacher burn-out is the modern case of the enduring problem of nihilism: the higher values are losing their value. The ends are lacking, said Nietzsche; there is no answer to this question: "What's the use?" And actually the nihilistic "what's the use" is less a question than a sigh, a shrugging-off of any suggestion that there might be cause for hope. Teacher burn-out is not necessarily a symptom of excessive output of effort, of being overworked. It may be the condition that ensues when as teachers we no longer know why we are doing what we are doing. Teacher burn-out is hopeless in that nobody can make us believe there is an answer to the sigh, "What's the use?" The only way such teacher burn-out can be overcome is by recapturing in ourselves the knowledge that life is bearable—not in the sense that we can bear it, as we bear a burden which weighs us down, but in the sense that we know that life is there to bear us—as in the living with hope. We can do this, once again, by seeing the child as child, by giving birth and bearing to children, rather than aborting the child in the middle of the abstracted rhetoric of our theorizing.

Writing Mediates Reflection and Action

In an oral culture, in a society dominated by orality, phenomenology would be quite impossible. Why? Not only because phenomenology is a certain mode of reflection done traditionally by scholars who write. But also because a certain form of consciousness is required, a consciousness that is created by the act of literacy: reading and writing. Ong (1982) has argued that the cultural and historical fact of literacy has led to a transformed consciousness that has created a certain distance and tension between understanding and experience, reflection and action. So when we speak of "action sensitive understanding" then we are orienting ourselves to this tension. One place where this tension is experienced in an acute form is in the act of human science research as writing. In other words, it is a certain kind of writing that we are concerned with here. It is the minded act of writing that orients itself pedagogically to a notion that is a feature of lived experience.

Writing is our method

What relation exists between research and writing? When we examine the earlier human science literature produced by the *Geisteswissenschaftliche Pädagogik* (see Hintjes, 1981) and the more phenomenological pedagogical tradition in Germany and the Netherlands we notice a general neglect of discussion of the relationship between research and writing. The same is true for the contemporary literature of research in the social and human sciences; writing as a methodological concern is usually only discussed (if at all) for the purpose of research report writing and publication of scholarly articles. Educators have written about the formative value of reading for the development of literacy and critical consciousness (see, for example, Freire, 1987). But the connection between research and writing is surprisingly little understood. An exploration of both the epistemology and the pedagogy of writing shows the importance of this relation.

In all research, including in traditional (experimental or more positivistic) research, there comes a moment when the researcher needs to communicate in writing what he or she has been up to. One speaks here of the "research report" which suggests that a clear separation exists between the activity of research and the reporting activity in which the research is made public. Also in the work of various contemporary human science researchers, writing is conceived largely as reporting process. With them the aim is to make human science methodologically "rigorous," "systems based," and "hard." In such framework there is no place for thinking about research itself as a poetic textual (writing) practice. But there may be a price to be paid for the desire to be respectable in the traditional "scientific" sense. And that has to do with the quality of the insights generated by a preoccupation with epistemology and method. Barthes expressed this well with a warning:

> Some people speak of method greedily, demandingly; what they want in work is method; to them it never seems rigorous enough, formal enough. Method becomes a Law . . . . the invariable fact is that a work which constantly proclaims its will-to-method is ultimately sterile: everything has been put into the method, nothing remains for the writing; the researcher insists that his text will be methodological, but this text never comes: no surer way to kill a piece of research and send it to join the great scrap heap of abandoned projects than Method. (Barthes, 1986, p. 318)

Other researchers have given more prominence to the textual nature of phenomenological inquiry but even these authors have not squarely addressed the relation between phenomenological reflection and the writing process. Yet for the human sciences, and specifically for hermeneutic phenomenological work, writing is closely fused into the research activity and reflection itself. We might argue that even for traditional social science research the cognitive stance required to do research is closely related to the cognitive style of writing.

Writing fixes thought on paper. It externalizes what in some sense is internal; it distances us from our immediate lived involvements with the things of our world. As we stare at the paper, and stare at what we have written, our objectified thinking now stares back at us. Thus, writing creates the reflective cognitive stance that generally characterizes the theoretic attitude in the social sciences. The object of human science research is essentially a linguistic project: to make some aspect of our lived world, of our lived experience, reflectively understandable and intelligible. Researchers recognize this linguistic nature of research in the imperative reminder: "Write!" Human science research requires a commitment to write. But writing for a human science researcher is not just a supplementary activity. The imperative "Write", as Barthes put it, "is intended to recall 'research' to its epistemological condition: whatever it seeks, it must not forget its nature as language—and it is this which ultimately makes an encounter with writing inevitable" (Barthes, 1986, p. 316).

For Barthes, research does not merely *involve* writing: research is the work of writing—writing is its very essence (1986, p. 316). In the human sciences no research that has failed to write itself has understood its fundamental mandate. For scholars such as Husserl, Heidegger, Sartre, and Merleau-Ponty the activities of researching and reflecting on the one hand, and reading and writing on the other hand, are indeed quite indistinguishable. When one visits the Husserl Archives at the University of Louvain this close connection between research and writing becomes evident in the symbolic value of Husserl's desk which occupies a prominent place in the archival room. It is at this desk where phenomenology received its fundamental impetus.

More so than Husserl, Sartre was a phenomenologist who stood and acted in the middle of the hustle and bustle of social and political life. But as writing became very difficult for the aging Sartre, thinking became difficult as well. "I still think," the seventy-year-old Sartre (1977) said once in an interview, "but because writing has become impossible for me the real activity of thought has in some way been repressed" (p. 5). Sartre was speaking about the difficulty that the loss of sight created for him as reader and author. It is obvious that for Sartre writing was not just a mere moment in the intellectual life of the thinker. Writing was somehow at the center of this life. "The only point to my life was writing," he said. "I would write out what I had been thinking about beforehand, but the essential moment was that of writing itself" (p. 5). With this line Sartre has given us his most succinct definition of his methodology. Writing is the method. And to ask what method is in human science is to ask for the nature of writing. What is writing? How is writing research (thinking, reflecting)? Certainly, writing is a producing activity. The writer produces text, and he or she produces more than text. The writer produces himself or herself. As Sartre might say: the writer is the product of his own product. Writing is a kind of self-making or forming. To write is to measure the depth of things, as well to come to a sense of one's own depth.

To Write is to Measure Our Thoughtfulness

*Writing separates us from what we know and yet it unites
us more closely with what we know.*

Writing teaches us what we know, and in what way we know what we know. As we commit ourselves to paper we see ourselves mirrored in this text. Now the text confronts us. We try to read it as someone else might, but that is actually quite impossible, since we cannot help but load the words with the intentions of our project. Yet, the text says less than we want, it does not seem to say what we want: we sigh: "Can't we do any better than this?" "This is no good!" "We are not coming to terms with it." "Why do we keep going when we are not getting anywhere?" "We need to scrap this." "Let's try it again that way." Writing gives appearance and body to thought. And as it does, we disembody what in another sense we already embody. However, not until we had written this down did we quite know what we knew. Writing separates the knower from the known (see Ong, 1982, for some distinctions in this section), but it also allows us to reclaim this knowledge and make it our own in a new and more intimate manner. Writing constantly seeks to make external what somehow is internal. We come to know what we know in this dialectic process of constructing a text (a body of knowledge) and thus learning what we are capable of saying (our knowing body). It is the dialectic of inside and outside, of embodiment and disembodiment, of separation and reconciliation.

*Writing distances us from the lifeworld, yet it also draws
us more closely to the lifeworld.*

Writing distances us from lived experience but by doing so it allows us to discover the existential structures of experience. Writing creates a distance between ourselves and the world whereby the subjectivities of daily experience become the object of our reflective awareness. The writer's immediate domain is paper, pen or keyboard on the one hand and language or words on the other hand. Both preoccupations have an alienating effect. The author who writes about the experience of parenting must, temporarily at least, "slacken the threads" between himself or herself and the world. Every parent/author knows the tensions between the demands made by the two roles even if the object of interest in both cases is the child. Whereas, on the one hand, writing gets me away from immediate involvement with my child, on the other hand it allows me to create a space for pedagogic reflecting on my parenting relation with this child so that I may return to this child with a deepened understanding of the significance of certain realities of the lifeworld.

Writing decontextualizes thought from practice and yet it returns thought to praxis.

Writing tends to orient us away from contextual particulars toward a more universal sphere. As we try to capture the meaning of some lived experience in written text, the text in turn assumes a life of its own. Thus writing places us at a distance from the practical immediacy of lived life by being forgetful of its context. Or rather, writing focuses our reflective awareness by disregarding the incidentals and contingencies that constitute the social, physical, and biographic context of a particular situation. But as we are able to gain in this manner a deeper sense of the meanings embedded in some isolated aspect of practice, we are also being prepared to become more discerning of the meaning of new life experiences. And thus reflectively writing about the practice of living makes it possible for the person to be engaged in a more reflective praxis. By praxis we mean thoughtful action: action full of thought and thought full of action.

Writing abstracts our experience of the world, yet it also concretizes our understanding of the world.

Because language is itself abstractive, writing tends to abstract from the experience we may be trying to describe. This abstractive tendency is a problem for human science research since its aim is precisely to return "to the things themselves," which means to return to the world as lived: "that world which precedes knowledge, of which knowledge always *speaks*, and in relation to which every scientific schematization is an abstract and derivative sign-language" (Merleau-Ponty, 1962, p. ix). What is the great paradox of language? That it always abstracts from the concreteness of the world which it was responsible for creating in the first place. Writing intellectualizes. We recognize this intellectualizing in the image of Kien, Canetti's bookish person, who appears thoroughly alienated from real existence (Canetti, 1978). And yet, writing, true writing can concretize the experience of the world more pithily it seems, more to the shaking core (however strange it may seem) than the world as experienced. The narrative power of story is that sometimes it can be more compelling, more moving, more physically and emotionally stirring than lived-life itself. Textual emotion, textual understanding can bring an otherwise sober-minded person (the reader but also the author) to tears and to a more deeply understood worldly engagement.

Writing objectifies thought into print and yet it subjectifies our understanding of something that truly engages us.

On the one hand, the inscribing, the writing of the text *is* the research. One writes to make public, to make conversationally available what the author lives with: an idea, a notion being questioned. On the other hand, the text once completed and in print-circulation is now a testimonial, a relic of embodied reflections. More so than long-hand writing, printed text is an object. We sense this in the greater ease with which we can take distance from our text once it has been converted into type-faced print. So there is an subjectifying and an objectifying moment in writing and in the way that the word allows us to understand the world. Research is writing in that it places consciousness in the position of the possibility of confronting itself, in a self-reflective relation. To write is to exercise self-consciousness. Writing plays the inner against the outer, the subjective self against the objective self, the ideal against the real.

Writing Exercises the Ability to See

Writing involves a textual reflection in the sense of separating and confronting ourselves with what we know, distancing ourselves from the lifeworld, decontextualizing our thoughtful preoccupations from immediate action, abstracting and objectifying our lived understandings from our concrete involvements (cf. Ong, 1982), and all this for the sake of now reuniting us with what we know, drawing us more closely to living relations and situations of the lifeworld, turning thought to a more tactful praxis, and concretizing and subjectifying our deepened understanding in practical action. Writing has been called a form of practical action. Writing is action in the sense of a corporeal practice. The writer practises his or her body in order to make, to "author" something. In one sense, the text is the product of the writer's practical action. But writing exercises more than our mere redactive skills. Writing exercises and makes empirically demonstrable our ability to "see." Writing shows that we can now see something and at the same time it shows the limits or boundaries of our sightedness. In writing the author puts in symbolic form what he or she is capable of seeing. And so practice, in the lifeworld with children, can never be the same again. My writing as a practice *prepared* me for an insightful praxis in the lifeworld. (I can now see things I could not see before.) Although I may try to close my eyes, to ignore what I have seen, in some way my existence is now mediated by my knowledge. And because *we* are what we can "see" (know, feel, understand), seeing is already a form of praxis—seeing the significance in a situation places us in the event, makes us part of the event. Writing, true writing, is authoring, the exercise of authority: the power that authors and gives shape to our personal being. Writing exercises us in the sense that it empowers us with embodied knowledge which now can be brought to play or realized into action in the performance of the drama of everyday life.

To Write is to Show Something

Phenomenological text succeeds when it lets us see that which shines through, that which tends to hide itself. And how can research as writing "let us see?" Phenomenology is heedful of our propensity to mistake what we say (our words) for what we talk about (the *logos*). Phenomenological writing is not found in the colorful words of the story-teller, nor in the fanciful phrases of the person with a flair for writing. The words are not the thing. And yet, it is to our words, language, that we must apply all our phenomenological skill and talents, because it is in and through the words that the shining through (the invisible) becomes visible.

The language of human science writing discloses reflectively ("shows" us) how phenomenological knowledge is held and what it is like to know things pedagogically. In other words, pedagogical writing requires a responsive reading. One does not read poetry as if it were a mathematical treatise, or a logical argument, or even a story line. The person who reads poetry as if it were prosaic discourse misses a full understanding of the poem. Similarly, the person who cannot see how a phenomenological use of words is a function of the things being described in the words, will be unable to understand the description. The reader must be prepared to be attentive to what is said *in* and *through* the words. While a text possesses literal content or lexical meaning, there is also meaning in the form or rhetorical structure of a text. Certain meaning is better expressed through *how* one writes than in *what* one writes. Content may be visible as form but for that reason concealed as content, says Rosen (1969). So that attentiveness to form is also attentiveness to content. Phenomenology is like poetry, in that it speaks partly through silence: it means more than it explicitly says.

Phenomenology, like poetry, intends to be silent as it speaks. It wants to be implicit as it explicates. So, to read or write phenomenologically requires that we be sensitively attentive to the silence around the words by means of which we attempt to disclose the deep meaning of our world. For this reason Brown (1966, p. 258) says:

> Speech points beyond itself to the silence, to the word within the word, the language buried in language, the primordial language, from before the Flood or the Tower of Babel; lost yet ready at hand, perfect for all time; present in all our words, unspoken. To hear again the primordial language is to restore to words their full significance.

To Write is to Rewrite

Thus, in spite of the seemingly instrumental or step-wise character of the approach outlined in this text, the methodology of phenomenology is more a carefully cultivated thoughtfulness than a technique. Phenomenology has been called a method without techniques. The "procedures" of this methodology have been recognized as a project of various kinds of questioning, oriented to allow a rigorous interrogation of the phenomenon as identified at first and then cast in the reformulation of a question. The methodology of phenomenology requires a dialectical going back and forth among these various levels of questioning. To be able to do justice to the fullness and ambiguity of the experience of the lifeworld, writing may turn into a complex process of rewriting (re-thinking, re-flecting, re-cognizing). Sartre describes how writing and rewriting aims at creating depth: constructing successive or multiple layers of meaning, thus laying bare certain truths while retaining an essential sense of ambiguity. This depthful writing cannot be accomplished in one straightforward session. Rather, the process of writing and rewriting (including revising or editing) is more reminiscent of the artistic activity of creating an art object that has to be approached again and again, now here and then there, going back and forth between the parts and the whole in order to arrive at a finely crafted piece that often reflects the personal "signature" of the author.

Sartre calls this crafted aspect of a text "style" (1977, pp. 5-9). Naturally, he alludes to something more complex than mere artistic idiosyncracy or stylistic convention. One is reminded of Schleiermacher's use of the notion of "style" to refer both to the essential genius of a text and to the thoughtfulness of the author as the producer of the text (1977, pp. 166-173). To write, to work at style, is to exercise an interpretive tact, which in the sense of style produces the thinking/writing body of text. For Schleiermacher "style" was an expression of *Geist* (mind, culture, spirit), a *geistig* phenomenon. More modern phenomenological formulations see style as the outward appearance of the embodied being of the person. In writing, the author stylizes in textual form the truth that is given signification in his or her contact with the world (Merleau-Ponty, 1973, p. 59). "Style is what makes all signification possible," says Merleau-Ponty (p. 58). But we should not confuse style with mere technique or method, rather style shows and reflects what the author is capable of seeing and showing in the way that he or she is oriented to the world and to language. It is this blessed moment where style gathers language to "suddenly swell with a meaning which overflows into the other person when the act of speaking [or writing] binds them up into a single whole" (Merleau-Ponty, 1964b, p. 235).

To write means to create signifying relations—and the pattern of meaningful relations condense into a discursive whole which we may call "theory." To write/theorize is to bring signifying relations to language, into text. Language is a central concern in phenomenological research because responsive-reflective writing is the very activity of doing phenomenology. Writing and rewriting is the thing. Phenomenologists have commented on the reflexive character of writing. Writing is a reflexive activity that involves the totality of our physical and mental being. To write means to write myself, not in a narcissistic sense but in a deep collective sense. To write phenomenologically is the untiring effort to author a sensitive grasp of being itself—of that which authors us, of that which makes it possible for us to be and speak as parents and teachers, etc., in the first place. As an aspect of the methodology of phenomenology, the experience of recalling has been described as a form of recollecting (Heidegger, 1968), a gathering of the kinds of understanding that belong to being. This is the search for the ontological difference; it is a search for the understanding of the *logos* that lets us be mothers and fathers. And herein lies a responsibility for phenomenology. This recollective thinking needs to be brought to speech, rather like what happens in the poetizing writing of the poet who gives form to an authentic speaking. Rilke called this thinking a kind of "blood remembering" (in Mood, 1975, p. 94)—an appropriate term, since for us parents and teachers the blood remembering implies a recognition of the memory that children are indeed of our blood: a recognition that, like a vow, becomes full of an unconditional quality, a recognition that is a heeding of the sign of a presence. And we experience the incarnation of this presence in the "us" from which our hope in this child derives its meaning—that is to say, a togetherness of which we proclaim the indestructibility.

CHAPTER 6

Maintaining a Strong and Oriented Relation

The Relation Between Research/Writing and Pedagogy

Few educational theorists have addressed the question of how to apply the measure of pedagogy to the standard of one's own work. To be unresponsive to pedagogy could be termed the half-life state of modern educational theory and research which has forgotten its original vocation: that all theory and research were meant to orient us to pedagogy in our relations with children. In this chapter the relation between research and vocation, between theory and life will be examined—not forgetting, of course, that in the process of this examination the question of what is the meaning of the pedagogy of parenting and teaching will be constantly posed.

Modern educational theory and research seems to suffer from three main problems: (1) confusing pedagogical theorizing with other discipline-based forms of discourse; (2) tending to abstraction and thus losing touch with the lifeworld of living with children; and (3) failing to see the general erosion of pedagogic meaning from the lifeworld.

(1) Educational research is notoriously eclectic. It borrows freely from other disciplines their language and techniques. But the connection of research to pedagogy may become rather tenuous. For example, the trendy surge of ethnographic research in education has produced numerous studies of children's lives (and of the educators who figure significantly in their lives): children in classrooms, on playgrounds, in their neighborhoods, adolescents in shopping malls, teachers in various settings, and so forth. But what we are offered on the basis of these studies are texts of the lives of children, teachers, administrators, and so

forth, that distance and estrange us from those lives rather than bring these lives closer into the field of vision of our interest in children as teachers, parents, educational administrators, and so on.

Why this fear of pedagogy? Researchers in education may object that it is one thing to try to understand the child's experience and quite another thing to act pedagogically upon this understanding. But one should wonder, is it ever possible to observe a child closely and to see the child's experience in a pure way? Outside of our relation to this child? Is it possible to describe a child, and his or her lifeworld, in a fashion that is disinterested, that lacks orientation? This would be difficult to imagine. Description would always seem to be animated by a certain interest. And this interest defines the relation in which I stand with respect to this child or these children. For example, an adult's interest in a child may involve a kind of biographic glimpse of the child's experience.

> I see a child skipping rope in the street, and I pause and smile. I see a youthful bounce, the commanding rhythm of a rope — and perhaps a memory. I recognize this rhyme. Times do not change. When the child stops, I still feel the snap against my feet. Regret fills me. I wish I could revisit the old school playground. But then I come to myself. My childhood place is thousands of kilometers away. It is not likely I would see it again as I knew it. I turn away from that child and resume my walk. I saw a child, a rope, a game. Sight and sound collaborated to make me feel the rope against my feet. Then I saw regret, nostalgia. Then I went on my way. (van Manen, 1986, p. 16)

Did I see anything of this child's experience? Not likely. As mere passer-by I do not even know this child. At best, I recaptured something of my own childhood. But understanding a child's experience of skipping is not accomplished by reducing the child's experience to one's own. What would it involve to understand a child's experience of skipping? From a human science point of view we may try to explore the cultural experience of such play or we may attempt to describe the physiological quality of the skipping activity. We may try to understand how the body feels for the child, the quality of the rope, the rhythmic experience of different skipping songs and associated skills, the preferred sensation of the ground's surface, and very importantly the social significance of others in skipping games. As an ethnographer then I may ask the girl to tell me about skipping. I may discover that skipping is a game that has consequences for children's peer relations, their friendships, their communicative abilities, their sense of social stratification, and so forth. Similarly, a historian of children's games may see other aspects of the children's experiences. How may a teacher understand this child's experience of skipping? A teacher may have an eye for the phenomenological or ethnographic meaning dimensions of this child's experience. But a teacher's eye would first of all be trained by a pedagogic orientation.

> The teacher sees Diane skipping rope. He sees much more than a passer-by can see, for he has known her for more than a year. She skips away from the other children, and he wonders what it will take for Diane to become one of them. She is academically the best achiever of her class, but her achievements are not the product of some irrepressible raw intelligence. Diane earns her accomplishments with a grim fervor that saddens the teacher. She has an over-achieving mother who fosters ambitious goals. Diane's mother intends to have herself a gifted daughter. Diane complies. She earns her mother's favor, but at the price of childhood happiness, her teacher thinks. As he sees her skipping, he observes her tenseness and contrasts it with the relaxed skipping of the others. It is the same tenseness that betrays her anxiety with every assignment, every test. Diane marches rather than skips through the hoop of the rope.
>
> The teacher also sees how Diane's eyes are turned to a half dozen girls who skip together with a big skipping rope. One of the girls returns her glance and gestures for Diane to come. Diane abruptly stops. The rope hits her feet and she turns toward the school door.
>
> What does the teacher see? A lonely girl who can relate to class mates only by constantly measuring herself by competitive standards. If only she could develop some personal space, some room to grow and develop social interests just for herself, away from her mother. The teacher is hopeful, for in Diane's eyes he has spotted desire — a desire to be accepted by her classmates. (van Manen, 1986, p. 17)

An adult's understanding of a child's experience has something to do with the way this adult stands in the world. So we need to ask, what does it mean to be an educator *and* a human science researcher? Can we conveniently separate the two forms of life? I am not suggesting that something is inherently at fault with ethnography, ethnomethodology, or other methodological perspectives derived from the various social sciences. Rather, there is a problem when a scientific research perspective is confused with pedagogic understanding (for a case in point compare Wolcott, 1988). Is educational research *educational* when it fails to present itself in both form and content as an educational form of life? What happens to our voices when we are living the half-life? I have seen thoughtful educators involve themselves in graduate work and adopt some research perspective and language that strangely transforms them, leading them *away* from a pedagogic orientation toward an orientation that is typical of some other scientific discipline. Now this educator, who once could offer such sensitive insights into the processes of teaching and parenting, speaks with an altered voice. It is the voice of the ethnographer, the biographer, the critical theorist, the ethnomethodologist, the journalist, the phenomenologist, the critic, or the hermeneutic philosopher, and so forth—but one wonders: Where in all this research can we still hear the adult speak with a pedagogic voice? Where in this text is the connection with the everyday lifeworld which for this educator used to be invested with a pedagogic interest?

A researcher who sees himself or herself as educator and who wants to arrive at better pedagogic understandings of questions concerning children's experiences—children reading, children at play, children learning in classrooms, children experiencing family break-up, children having difficulties, children experiencing loss, and so on—needs to inquire (reflect, speak, and write) in a manner that is both *oriented* and *strong* in a pedagogic sense. In other words, as we speak or write (produce text), we need to see that the textuality of our text is also a demonstration of the way we stand pedagogically in life. It is a sign of our preoccupation with a certain question or notion, a demonstration of the strength of our exclusive commitment to the pedagogy that animates our interest in text (speaking and writing) in the first place. We tend to live the half-life, unresponsive to pedagogy, when our scholarly activities are cut off from the pedagogic reason for this scholarship. In the domain of this half-life we may see forms of theorizing that are severed from the moral life, the ordinary pedagogic practices, of which these forms of theorizing too are ultimately a part. And so, there seems to exist much theory in education that lacks education. Educational theorists (of various cloth) may have become unresponsive to their pedagogic responsibility to their readers and to the children with respect to whom their theories are constructed in the first place.

(2) The tendency to abstraction is a common hazard of all academic activity. It is, in part, the reason for the disdain that practitioners hold

for university-based theorists who have lost touch with "the real world of children." Flitner (1982) recounts how Langeveld once likened the products of much of educational research to a puzzle—each puzzle carries the same caption: "Can you find the child?" Where does all this theorizing and research still connect with the lifeworlds of children? Rather than teaching us to live our lives with children more fully, educational research so often seems to be cutting us off from the ordinary relation we adults have with children. Traditional research in education has tended to abstract and fragment the realities of everyday acting and dealing with children. In modern forms of human science research in education, children may once again be recognizably present; however, their representation often betrays a lack of true pedagogic commitment to them. The children may be there as objects of our human science interest in them—but they are frequently not concretely and morally present in that they force us to reflect on how we should talk and act with them and how we should live by their side.

Probably the most severe damnation of the tendency to abstract theorizing is the accusation that educational researchers and theorists run the danger of forgetting their original mandate or vocation: to help bring up and educate children in a pedagogically responsible manner. Researchers and theorists tend to forget that pedagogy is an embodied practice and that pedagogical research and theorizing, too, are pedagogic forms of life. When as parent or teacher I reflect on the way I raise or teach my children, this reflective process is animated by the same pedagogic commitment that animates the concrete practice of my parenting and teaching these children in the first place.

Jean-Jacques Rousseau, who is often considered the first modern pedagogical theorist, of course would have agreed that abstract theorizing should not detract us from seeing the real flesh and blood child. And he should have known—I mean, actually, he should have known better! That is clear to anyone reading his confessions. He says, "The manner in which I had disposed of my children, however reasonable it had appeared to me, had not always left my heart at ease. While writing my *Treatise on Education*, I felt I had neglected duties with which it was not possible to dispense. Remorse at length became so strong that it almost forced from me a public confession of my fault at the beginning of my *Emile*" (Rousseau, 1980, pp. 572, 573). Rousseau immortalized himself with trail-blazing texts on education. It is Rousseau who said that the heart often provides surer insight than reason: heartless knowledge is dead knowledge. Knowledge without love, respect, and admiration for the being of a child cannot come to a full understanding of the child. Against the social forces of hypocrisy and selfish interests, Rousseau pitted belief in the virtue and goodness of human nature. And yet . . . the five illegitimate children he fathered he relinquished to *une maison pour des "enfants trouvés"*—a home for foundlings. (Rousseau's own mother died shortly after his birth and his father apparently deserted him.)

Strange. The man who, as theorists say, first saw the child as child did not know what his vision required of his body. (Aries, 1962, has argued that there was no concept of childhood until the age of Rousseau—but this has been contested by Pollock, 1983, and others.) In life Rousseau apparently failed as teacher, as governor of the sons of Monsieur de Mably. But Rousseau tried to reclaim his honor by showing that, theoretically at least, he knew what he could not embody. Thus appeared his justification: *Projet pour l'éducation de M. de Sainte-Marie.* It was his first scholarly paper. We have been writing scholarly papers in education ever since. So where are we now? As followers of Rousseau, we see ourselves mirrored in scholarly activities. In the name of children, we gather at learned conferences where we give speeches, proclaim truths, and study or listen to those so much wiser than we are. For the sake of our children, we teach teachers, read and write articles, purchase and publish books. We feel humbled at the powerful surge of influence. In these texts, in these spaces, great teachers of teachers assemble to influence those who influence children. Incredible arrogance or pitiful drama?

In spite of the fact that academics tend to be abstract and their texts tend to be cut off from the ordinary lifeworld, Rousseau also provides the example of how with his *Emile* he managed to break through the alienating effects of abstraction. Although Rousseau was contradictory or ambiguous about his exact intentions with the *Emile*, it is possible to argue that the text was written as a child-rearing manual of an imaginary child, Emile. It contained much concrete advice on the practice of caring for babies and young children. And yet, *Emile* was written less on the basis of personal experience and observation than on the basis of theory, some of it derived from the philosophical theories of Locke. Shortly after publication, *Emile* became a best-seller among the upper-class women of Europe. And as a result of Rousseau's persuasive discourse many of these women discontinued the practice of swaddling their babies and many began to breast-feed their own babies rather than handing them over to wet-nurses.

(3) It is estimated that in North America alone more than four million children are regularly abused and assaulted by their natural parents. Many teachers and childcare workers are distressed at their daily encounters with child neglect, abuse, or abandonment. Child suffering and exploitation is not just a third-world phenomenon. Both Canadian and United States societies seem to have tacitly accepted the existence of "throw-away kids," young children living on and off the streets of urban society, kids living lives of drug-dependency, and youths wasting their lives in prostitution or crime. In addition, there are the child-rearing problems associated with the many (often single parent) families who exist on the drudgeries of poverty and the welfare cycle. And add to that the well published modern phenomenon of family break-down or divorce, and in contrast, life in the career family in which often there is neither time nor space for the commitment of parenting by either the father or the mother—thus the demands, for example, for universal day-care, the institutionalization of young children in what are frequently profit-making enterprises where children of very young age are cared for in the employ of pseudo-parents, called "child care workers," many of whom themselves are often hardly of child-bearing age.

As this century closes, a general cynicism (Sloterdijk, 1983) and narcissism (Lasch, 1979) have tended to reduce and erode the meaning and significance that children have or could have in our lives. Modern men and women seem to place low priority on the value of children in their lives. Our relation to our children has turned into a cultural question mark—witness, for example, the new type of popular cinematography as *Kramer versus Kramer, Raising Arizona*, etc. The irony is that it is difficult in this age of relativism to be seen to defend the family and familial relations without being accused by the more critically-minded theorists of wide-eyed romanticism and naivety. Of course, no modern human science should fail to provide a critical perspective in this post-modern age. But can critical theory afford to develop itself largely in abstraction from the concrete world of living meanings? Unfortunately critical educational theory has been largely inconsequential in the efforts to improve the lives of children. Too often pedagogic concerns tend to be reduced to political ones while the question of what is good for children rarely gets raised. And to be critical means also to be suspicious of potentially self-serving discourses which allow the theorists/academics the luxury of criticism while showing a curious lack of concrete commitment to their causes in their own comfortable daily lives.

At any rate, it appears that the life of our active pedagogic involvements with children is growing thin and arid. The deeper questions of what children mean to us (Smith, 1984) are more likely to be met with indifference, impatience, or incomprehension. And as we aim to recover, by a process of reflection on lived experience, the living meaning of mothering, fathering, teaching, then we may discover to our horror that the pre-reflective life has indeed eroded and shallowed. New parents are unsure of their tasks. Family traditions have lost their authoritative normativeness. And so new mothers and fathers enroll in "parent skill training" courses (there are even a variety of "advanced parenting" programs!) to learn what they once acquired from their parents. Where is the common sense, the sense we have in common, the basic assumptions and values that constitute the indices of the rich resource, the inexhaustible layers of meaning, of everyday living with children? Who is willing to defend the need for the living meaning of living itself that ante-dates all forms of reflection?

On the Ineffability of Pedagogy

Many North American educational researchers are brought by their understanding of the meaning of research to ignore the very thing they are supposed to study in the first place. They will talk or write about anything faintly reasonable or absolutely absurd in relation to its association with the enterprise of educating real children, but not about the question of the nature of pedagogy. Yet, still, the word "pedagogy" has crept into recent North American literature dealing with curriculum, teaching, teacher education, and so forth. The term has been roughly equated with the act of teaching, instructional methodology, curriculum approach, or education in general. There has been little attempt to pose the question of the nature of pedagogy, to dialogue about the meaning of pedagogy in our everyday lives. The reason for this may be the elusiveness of the meaning of the notion of pedagogy. Where should we attempt to find the location or the space where pedagogy may be seen to reside? In the educator's acting? In the educational intention? In the theory or knowledge forms that teachers or parents use? In the effects that teachers have on children? Can pedagogy be observed? Can it be experienced? What does it mean to ask for the nature of pedagogy in this way?

We may have to accept the possibility that the notion of pedagogy is ineffable, and that no scientific observation or conceptual formulation will lead to an unambiguous definition of pedagogy. If pedagogy is ineffable then it may also be beyond the effort of behavioral teacher competence or parent skill-training, since it is not definable or teachable in a direct or straightforward manner. But this characteristic of un-teachability does not make pedagogy any less a desirable object for our understanding, since a hermeneutic phenomenological grasp of the meaning of pedagogy is practical in a different sense. Learning to understand the essence of pedagogy as it manifests itself in particular life circumstances contributes to a more hermeneutic type of com-petence: a pedagogic thoughtfulness and tact. And it is characteristic of pedagogic thoughtfulness and tact that it always operates in unpre-dictable and contingent situations of everyday living with children.

Let us now see how the meaning of pedagogy, although elusive and ineffable, may be grasped indirectly through the dialogic type of text of human science discourse. We first must consider that the use of the word "pedagogy" as a noun is already somewhat ambiguous. How may we come to an understanding of the ineffable nature of pedagogy while recognizing that pedagogy is something that animates our living with children?

For a start there is a classic approach suggested in Plato's *Meno*. What we need to do is read Plato's *Meno* as if it asks what the meaning is of pedagogy. This is a good starting point because, in spite of Plato's apparent reservations about the adequacy of written text to represent life, his *Dialogues* are the great prodigy of the philosophic tradition. There is no other text that has so effectively penetrated into the lifeblood of philosophy and the human sciences. No other human science text has so dramatically resisted all polemic efforts to deal with it in a final and conclusive way. No other text has remained so fresh and untainted in spite of many hundreds of years of dogmatic exegesis and analytic assault. How can any teacher fail to marvel at this incredible textual power to teach those willing to read? I ask this because even a non-philosophic reading of Plato may prompt questions so deep that it leaves one profoundly stirred.

Socrates engages Meno on the question of the nature of virtue
(1961, pp. 354-384). Is virtue a form of knowledge and therefore
teachable, or acquired by practice? Or is it granted by divine dispensa-
tion? As we know, the *Meno* dialogue still ends in perplexity. Socrates
retracts whatever conclusions seem warranted. Meno meets Socrates
in the street and strikes up a conversation: "Can you tell me, Socrates—
can virtue be taught?" The reader of Plato's dialogue has come to
expect Socrates' answer. He claims ignorance. There is nothing to tell
about virtue or pedagogy in a propositional sense. Meno answers slyly,
"But Socrates, you are supposed to be so smart. You can't do better
than that?" Meno asks Socrates for an expert opinion, but Socrates
rejects this role. The meaning of virtue and pedagogy cannot be captured by definitions, by polemical arguments or by giving speeches.
Socrates needs to establish a dialogical relation with Meno to open the
question of the teachability of virtue or pedagogy in a teachable way.
And just as Socrates needs to establish a dialogic relation with Meno,
so Plato (or rather Plato's text) needs to establish a dialogic relation
with the reader. Dialogically constructed texts allow us to recognize our
lives in the mimicry of stories and conversational anecdotes. Thus
dialogic texts allow for a certain space, a voice, which teaches by its
textuality what the sheer content of the text only manages to make
problematic.

So we look in Plato's dialogues on the expressibility and teachability
of virtue or pedagogy for this space. In other words, when we read Plato
on the topic of pedagogy, we are disappointed if we fail to recognize
that the real understanding of virtue or pedagogy is not captured by
definition or by way of a conclusive statement such as, "Yes (or No)
virtue and pedagogy is (not) a kind of knowledge." The pedagogy or
teachability of virtue has a sphere of ineffability associated with it.
Socrates appears to waffle in the end. Yet the reader has gained
something more important than a definition. He or she has had the
experience of being *oriented* (turned around) to the notion of virtue in
a way that is profoundly conclusive. It is important to see that poetic
texts such as Plato's dialogues practice a certain textuality; a dialogic
textuality that asks for a mimetic reading. Dialogic text can teach
indirectly what monologic text fails to achieve.

Another way of showing how the meaning of pedagogy is ineffable
and yet can be grasped indirectly is by referring to the most modern sort
of text: post-modernism. Post-modernists such as Foucault (1977),

Barthes (1975), Derrida (1978), and Kristeva (1980), also see the textuality of text as essentially dialogic. The post-modern position would say that pedagogy is not really any-"thing." It is not something inside the text, as if words on a page could provide pedagogy to the reader, nor is pedagogy something outside the text, as if it were summoned by the text. Pedagogy, like textuality itself, is neither a *this* nor a *that*.

From a post-modern point of view pedagogy is neither the theory we have of teaching nor is it its application. We all know that theoretical scholarship in education does not vouch for pedagogic competence. One may be steeped in theories of education and yet be a poor educator. The meaning or essence of pedagogy does not reside in theory. But neither is pedagogy located in the application of theory. One may be an expert on translating learning theory into particular curriculum programs. However, it is doubtful that any curriculum (or learning theory application) could ever be sensitive to the way a particular child or group of children could and should learn something specific.

We often seem to equate the meaning of pedagogy with the aims of teaching or with the activity of teaching. But the post-modernist would say that pedagogy can neither be the intention nor the action. When a child complains that he or she is not understood or properly treated and loved, then no set of good intentions, aims, or curriculum objectives on the part of the parent or teacher will alter this fact. Regardless of the teacher's intention, the pedagogically important questions are always: "What is this situation or action like for the child?" "What is good and what is not good for this child?" Similarly, pedagogy does not reside in certain observable behaviors or actions. If it did, then all we would need to do would be to copy those relevant actions or observable behaviors. But a positivistic orientation tends to confuse pedagogy with what teachers or parents *do*. It tends to judge teachers almost entirely in terms of the ability to demonstrate certain productivity, effectiveness, or the competencies which are presumed to serve these values. A positivist orientation has difficulty discerning whether the contact a teacher has with his or her children is indeed a "real" contact, that is, a pedagogic contact. For example, positivism can teach teachers about the effectiveness of eye-contact in the "management of classroom behaviors." And positivism can assess the incidence of eye-contact in empirical situations, by means of categorical interaction-analysis systems or other such instruments. However, the function of optimum frequency of eye-contact in the completion of specific learning tasks entirely glosses over the pedagogic meaning of the "meaningful look" between teacher and students. In other words, pedagogy is not identical to observable action; rather, it resides in that which makes the action pedagogic in the first place.

Further, post-modernism would say that pedagogy is neither the body nor the heart. Pedagogy does not magically ensue from the corporeal. The fact that I am the biological parent or the *in loco parentis* teacher of this child does not make me necessarily a true parent or teacher. Nor is pedagogy secured by sheer love, as we know from the tragic lives of children who were loved to death.

So a post-modern perspective alerts us to the mistaken tendency to confuse pedagogy with text or its reference, with process or content, with its medium or its end. Pedagogy is neither one nor the other; rather it constantly and powerfully operates in between.

Stepping out of the post-modern perspective and back into the practice of living we must ask, "Don't we already know what pedagogy is?" The answer is paradoxical: we do and we don't. We do, because parenting (and teaching) is the oldest profession in the world. Child rearing is as intrinsic to human life as is feeding, clothing, caring, and sheltering. Pedagogy inheres in our phenomenological response to the child's natural helplessness. In spite of the historical atrocities human beings have inflicted on their offspring, we recognize that there is a natural need to do right with the young child. (Call it instinct, sentimentality, culture, motherhood, or paternity; call it whatever you wish.) It is the poverty of social science that it fails to see an obvious fact. The young child, by virtue of its very vulnerability, tends to bring out the best in grown-ups. The parent experiences the newly born as an appeal, as a transforming experience to *do* something: to hold the child, to protect the child, to make personal sacrifices for the benefit of the child, and to worry perhaps if everything is all right. The first overwhelming sense a new parent experiences is often this ability of a natural responsiveness: response-ability, the unfolding of our pedagogic nature. As new parents, before we have a chance to sit back and reflect on whether or not we can accept this child, the child has already made us act. And, luckily for humankind, this spontaneous needfulness to do the right thing usually is the right thing. As we reach to hold the child (rather than turn away and let it perish), we have already acted pedagogically. This is our practical "knowledge" of pedagogy. It is pre-theoretic, pre-reflective. It is the knowledge of our motherly and fatherly bodies—the knowing body.

And it is important to see that the "natural" pedagogic relation between parent and child is from the very beginning a moral or normative one. *Responsibility* is a living norm that the parent experiences in the birth of a child. (In our culture an adult who would leave a newborn child to perish would be charged with murder.) But then the question arises whether the parent who takes responsibility for the child can indeed be trusted to continue to act responsibly (rather than neglectfully or abusively). And Langeveld argues that herein lies the norm of *reliability* or *dependability*. Is this adult reliable? Can he or she be depended upon to continue taking care of the child? And this question of dependability leads automatically to the next question: is this person *competent* or *capable* of taking care of the child? The requirement of competence is the third living norm, since dependability is no assurance of competence. And so we see that from a lifeworld or phenomenological view the norms of responsibility, reliability, and competence arise naturally in our living with children.

So, when living side by side with adults, children soon prompt increasingly reflective questions. In other words, as soon as we gain a lived sense of the pedagogic quality of parenting and teaching, we start to question and doubt ourselves. Pedagogy *is* this questioning, this doubting. We wonder: Did I do the right thing? Why do some people teach or bring their children up in such a different manner? We are shocked when we see or hear how children are physically or psychologically abused. We also may notice in distress how many children are more subtly ill-treated or abused. We see this all around us in shopping places, in public transportation locations, in the neighborhood, and on the street. We wonder how children experience being kept (abandoned?) for long hours in day-care institutions. What should we do about this? What can I do about this? Educational theory offers models for teaching, approaches to discipline, techniques for teacher effectiveness, methods for curriculum, management procedures for effective parenting, rationales for modern child care, and so on. And yet we suspect that it is not enough to apply some techniques, follow a program, or trust social policy. As Langeveld (1965) once said, something more fundamental to our being human is required. To be able to *do* something, you have to *be* something! We know how George Bernard Shaw once satirized, "He who can, does. He who cannot, teaches." But, teachers always utter the well-worn repartee: "He who cannot teach, teaches teachers." I have often had the feeling that teachers have hinted at a stronger point than George Bernard Shaw. As if the task to parent and to teach children is not difficult enough! Shouldn't we shudder at an incredible arrogance and inevitable sophistry implied in the idea of teacher education? Who dares to elevate himself or herself to such exalted status?

Someday, someone may be brave enough to do a mischievous study. It would test the pedagogic worth of dominant educational perspectives and theories. It would examine the lives of the people who produce scholarly writings about education. It would study the pedagogical value of the personal lives of those with high reputations. One might imagine the preposterous but true allegations: This one has abandoned his wife and children for the sake of an academic career in education. That one leaves two children in day-care from eight to five in order to free up time to write about teaching kids. This one is so confused at home that she no longer knows how to talk to her daughter, who metes out her daily revenge. That one admits, with regret, that he cannot remember much of his children's childhoods. (Absentee fatherhood, so the author may need to argue, has been a common illness among the greats of educational theory.) This one needed to break out, to experiment with life, with sex. His child has a chance at so-called "quality time" with a part-time parent during summer vacations. That one (though childless) claims a fascination with researching children's lives, but is not able to risk a personal pedagogic relation with a child. Each anecdote would turn into a paradigm case of pedagogic parody.

But why might it be that so many people who preoccupy themselves daily with profundities about educational theory themselves seem so shockingly neglectful or incompetent? Does it mean that what we say about children finds no reverberation in lived life, that living with children is one thing and talking about how we are to live with them is something else? What is the significance of theorizing and research and scholarly thought if they absolutely fail to connect with the bodily practices of everyday life? What does it mean to stand for something if it does not make a person stand out? So while acknowledging the ineffability of pedagogy we know that nevertheless we need to see or to listen to pedagogy itself. Of course, no sooner have we "seen" pedagogy or caught a glimpse of our pedagogic being than we are prompted to reflect questioningly on the way we live with children, as we should do.

We need to *act* in the lives we live, side by side with our children, but then also *wonder*, always wonder whether we did it right. We need to "listen" to pedagogy so as to be able to act in a better way pedagogically tomorrow.

"Seeing" Pedagogy

What does it mean to "listen" to pedagogy? What does it mean to "see" pedagogy in our daily lives? So much of traditional (more positivistic) educational research and theorizing suffers from a certain deafness and blindness. It confuses categorical or operational instances of some rational conceptualization of pedagogy for the "real" thing. It fails to see that we cannot "see" pedagogy if "to see" means to observe operational or measurable instances of pedagogic teaching. It fails to see that the meaning and significance of pedagogy remains concealed as a consequence of the theoretical overlays and perspectival frameworks we construct in the paradoxical effort to see more clearly the significance of certain pedagogic practices (usually called "teaching behaviors," "curriculum effects," etc.).

To the extent that we are trapped by a positivistic perspective we confuse the meaning of teaching or parenting with what we see teachers or parents *do*. If pedagogy were absent in a particular situation, how would we be able to tell the difference? But in a deep sense too positivism fails to perceive the absence of pedagogy. It fails to see the absence of pedagogy by mistaking concrete descriptions or case studies of teaching with what constitutes its ground. It fails to see that in a deep sense pedagogy absents or "hides" itself by virtue of its own activity: in the process of showing itself it also shows its hidden character.

This argument implies that one can *be* a pedagogue and yet not *have* pedagogy. Pedagogy is not something that can be "had," "possessed," in the way that we can say that a person "has" or "possesses" a set of specific skills or performative competencies. Rather, pedagogy is something that a parent or teacher continuously must redeem, retrieve, regain, recapture in the sense of recalling. Every situation in which I must act educationally with children requires that I must continuously and reflectively be sensitive to what authorizes me as pedagogic teacher or parent. Exactly because pedagogy is in an ultimate or definitive sense unfathomable, it poses the unremitting invitation to the creative activity of pedagogic reflection which brings the deep meaning of pedagogy to light.

The Pedagogic Practice of Textuality

In education, we often confuse what is possible with what is pedagogically desirable. For example, even if it were possible for many children to *be able* to read by age four, that does not mean that children *should* be reading at that early age. The understanding and skill required to teach children to read early is not the understanding and skill required for knowing what is appropriate for this or that particular child. The first kind of knowledge may be the expertise of reading theorists; the second kind of knowledge is pedagogic.

My point is that, no matter how challenging it may be to develop theories or models of learning, reading, doing mathematics, and so forth, no learning theories, teaching methods, or reading models will tell us what is appropriate for this child in this situation (van Manen, 1988). That is the task of pedagogical theory. Pedagogical theory has to be *theory of the unique*, of the particular case. Theory of the unique starts with and from the single case, searches for the universal qualities, and returns to the single case. The educational theorist, as pedagogue, symbolically leaves the child—in reflective thought—to be with the child in a real way, to know what is appropriate for this child or these children, here and now.

A child's learning experience usually is astonishingly mercurial and transitional in terms of moods, emotions, energy, and feelings of relationship and selfhood. Those who absorb themselves in their children's experiences of learning to read, to write, to play music, or to participate in any kind of in or out of school activity whatsoever, are struck by the staggering variability of delight and rancor, difficulty and ease, confusion and clarity, risk and fear, abandon and stress, confidence and doubt, interest and boredom, perseverance and defeat, trust and resentment, children experience as common everyday occurrences. Parents may know and understand this reality. Some teachers do. But how many curriculum theorists or teaching specialists know what the child's lived experience is like? How many teacher-educators know how a single child learns? Can classroom methodology be responsive if it does not understand the ups and downs of one child's experience? And what must we do? What knowledge must we pursue? What research texts must we produce that are sensitive to the peculiar question of the nature of pedagogy?

To do research, to theorize, is to be involved in the consideration of text, the meaning of dialogic textuality and its promise for pedagogy— for pedagogical thinking and acting in the company of children. In this book we have at various times discussed conditions for a dialogic textuality—methodological requirements that render a human science text a certain power and convincing validity. These conditions for research/writing may be summarized as follows: our texts need to be oriented, strong, rich, and deep.

We might say that these four conditions are also evaluative criteria of any phenomenological human science text. Throughout the previous chapters these four notions have been mentioned. I will now attempt to capture their meaning:

Our text needs to be oriented.

Whatever approach we seek to develop, it always needs to be understood as an answer to the question of how an educator stands in life, how an educator needs to think about children, how an educator observes, listens, and relates to children, how an educator practices a form of speaking and writing that is pedagogically contagious. The idea of *orientation* may seem trivial. Isn't the very fact that we write about curriculum, teaching, or education not already a manifestation of ped- agogic orientation? My suspicion is that few educators display an understanding of the need for orientation in a reflexive and ontological sense. To say that our text needs to be oriented in a pedagogic way is to require of our orientation to research and writing an awareness of the relation between content and form, speaking and acting, text and textuality. To be oriented as researchers or theorists means that we do not separate theory from life, the public from the private. We are not simply being pedagogues here and researchers there—we are re- searchers oriented to the world in a pedagogic way.

Our text needs to be strong.

Whatever interest we develop in talking and thinking about children, teaching, or parenting, it always needs to aim for the strongest pedagogic interpretation of a certain phenomenon. As we try to gain clarity about a certain notion—let it be reading, writing, discipline, play, the child's experience of difficulty, responsibility, risk, wonder, or the teacher's sense of motivation, application, method, or planning—we should use our orientation as a resource for producing pedagogic understandings, interpretations, and formulations, and strengthen this resource in the very practice of this research or theorizing. It requires that we do not treat our orientation as just one approach among many (as if pedagogy were a relativistic praxis), but that we try to formulate a pedagogic understanding that is exclusive of other interests. As Nietzsche (1984) said about the art of reading (and writing), "every strong orientation is exclusive" (p. 164). A strong pedagogic orientation requires that one reads any situation in which an adult finds himself or herself with a child as a pedagogic situation, as an answer to the question of how we should be and act with children.

Our text needs to be rich.

An educator who is oriented in a strong way to the world of real children develops a fascination with real life. The meanings of the lived sense of phenomena are not exhausted in their immediate experience. A rich and thick description is concrete, exploring a phenomenon in all its experiential ramifications. The educator, as author, attempts to capture life experience (action or event) in anecdote or story, because the logic of story is precisely that story retrieves what is unique, particular, and irreplaceable. So, in textual terms, these epistemological considerations translate into an interest in the anecdotal, story, narrative, or phenomenological description. The dialogic quality of these devices is obvious, for they engage us, involve us, and require a response from us.

Our text needs to be deep.

Depth is what gives the phenomenon or lived experience to which we orient ourselves its meaning and its resistance to our fuller understanding. Or as Merleau-Ponty (1968) expressed it: "Depth is the means the things have to remain distinct, to remain things, while not being what I look at at present" (p. 219). As we struggle for meaning, as we struggle to overcome this resistance, a certain openness is required. And the measure of the openness needed to understand something is also a measure of its depthful nature. Rich descriptions, that explore the meaning structures beyond what is immediately experienced, gain a dimension of depth. Research and theorizing that simplifies life, without reminding us of its fundamental ambiguity and mystery, thereby distorts and shallows-out life, failing to reveal its depthful character and contours. Marcel (1950) discusses the notion of depth in reference to the idea of "the secret," of what is beyond the ordinary, this "dazzling yonder." What do we mean when we talk of a "deep thought" or a "profound notion?" We should not confuse depth with the unusual, the strange, or the odd:

> A profound notion is not merely an unaccustomed notion, especially not so if we mean by "unaccustomed" simply "odd." There are a thousand paradoxes that have this unaccustomed quality, and that lack any kind of depth; they spring up from a shallow soil and soon whither away. I would say that a thought is felt to be deep, or a notion to be profound, if it debouches into a region beyond itself, whose whole vastness is more than the eye can grasp . . . (p. 192)

This kind of depth can be sensed at many levels and in many regions of our lives; certainly at the level of our living with our children and at the level of our own childhood and of our own life. And especially, says Marcel, "when one ceases to conceive of that life as something that could be adequately expressed in terms of story or film; for story and film are merely flimsy, makeshift bridges flung by us across a gulf that is always there" (p. 192). Deep thought may be reached for by means of text but it should not be confused with the text itself.

And so any text that may teach us something about the depthful character of our pedagogic nature is bound to aim for a certain hermeneutic: reaching for something beyond, restoring a forgotten or broken wholeness by recollecting something lost, past, or eroded, and by reconciling it in our experience of the present with a vision of what should be. This kind of text cannot be summarized. To present research by way of reflective text is not to present findings, but to do a reading (as a poet would) of a text that shows what it teaches. One must meet with it, go through it, encounter it, suffer it, consume it and, as well, be consumed by it.

In the work of writing and reading text we must always ask: how can we invent in the text a certain space, a perspective wherein the pedagogic voice which speaks for the child can let itself be heard? And, as we hear it speak, of course, it may be bitter, accusing, or cynical about our pretensions and about the way we are, or should be, with our children.

Human Science as Critically Oriented Action Research

Whereas hermeneutic phenomenology has often been discussed as a "mere" descriptive or interpretive methodology, it is also a critical philosophy of action. First, human science is concerned with action in that hermeneutic phenomenological reflection deepens thought and therefore radicalizes thinking and the acting that flows from it. All serious and original thinking is ultimately revolutionary—revolutionary in a broader than political sense. And so to become more thoughtfully or attentively aware of aspects of human life which hitherto were merely glossed over or taken-for-granted will more likely bring us to the edge of speaking up, speaking out, or decisively acting in social situations that ask for such action. And while phenomenology as form of inquiry does not prescribe any particular political agenda suited for the social historical circumstances of a particular group or social class, the thoughtfulness phenomenology sponsors is more likely to lead to an indignation, concern, or commitment that, if appropriate, may prompt us to turn to such political agenda. It is on the basis of understanding what serves the human good of this child, or these children in need, that one may engage in *collective* political action: action against political, bureaucratic, or ideological structures. Or perhaps more down to earth: one may engage in *personal* action which will help specific children in predicaments, for example, to escape the cycle of poverty in which the child and family are trapped.

Second, phenomenology is a philosophy of action especially in a pedagogic context. Pedagogy itself is a mode of life that always and by definition deals with practical action. We must forever and ongoingly act in our living with children or with those for whom we have pedagogic responsibility. What the phenomenological attitude gives to educators is a certain style of knowing, a kind of theorizing of the unique that sponsors a form of pedagogic practice that is virtually absent in the increasingly bureaucratized and technological spheres of pedagogic life. I have called this knowing and acting, "pedagogic thoughtfulness" and "pedagogic tact" (van Manen, 1986, 1988).

Finally, phenomenology is a philosophy of action always in a personal and situated sense. A person who turns toward phenomenological reflection does so out of personal engagement. If a child seems overly fearful or anxious about being left alone then I want to know the meaning of this fear or anxiety, because this child and any child figures importantly in my life. As I act towards children, I feel responsible to act out of a full understanding of what it is like to be in this world as a child. And so, for the sake of this child or these children I want to be suspicious of any theory, model, or system of action that only gives me a generalized methodology, sets of techniques or rules-for-acting in predictable or controllable circumstances.

Pedagogic situations are always unique. And so, what we need more of is theory not consisting of generalizations, which we then have difficulty applying to concrete and ever-changing circumstances, but *theory of the unique*; that is, theory eminently suitable to deal with this particular pedagogic situation, this school, that child, or this class of youngsters. We can move toward theory of the unique by strengthening the intimacy of the relationship between research and life or between thoughtfulness and tact:

(a) One can strengthen the intimacy of the relation between knowledge and action by re-instating lived experience itself as a valid basis for practical action. This means also that as researchers in education we need to discover and rediscover new sources for informing our research activities: lived experiences, philosophy, literary novels, poetry, art forms, personal experiences, and so on.

(b) We can further strengthen the intimacy between knowledge and action by moving toward a personal and lived sense of principled knowledge. Educational research and theorizing should not be only oriented to producing systems of decision-making procedures or rules-for-acting but also toward a continual clarification of the guiding principle which turns any kind of social situation or relation of adults and children into a pedagogic one. In any adult-child situation we should always ask what is pedagogically the responsible or right thing to do for the children entrusted to our personal care.

(c) Also, research and life are drawn more closely together in our understanding of research/writing as a form of thoughtful learning. And thoughtful learning has the dialectic effect of making us more attentively aware of the meaning and significance of pedagogic situations and relations.

(d) We should remind ourselves that, from a reflexive point of view, research and theorizing themselves are a pedagogic form of life and therefore inseparable from it. By the very knowledge forms we pursue and the very topics to which we orient ourselves, we do in fact show how we stand in life. As researchers and theorists, we recommend in the forms of knowledge in which we partake whether one should orient oneself to children bureaucratically or personally, paternalistically or authentically, instrumentally or humanistically, etc.

(e) Finally, if we think of phenomenology as a kind of action oriented research, then an intimacy between research and life immediately suggests itself. Phenomenological human science is not external, top-down, expert, or contract research. It is done *by* rather than *for* the people, as critical theorists would say. Phenomenological engagement is always personal engagement: it is an appeal to each one of us, to how we understand things, how we stand in life, how we understand ourselves as educators, etc. Even to the extent that we are as authors/readers dialogically involved with human science literature, we are involved with it hermeneutically: personally, biographically, situationally, that is, as parent or teacher of this child or these children.

Action Sensitive Knowledge Leads to Pedagogic Competence

When we compare the pragmatic consequence of behavioral social science with phenomenological human science we note that traditional behavioral research leads to instrumental knowledge principles: useful techniques, managerial policies, and rules-for-acting. In contrast, phenomenological research gives us tactful thoughtfulness: situational perceptiveness, discernment, and depthful understanding. The fundamental thesis is that pedagogic thoughtfulness and tact are essential elements of pedagogic competence. But we should be mindful as well that in everyday life circumstances, knowledge is like living: *things are always more complex!* As teacher, parent, principal, counsellor, or psychologist, we act pedagogically by mobilizing in unique and complex ways all aspects of pedagogic competence.

Human science research produces theory of the unique. And it is a feature of theory of the unique that it appropriates the particular case, not prospectively or introspectively, but retrospectively. Our living with children in natural situations of parenting and teaching is much less characterized by constant choice and rational decision making than theories of the teacher as "reflective practitioner" and "deliberative decision maker" have made us believe. Rather, in concrete and particular contexts we much more accurately are involved in actions immediately and directly.

The increasing bureaucratization of pedagogic institutions and the technologizing effect of educational research and knowledge forms tend to erode our understanding and praxis of pedagogic competence in everyday life. Moreover the lifeworld of parents living with children seems to become more shallow as the family structure weakens and as children are increasingly turned over to institutional care. Day-care and schools seem to absorb more and more pedagogical responsibilities once thought to belong to the task of parenting. Thus, human science research has radical consequences in that phenomenology edifies serious thinking on the meaning of living and acting in concrete pedagogic situations and relations. Phenomenology responds to the need for theory of the unique, and phenomenological reflection makes possible a neglected form of pedagogic learning: thoughtful learning. More fundamentally than skill learning, it is thoughtful learning which is at the heart of our pedagogic life as mother, father, teacher, psychologist, social worker, educator.

Some people bring children into this world and then abandon them. Others hold on to them but do not know how to love. Then there are parents who love their children and make an effort to raise them but they make a mess of it anyway. So we need laws to protect the child from neglect, or worse, from child abuse. The same kind of scenario can be sketched for teachers. It seems easier to talk about pedagogic incompetence than about competence. (We might boldly say that those who do not find the topic of competence difficult do not know in a serious way what they are talking about.) What makes it possible for us to speak (theorize) of competence when it comes to raising or teaching (educating) children? It means that we are able to do things in children's lives and that we are able to do things right. But modern (positivistic) conceptions of research and theorizing no longer permit us to speak of certain forms or kinds of theories as right or wrong, good or bad, reasonable or unreasonable. Modern conceptions of theorizing are more often guided by the useful (the manageable, the pragmatic, the efficacious) than by the good. Indeed Nietzsche (1962), Heidegger (1968), and others have shown that our conception of knowledge and rational thinking has been detached from its traditional affiliation with the conception of the "good." And yet we have to understand the "good" in order to give content to the meaning of competence when we speak of an adult as a "good" teacher or "good" parent.

We are interested in pedagogic competence because we realize that it is not enough to bring children into the world and to love them, or to accept a job as a teacher and to lecture about history or science. We also have to be able to help the child grow up and give shape to life by learning what is worthwhile knowing and becoming. So we are interested in competence because we want to know what to do and we want to be able to distinguish what is good and what is not good for a child: as pedagogues we must act, and in acting we must be true to our calling. If we are expected to do the right thing in our pedagogic relationship with children we may require an idea of pedagogic competence that makes pedagogic praxis possible. However, to spell out the conditions of adequate pedagogic performance by formulating a concept, theory, or model of pedagogic competence is an idle endeavor, because such effort presumes that we know conceptually what is essentially unknowable in a conceptual or positive sense. And yet, we do know in what directions the significance of pedagogic competence must be sought.

> Mark is quietly playing on the floor while his Mom is reading a magazine. But the little boy has begun to crawl speedily toward the door while chuckling with pleasure. Then he stops, sits up, and looks at his mother who casts a furtive glance. The next moment Mark is back on all fours and now his movements are even faster while his laughter turns into an excited panting. Mark stops again and looks back at Mom. The excitement is impossible to ignore and mother tears herself out of her reading and proceeds noisily and playfully into the direction of Mark. The chase is now fully on! And Mark is getting beyond himself with excitement, so that his laughter turns into hick-ups and high-pitched screams. "I'll get you! I'll get you!" laughs Mom and stamps her feet and claps her hands. Mark can hardly control himself. His delighted laughter virtually immobilizes him and instead of crawling faster his limbs now move awkwardly slowly. He just cannot get away from his mother—who'll grab him in her next move. And then she fetches him and pulls him into a playful embrace. "I gotch'a!" This is all too much and the little boy shrieks with pure exaltation. It's good that Mom's tactful kisses are so sweet because one gets the uncanny feeling that Mark's joyful excitement could have climaxed into a confused crying bout. Some more hugging and face-rubbing in Mom's hair and Mark is back on the floor. Mom sits down but she leaves the magazine alone. She knows the next "come and get me" is only a few seconds away.

Are we still talking of pedagogic competence here? But of course. A good mother knows that Mark's so-called "initiation behavior" is really an invitation. An invitation to show that she really cares—enough to drop what she is doing to show the little boy tactfully that he cannot get away as yet. And so mother's confirmation of her care turns into an adventurous pursuit. When Mark runs away from his mother his escape experience turns into a primitive mock-up of independence. For just a few moments Mom turns into a stranger who is out to get this little boy. Precisely because Mom is so familiar, it is possible to imagine her to turn into a strange other; children do not play "come and get me" with real strangers! And Mark is thrilled in the realization of his own vulnerability in the conduct of this imaginary hunt. How could he possibly outrun this big and powerful person? So there is a tension created here between security and risk, intimacy and foreigness, the security of the intimate sphere of the parent which is temporarily suspended and traded for an atmosphere of risk. Although being chased and caught borders on playful fright, in reality it would be more frightening if no one cared enough to come and claim you. Both mother and child are showing each other that they cannot do without each other. So the chase becomes a playful testing of Mom's dependability. And yes, "security," and "love," and "independence" are also the pedagogic categories of this relationship. But if these words are to communicate more to us than the theoretic-didactic precepts of child-development literature, then we need to learn that pedagogic competence involves a kind of thoughtfulness, a form of praxis (thoughtful action: action full of thought and thought full of action) wherein the themes of the pedagogic significance of the chase are experientially understood and actualized in real and concrete situations. Competence means that mother knows tactfully when to do what and how, and when to stop the chase game, "because too much excitement is too much!"

And pedagogic competence involves the anticipatory and reflective capacity of fostering, shaping, and guiding the child's emancipatory growth into adulthood: what you should be capable of, how you should have a mind of your own, and what you should be like as a person (Langeveld, 1965). The emancipatory interest of pedagogy in the educational development of children does not require that children are "educated" to become like the adults who educate them. Adults themselves are challenged by the emancipatory interest of pedagogy to see their own lives as a potentiality, that is, as lives of oriented being and becoming.

Pedagogic competence manifests itself not only in praxis, in our concrete relationships, activities, and situations with children. It manifests itself as well in theorizing, in which the parent or professional educator reflectively brings to speech the meaning of pedagogic situations. This everyday form of pedagogic theorizing usually happens when the children have been tucked in bed or when the class has been dismissed; then the pedagogic life of parents and teachers finds reprieve. Friends come over for a visit, teachers retire to the staffroom, or join their spouses at home. On these occasions adults talk "kids" with adults—a mundane or occasional form of pedagogic theorizing.

CHAPTER 7

Balancing the Research Context by Considering Parts and Whole

The Research Proposal

Experimental or survey research projects can often be carefully planned (for approval by committee or funding agency) by outlining the nature of the statistical design and analysis, by presenting the research questionnaire, test instruments, etc. Human science of the type described in this book cannot be so readily captured in a research plan or proposal. A human science research proposal may be best prepared by presenting in narrative form an introduction to the nature and significance of the research question, and an exemplary presentation of what the actual research text will look like. For instance, one may show a sample of an interview transcript. By dividing the work in side-by-side columns one may provide an example of how the transcript is worked on, what an interpretation looks like, and what kind of writing one is capable of producing on the basis of such and other texts. The research plan may be able to offer a tentative discussion of the themes that are emerging on the basis of the preliminary work, and one may be able to indicate what scholarly sources will be studied and how these sources relate to the fundamental research question. Since in this kind of research the research activity is closely intertwined with the writing activity, one may need to show that one is indeed capable of such descriptive-interpretive writing and that one is capable of generating original insights in narrative form.

It is very important to have certain concrete research plans such as "I am planning conversational interviews with six elementary school children about their favorite play space," "I will accompany and play with the children in their play spaces," "I will ask the children to write about and do drawings of their favorite play spaces," and "I will take photographs of the children's play environments," etc. It may be less important to write a detailed methodological excursus of the study until after the actual study has been completed. A certain openness is required in human science research that allows for choosing directions and exploring techniques, procedures and sources that are not always foreseeable at the outset of a research project. Similarly, a philosophical treatise about the history or nature of hermeneutics or phenomenology in general may be less helpful for making a study acceptable to an external committee than a carefully initiated discussion on the phenomenology of the topic of the proposed study.

Effects and Ethics of Human Science Research

The tasks and challenges implicit in human experiences are varied. These tasks may be to educate school children, to help abused youngsters, to minister the sick, to give psychological care to those who grieve, to mobilize the politically disadvantaged, and so forth.

The argument in the previous chapter has been that pedagogical research becomes truncated from its own life if it fails to connect with the pedagogic challenges which inhere in the human experiences to which it has oriented itself. Pedagogical research cannot step outside the moral values that grant pedagogy its meaning. At the very least the pedagogically oriented human science researcher needs to be aware of the following:

(1) The research may have certain effects on the people with whom the research is concerned and who will be interested in the phenomenological work. They may feel discomfort, anxiety, false hope, superficiality, guilt, self-doubt, irresponsibility—but also hope, increased awareness, moral stimulation, insight, a sense of liberation, a certain thoughtfulness, and so on.

(2) There are possible effects of the research methods on the institutions in which the research is conducted. For example, health practices may be challenged or changed as a consequence of the increased awareness of the experience of birth by the mother, child, and father.

(3) The research methods used may have lingering effects on the actual "subjects" involved in the study. For example, intense conversa-

tional interviews may lead to new levels of self-awareness, possible changes in life-style, and shifting priorities of living. But, if done badly, these methods may instead lead to feelings of anger, disgust, defeat, intolerance, insensitivity, etc.

(4) Phenomenological projects and their methods often have a transformative effect on the researcher himself or herself. Indeed, phenomenological research is often itself a form of deep learning, leading to a transformation of consciousness, heightened perceptiveness, increased thoughtfulness and tact, and so on.

Plan and Context of a Research Project

In conceiving and planning a human science research study, the context needs to be articulated since context places certain limitations on the general applicability and acceptability of methodological procedures. Practically speaking, the researcher needs to be creative in finding approaches and procedures uniquely suited to this particular project and this individual researcher. To the extent that we wish to speak or write about an individual child, a particular event, a concrete practice, a specific interpersonal relationship or situation, we need to approach method always contextually, while keeping in view the fundamental research question. These contextual considerations and conditions may have to do with personal, institutional, and substantive aspects of the research question and project. The following questions may help in considering a practical research approach:

(a) *What is the object of human experience to be studied?* These objects can be very different and require approaches that are uniquely suited to the topic at hand. For example, to explore "the child's experience of favorite play spaces" we may do well to actually follow the children and participate in their play activities. A small tape recorder, frequent note-taking, photographs, drawings, etc., may provide the means to collect anecdotes and descriptions of significant moments and events (see Hart, 1979; Bleeker and Mulderij, 1978, 1984). Such material collected in the thick of lived life may be compared or augmented with more reflective recollections obtained by interviewing adults about favorite play spaces in their childhood. Sometimes individuals can be asked to write recollective personal descriptions of those experiences. And of course there are descriptions to be won from other literary or artistic resources.

A very different topic of human existence such as the study of "the experience of a chronic life-threatening illness" may require the invention of a unique method. Olson (1986) used selected anecdotes from literary sources as hermeneutic prompts for conversational interviews by those involved in the experience of illness. In order to study and reflect on the experience of the patient, Olson used *A Diary*. For reflecting on the experience of the medical doctor she used selections from Camus' *The Plague*. In order to explore the experience of the nurse she employed sections from Nightingale's *Notes on Nursing*. For reflecting on the minister's experience she chose anecdotes from Tolstoy's *The Death of Ivan Ilyitch*. And in order to explore the experience of illness from the point of view of a close relative (the mother of the patient) she used Tennyson's poem *In Memoriam*. Next she engaged a patient, a doctor, a nurse, a minister, and a mother with these literary anecdotes and excerpts in order to prompt them to reflect hermeneutically on their own experiences and to tell about their own life experiences by using the literary material as a resource for making sense of the meaning of being ill. These reflective interview transcripts in turn demanded interpretive analysis by the researcher in order to produce a human science description of the experience of illness.

Other phenomena of human experience may again require very different procedural methods. For example, when we try to understand the meaning and significance of "the experience of difficulty in the child's learning" we may talk with elementary school children or high school youths about selected learning experiences and we may ask the older children to describe their experiences in personal writing. In contrast, a mentally handicapped child cannot be engaged in this fashion. And one would need to possess sensitive observational and interactional skills to notice and interpret significant moments and events in the world of mentally handicapped youngsters (see Maeda, 1986).

A very different type of phenomenon, "the experience of writing on the computer" may require a variety of procedural activities and methods. Baldursson (1988) used a diary to keep track of his personal experiences of using the word processor in the production of different types of text. As well, this topic seemed to ask for a probing of the meaning and significance of reflective philosophical sources of the nature of orality and written literacy, and an examination of testimonials of professional writers of their experience of the writing process in longhand, by means of the typewriter, or on the word processor.

A phenomenon such as "the experience and significance of risk in the child's life" may proceed in several alternative directions, requiring different research approaches. Smith (1989) asked how parents experience risk when they see their children in certain situations or when they observe their children doing something that is dangerous or risky on the playground. The research question is formulated as such: "What is the parent's experience of seeing risk?" This question quickly becomes more complicated as one realizes that children see risk too. Moreover, children notice how their own parents respond to their experience of risk and danger. And in turn, the parents need to make something of this experience. So that, inevitably, a study of "seeing risk" assumes a dimension of pedagogic self-reflectivity. In Smith's study, as in most others with which I am familiar, difficult decisions sometimes had to be made regarding approaches to be taken for "data gathering," selecting "subjects" or "participants" for interview and observation, recording conversations, organizing and approaching transcripts for analysis and interpretation, how to integrate data gleaned from other sources, how to determine and formulate themes, and how to develop a textual (writing) practice for producing a carefully "argued" description.

Another way of focussing on an aspect of the experience of parenting is to raise the question of the beginning or genesis of the parental experience. Bergum (1986) asked: How does a woman experience the process of becoming a mother? Or how does a man experience the process of becoming a father? In her study of "the transforming experience of woman into mother," Bergum followed five women through their experience of pregnancy and through the experience of birthing. A series of unstructured conversational interviews allowed her to construct a life story about each woman. And each life story could be seen to contain a fundamental theme of the transformative experience of woman into mother. Those transformative themes were "The nature of the decision to have a child," "Carrying and experiencing the presence of the child," "The pain of birthing," "Living with the child on one's mind," etc.

(b) *What is the intelligibility of the experience to be studied?* The nature of the intelligibility of the experience with which we concern ourselves may be quite different from the ease with which other possible experiences can be intuitively and cognitively comprehended. Commonly shared experiences such as "reading a novel," "being evaluated," may be more easily approached and understood than less common experiences such as "parachute jumping," "rock climbing," or experiences belonging to certain life conditions such as "birthing pain," "old age forgetfulness," and so forth. Because most of us have read novels, there is an immediate realm of interpersonal experience that can be mobilized to explore and validate descriptions of "the reading experience." However, in the case of "the experience of birthing pain" fifty percent of people are by definition of nature unable to personally validate an interpretive account of such experience. And for the purpose of collecting interview material about the experience of birthing pain, one is obviously much differently constrained in terms of availability of persons to be interviewed, the timing of interviews, and so forth.

(c) *What is the experiential situation which the researcher enters?* The challenge of human science research is that the experiential situations may be drastically different. Thus it can be misleading to use one research study as a model for application in another research environment. Situations in which the studied phenomenon occurs may be as different as a particular schoolroom, a playground, a home, a hospital, a professional workplace, a youth centre, and so forth. And within the hospital, for example, the experiential situation of the patient, the nurse, the doctor, the technicians, etc., may again be quite different.

These questions hint at the contextual complexity of a human science research study. But it is important to be reminded of some basics: human science research is the study of lived human experience. The human science researcher asks: What is this lived experience like? What is the meaning and significance of this experience? Throughout this book the notion of pedagogy has often been employed exemplificatively to explore the meaning of the phenomenon of parenting and teaching. It is methodologically important to keep one's fundamental research question foremost in mind. The illustrative question for me, the author of this book, is: what is the experience of pedagogy? What is the meaning and significance of the phenomenon of parenting and teaching? This is a very broad and big question, certainly worth a life-time's work.

To make any study more manageable it is usually helpful to narrow one's focus to an identifiable and manageable topic or question. In fact, a study of the phenomenology of pedagogy necessarily would get one involved in certain aspects (categories) of the experience of parenting and teaching, etc. For example, one might wonder: How do parents *look* at children differently from other adults? What is the parent experience of *seeing* a child? What is the experience of parental *hope*? How does parental hope differ from the hopes that teachers have for their children? What is the nature of the experience of pedagogic *responsibility*? (see, for example, van Manen, 1986).

For the purpose of any particular research project, therefore, it is most helpful to be well-defined and well-focused in the choice of one's topic, otherwise one is quickly lost in the sheer expanse and depth of one's question.

Working the Text

Traditionally, research studies in the social and behavioral sciences are presented in certain textual form. We need not document these conventions here. In phenomenological human science, too, there have emerged some patterns of "presenting" the research. However, the studies that have followed such presentational formats are not always the most interesting or the most insightful. Some qualitative studies consist of little more than endless reproductions and fragments of transcripts under the guise that the researcher has decided "to let the data speak for themselves." The approach of this book has been that the research process itself is practically inseparable from the writing process. Thus studies which do little more than present and organize transcripts fall short of their interpretive and narrative task.

It is useful, however, to think carefully about the structure or form of one's research study, even though that structure in its decisive form only emerges as one textually progresses with the work. Sometimes a researcher is unsure what direction to take. And because there is no research design or blueprint to follow, this feeling of frustration can effectively halt the work. This situation is not unlike the writer's block that authors sometimes experience. To get out of this predicament try to keep the evolving part-whole relation of one's study in mind. While it may not be possible to anticipate one's study with a fixed outline or table of contents, it should be possible to organize with broad brushstrokes the overall sense of the approach required by the fundamental question or notion one is addressing. Compare this approach to what a painter does in the preparation of a canvas for the imagery it is to serve.

Although there is no compelling reason for structuring a phenomenological study in any one particular way, it may be helpful to organize one's writing in a manner related to the fundamental structure of the phenomenon itself. Of course by "organizing one's writing" we do not merely concern ourselves with the problem of superficially ordering or arranging the text. Rather, we search for a sense of organizational form and organic wholeness of the text consistent with the methodical emphasis of the research approach. Here follow some alternative ways of structuring one's research studies:

Thematically

First, one may use the emerging themes as generative guides for writing the research study. In other words, the entire study—or at least the main body of the study—is divided in chapters, parts, or sections which elaborate on an essential aspect of the phenomenon under study. Each section heading articulates the theme that is being described in that section. And of course, complex phenomena would be further subdivided in subsuming themes. For example, on the basis of some themes derived from the illustrative sections of this study one may describe the lived experience of parenting by organizing one's writing around the themes of

- Bearing children
- Preparing the child's world as a place to be and to become
- Living with children as living with hope
- Exercising parental responsibility
- The need to act tactfully toward children

These themes are not exhaustive of the phenomenon of parenting but they allow a systematic investigation.

Human science is a *systematic* study of human experience. It is difficult sometimes to persist with a theme and systematically explore its meaningful aspects. One must resist the temptation to take a stab at meaning here, and then there, and then drift to another theme, thus producing a description that has no overall structure. Every phenomenological description has in some sense a forced quality to it. If one uses themes to organize the writing then the challenge becomes how to treat each of the themes systematically, even though one theme always implicates the meaning dimensions of other themes. For example, if one were to follow through systematically with the theme of pedagogic tact, then the following questions and organization might emerge (see van Manen, 1988):

What Are Aspects of Tact?
There is a self-evidence about tact in everyday living.
To be tactful is to "touch" somebody.
Tact cannot be planned, is unplannable.
Tact is governed by the sentient faculty.
Tact rules praxis.

How Does Pedagogic Tact Manifest Itself?
Tact shows itself as openness to the child's experience.
Tact shows itself as attunement to subjectivity.
Tact shows itself as subtle influence.
Tact shows itself as holding back.
Tact shows itself as situational confidence.
Tact shows itself as improvisational gift.

What Does Pedagogic Tact Do?
Tact preserves a child's space.
Tact saves what is vulnerable.
Tact prevents injury or hurt.
Tact heals (makes whole) what is broken.
Tact strengthens what is good.
Tact enhances what is unique.
Tact sponsors personal growth and learning.

How Does Pedagogic Tact Do what it Does?
Tact mediates through speech.
Tact mediates through silence.
Tact mediates through the eyes.
Tact mediates through gesture.
Tact mediates through atmosphere.
Tact mediates through example.

What Is the Significance of Tact for Teaching?
Tact gives new and unexpected shape to unanticipated situations.
Tact converts incidence into significance.
The touch of tact leaves a mark on the child.

Evans (1989) has interviewed school principals in order to examine how the anecdotal stories of everyday routines, problems and occurrences in the life of school administrators may be treated as narrative (practical) definitions of educational administration. As noted in chapter 6, the stories that educators tell may be treated as recommendations for acting. In our theorizing, in bringing life to speech, we are in a manner recommending a certain way of standing in the world. And so to do justice to someone's "theory" we need to read the theory as a strong version of what it intends (Blum and McHugh, 1984). When a school principal is telling a story about the way he or she went about dealing with a student, a teacher, or a parent he or she is in effect saying: "This is what it is like to be a principal." "This is how a principal is to act." Evans' study involves thus a strong reading of the everyday stories that administrators tell in order to attempt to strengthen them. He finds that a strong reading of the anecdotal stories reveals various themes which explicate the need to restore the pedagogic or educational ground of educational administration.

Analytically

Alternatively, one may conduct one's writing analytically in an ever-widening search for ground. Such an approach may take the shape of following some of the methodical activities discussed in this text. For example, if the research involves in-depth conversational interviews with certain persons, then these interviews may be reworked into *reconstructed life stories*, or the conversations may be analyzed for relevant *anecdotes*, or one may use incidents described in the interviews for constructing fictionalized *antinomous accounts* that bring out contrasting ways of seeing or acting in concrete situations, and so forth. In reconstructing life stories or in selecting anecdotes one wants to be careful to include only material that illustrates or highlights a theme. And this theme becomes the hermeneutic tool by way of which the phenomenon under study can be meaningfully understood. The next major part of the study may take the form of examining systematically the various themes that each narrative (reconstructed life story, anecdote, interview, reflective response, hermeneutic reading, etc.) or set of narratives, reveals.

Another approach is to start with a singular description of some particular life situation or event taken from everyday life, thus showing the puzzling and depthful nature of a determinate research question. The task is then to follow through with the several investigative queries which the concrete life situation makes problematic.

A third analytic approach is to begin by describing how ordinary social science at present makes sense of a certain phenomenon. The object is to show how the experience as presented by traditional social science is ill-understood, and how the taken-for-granted or generally accepted conceptualizations gloss over rather than reveal a more thoughtful understanding of the nature of a certain topic (see the section, "Explicating Assumptions and Pre-understandings," pp. 46-51). Next, one may reflectively show how certain themes emerge from considering etymological and idiomatic sources, from examining experiential descriptions, literary and phenomenological material, and so forth.

Exemplificatively

Another way of proceeding in phenomenological writing is to begin the description by rendering visible the essential nature of the phenomenon and then filling out the initial description by systematically varying the examples. For instance, after explicating the essential structure of the phenomenon of parenting, one may proceed by showing how this description is illuminated by considering various modalities of parenting:

- Being an adoptive parent
- Being a stepmother or stepfather
- Parenting disabled children
- Being a young parent or an older parent
- Being a single or divorced parent
- Being a parent of a lost child, and so forth.

Each variation may enlighten some essential aspects of the nature of parenting.

Exegetically

Fourthly, a phenomenological description may be organized by engaging one's writing in a dialogical or exegetical fashion with the thinking of some other phenomenological author(s)—in other words, with the tradition of the field. This approach is often taken in the classic discussions of themes of phenomenology. For example, Richard Zaner's *Problem of Embodiment* (1964) is organized into chapters around the writings on the phenomenology of the body by Jean-Paul Sartre, Gabriel Marcel, and Maurice Merleau-Ponty.

In the case of the phenomenon of fathering one may begin by addressing directly the works of, for example, Marcel (1978) and Langeveld (1987) who see the essence of fathering to consist in "the vow" and in "the active declaration of responsibility." The exegetical approach orients itself first or primarily to the available phenomenological human science literature and organizes itself in terms of a discussion of those texts and the structural themes that their authors have already identified and discussed. The exegetical approach treats the works of other authors as *incomplete* conversational scripts that require a *strong reading* (Blum and McHugh, 1984) in order to overcome the limits of those texts. Thus, there is a definite hermeneutic quality to this way of organizing one's textual work. One should not mistake the exegetical approach to researching-writing as "simple" armchair philosophizing. While inserting himself or herself in the scholarly human science tradition, the researcher needs to bring to the reflective process his or her personal lived experience as well as other possible experiential sources and material as discussed in this book.

Existentially

A fifth way of proceeding in phenomenological writing is to weave one's phenomenological description against the existentials of temporality (lived time), spatiality (lived space), corporeality (lived body), sociality (lived relationship to others) (see the chapter, "Hermeneutic Phenomenological Reflection," pp. 77-109). In the case of our illustrative example of the question of the meaning of parenting one may structure the phenomenological description around the question of how parents experience *time* differently from non-parents, how parents experience *space* or place differently from non-parents, how people *embody* the experience of parenting, how parents experience their pedagogical *relation* to their children and with their spouses, and so forth.

Various scholars (see, for example, Bergum, 1986) have used the four existentials as interpretive guides in original and fascinating studies of human science phenomena. However, here as with any of the other approaches we discussed above, we must guard against the temptation to follow any of these suggestions in a mindless, slavish, or mechanistic manner. Nothing sound can come out of work that is not animated by the desire to orient to its topic of study in a strong, original and thoughtful manner.

Inventing an Approach

The above five suggestions for textually organizing one's phenomenological writing thematically, analytically, exemplificatively, exegetically, or existentially are neither exhaustive nor mutually exclusive. A combination of the above approaches may be used. Or a different organization may be invented. One should be mindful, however, that the textual approach one takes in the phenomenological study should largely be decided in terms of the nature of the phenomenon being addressed, and the investigative method that appears appropriate to it.

Human science research as writing is an original activity. There is no systematic argument, no sequence of propositions that we must follow in order to arrive at a conclusion, a generalization, or a truth statement, because that would be to see writing itself as technical method. Its claim to validity as a method of demonstrating truth would be by virtue of itself as method, as having satisfied certain steps or stages. Pedagogically oriented human science theorizing is the attempt to achieve pedagogical understanding that goes beyond language and description. If this textual research and theorizing finds by means of language the means to express the ineffable it is because the secret of our calling is expressed by the pedagogic work we do with children, which teaches us to recognize the grounds that make the work possible.

A human science approach to pedagogy differs from other methods of inquiry in that it is not offered as a "new" epistemology or as an alternative research methodology that problematizes the topic of children and pedagogy in certain ways. Rather, the hermeneutic phenomenological human science attitude reminds us that children are already or mundanely a pedagogic concern to us prior to any epistemological choice point. Hermeneutic phenomenological human science in education is, therefore, not simply an "approach" (alongside other approaches) to the study of pedagogy. That is, phenomenology does not simply yield "alternative" explanations or descriptions of educational phenomena. Rather, human science bids to recover reflectively the grounds which, in a deep sense, provide for the possibility of our pedagogic concerns with children.

Glossary

The purpose of this glossary is not only to explain some technical terms and phrases that are used in this book, but also to highlight some common concepts and frequent phrases that the reader may encounter in human science sources.

Aletheia

Aletheia is the early Greek term for truth. In the human sciences truth is better seen as something that must be uncovered or as something that reveals itself into unconcealment. "Nature loves to hide," said the pre-socratic philosopher Herakleitos (Herakleitos and Diogenes, 1979, p. 14). This notion of truth contrasts with the more positivistic concepts of truth as a proposition corresponding to some state of affairs in the real world.

Being

Being is the most universal concept of Heidegger's hermeneutic phenomenology (1962). Being does not describe an entity or ultimate ground but rather it may be seen as Heidegger's fundamental term for his ontological analytic. "Being is always the Being of an entity" (p. 29), and so to ask for the Being of something is to inquire into the nature or meaning of that phenomenon. In other words, "Being" is a fundamental term of the human science research process itself.

Being-in-the-world

Being-in-the-world is a Heideggerian phrase that refers to the way human beings exist, act, or are involved in the world — for example, as parent, as teacher, as man, as woman, or as child.

bracketing

Bracketing (see the term "reduction") describes the act of suspending one's various beliefs in the reality of the natural world in order to study the essential structures of the world. The term "bracketing" was borrowed from mathematics by Husserl (1911/80), the father of phenomenology, who himself was a mathematician.

corporeality

The term "corporeality" refers to the notion of the lived body or embodiment (see the chapter, "Hermeneutic Phenomenological Reflection," pp. 77-109).

critical theory

Critical theory is now usually identified with the past work of representatives of the *Institut fur Socialforschung* at Frankfurt (often called the Frankfurt School), and especially with the work of Jürgen Habermas (Arato and Gebhardt, 1978). Critical theory has identified itself with the Marxist legacy of attempting to forge a dialectical synthesis of philosophy and a scientific understanding of society. Some features of this synthesis are: (1) an appeal to a widened notion of rationality, (2) a resistance to all forms of domination, (3) an orientation to praxis, and (4) the centrality of the concept of emancipation. In his book *Knowledge and Human Interests*, Habermas (1971) has distinguished among three forms of knowledge and associated cognitive interests: the technical, the practical, and the emancipatory. Each of these knowledge interests are seen to be rooted in primordial human activities: work, symbolic interaction, and power.

It is the empirical-analytic sciences which Habermas identifies as expressing the technical interest; the practical interest is seen to be incorporated in hermeneutics or the human sciences; and the emancipatory interest is served by the critically oriented sciences. Habermas thus places modern empirical-analytic social science in a more limited position of influence. And his critique of modern society becomes a critique of instrumental reason which is seen to govern dominant social science through which society understands itself and by way of which it legitimates its oppressive economic, political and social practices.

In education, research which has a critical theory thrust aims at promoting critical consciousness, and struggles to break down the institutional structures and arrangements which reproduce oppressive ideologies and the social inequalities that are sustained and produced by these social structures and ideologies.

Dasein

Dasein is a Heideggerian term which refers to that entity or aspect of our humanness which is capable of wondering about its own existence and inquiring into its own Being (Heidegger, 1962).

Erfahrung

Erfahrung is the German word for "life experience." This is the more general term. For example, we may say that a person has had many experiences (*Erfahrungen*) in life. Life experiences (*Lebenserfahrungen*) are more inclusive than lived experiences (*Erlebnisse*). Life experiences are the accumulation of lived experiences and the understandings and sense we may have made of these experiences (see Chapter 2, pp. 35-39).). Gadamer (1975) showed that certain *Erfahrungen*, for example in the case of aesthetic truth experiences, can have a transformative effect on our being. And thus we can speak of an "experienced" person when referring to his or her mature wisdom, as a result of life's accumulated experiences, *Erfahrungen*.

Erlebnis

Erlebnis is the German word for lived experience — experience as we live through it and recognize it as a particular type of experience (see the chapter "Turning to the Nature of Lived Experience," pp. 35-39). Dilthey (1985) used this term to show that there is a pattern of meaning and a certain unity to experience. Our language can be seen as an immense linguistic map that names the possibilities of human lived experiences.

essence

The term "essence" derives from the Greek *ousia*, which means the inner essental nature of a thing, the true being of a thing. The Latin *essentia*, from *esse* means "to be." Essence is that what makes a thing what it is (and without which it would not be what it is); that what makes a thing what it is rather than its being or becoming something else. In Plato's thought essence is the grasp of the very nature of something, of which any particular instance is only an imperfect example or imitation. *Eidos* is Plato's alternative term for Idea or Form (1961) which Husserl utilized to designate universal essences. With Aristotle (1941) the notion of essence is that something which some thing is to be in its final completed state; the essential nature (internal principle) of a thing. In Husserl's writings (1913/82) "essence" often refers to the *whatness* of things, as opposed to their *thatness* (i.e., their existence). Some phenomenologists make a distinction between *Grundwesen* (basic or fundamental essence) and *empirisches Wesen* (empirical essence). In this Husserlian distinction basic or ideal essence is accessible to phenomenological intuiting. For example, there is the empirical essence of actual "teachers" with all their inevitable peculiarities and inadequacies, and there is the fundamental or ideal essence of the Teacher as the essence which every real teacher is oriented to.

ethnography

Ethnography studies the culturally shared, common sense perceptions of everyday experiences. Ethnography is the task of describing a particular culture (ethnos), for example the form of life of an urban junior high-school class, the culture of school administrators in a certain school system, a particular day-care environment, or a certain ward in a hospital, and so forth. Ethnographers use an informant or participant-observation approach to study cultural "scenes" or cultural settings. They ask, "What do people do here? What kind of people are here?" Social situations are seen as places where human beings recurrently interact in particular ways (staff room, locker room, library desk, principal's office, etc.) and where people hold certain kinds of knowledge, ways of doing things, and perceptions that belong to those places. So the ethnographer wants to understand what one has to know, as a member of a particular group, to behave competently as a member of that group. A "good" ethnography describes a cultural reality in such a way that a non-member of the culture could "pass as an insider" if he or she had internalized the cultural features of the particular setting. To a certain extent ethnographers are interested in taxonomizing or categorizing the cultural perceptions in the ethnographic account. Thus, the lived-through or existential quality of personal experiences are sacrificed for the cultural, social, or scenic focus.

Thick Description may be seen as a methodological variation of ethnographic research. The term "thick description" borrows from the work of the anthropologist Malinowski and has been made popular by Geertz (1973). Ethnographic studies that aim for thick description tend to provide accounts not only that present and organize the "stories" as the informant(s) related them, but also that explore deeper meaning structures which the members of the social group may not be able to confirm or validate. In other words, thick description is more interpretive and analytic than mainstream ethnographic work.

ethnomethodology

Ethnomethodology studies the "methods" that people employ to accomplish or constitute a sense of objective or social reality. The purpose is to elucidate how taken-for-granted or seen-but-unnoticed "rules" lie at the basis of everyday communications and interactions among social actors. Garfinkel (1967) who coined the notion of ethnomethodology took certain ideas from the phenomenological sociology of Schutz (1973) and tied them in with certain structuralist interests and linguistic (semiotic) approaches. Ethnomethodologists show how people produce the facticity of the common sense reality of the social world and then experience it as independent of their own production. For example, Mehan (1974) has shown how interpretive skills on the part of children are crucial but unrecognized requirements for the normal conduct of classroom lessons. Ethnomethodologists are able to show how teachers "unknowingly" make certain normative demands on their students, implicitly assuming that certain communicative competencies on the part of the pupils are being employed in standard classroom procedures such as questioning, lecturing, testing, reading and achievement evaluation. For example, sometimes the level of sophistication students need and are able to show when they are required to handle a formal test situation is greater than the difficulty of the test material on which they may be "failing."

The central topic for ethnomethodology is the rational accountability of practical actions as ongoing, practical accomplishments. It focuses on the structuring activities of people in social situations and on the background expectancies and "rule use" or "members' methods" for making these social and structuring activities "visibly rational and reportable for all practical purposes."

Analytic Theory, as formulated by Blum and McHugh (McHugh, *et al.*, 1974), is not interested in describing (reporting), such as ethnography and ethnomethodology, but in analyzing (displaying). Analytic theory is a radical, less positivistic variation of ethnomethodology. The analytic theorist feels that there is no pressing need to do empirical data gathering or observational description (e.g., in using video-tape or audio-tape recording for analysis). They argue that life-topics for analysis are ready at hand in our own speech. Analytic theorists use a method of collaborative analysis in order to remind the conversational partner of that which he or she has to forget in order to speak (or write). To do research on a topic of concern (such as children's toys, special education, fatherhood, and so forth) the theorist formulates his or her interest as a problem and then develops a Socratic dialogue with this problem (and directly or indirectly with those who already have developed an approach to the problem). There are early Greek (neo-Platonic) and Heideggerian elements in the analytic approach (Blum, 1978). The theorist is interested in the reflexive character of his or her own inquiry. To theorize means that one orients oneself to that what makes it possible to be so oriented in the first place. Thus, theorizing is a kind of moral education: the theorist must show how any theorizing is an example of its own orientation to the Good, the good of theorizing.

hermeneutics

Hermeneutics is the theory and practice of interpretation. The word derives from the Greek god, Hermes, whose task it was to communicate messages from Zeus and other gods to the ordinary mortals. Hermeneutics is necessary when there is possibility for misunderstanding, said Schleiermacher (1977). He opened up the idea of hermeneutics as a theory or "technology" of interpretation, especially with respect to the study of sacred (biblical) and classical texts. Schleiermacher's program was critical (as the struggle against misunderstanding) and romantic (in the desire to recover the particularity, or the animating genius or notion of an author's thoughts). His aim was to understand an author as well or even better than he or she understands himself or herself.

The emphasis for Dilthey (1985) was not the fundamental thought of the other person but the world itself, the "lived experience," which is expressed by the author's text. Dilthey's hermeneutic formula is *lived experience*: the starting point and focus of human science; *expression*: the text or artifact as objectification of lived experience; and *understanding*: not a cognitive act but the moment when "life understands itself."

Heidegger, in turn, more radically de-psychologized the notion of understanding (1962). The notion of hermeneutic understanding for Heidegger was not aimed at re-experiencing another's experience but rather the power to grasp one's own possibilities for being in the world in certain ways. To interpret a text is to come to understand the possibilities of being revealed by the text. Heidegger's hermeneutics has been described as an interpretive phenomenology.

Gadamer (1975) adds that in interpreting a text we cannot separate ourselves from the meaning of a text. The reader belongs to the text that he or she is reading. Understanding is always an interpretation, and an interpretation is always specific, an application. For Gadamer the problem of understanding involves interpretive dialogue which includes taking up the tradition in which one finds oneself. Texts that come to us from different traditions or conversational relations may be read as possible answers to questions. To conduct a conversation, says Gadamer, means to allow oneself to be animated by the question or notion to which the partners in the conversational relation are directed.

Hirsch (1967) provides a more positivistic explanation of hermeneutics. For him text interpretation aims at reconstructing the author's intended meanings. Understanding is a dialectical process between the reader and writer. And Hirsch argues that the validity of any particular textual interpretation is increased by knowing something about the person who wrote it.

Ricoeur (1976) widens the notion of textuality to any human action or situation. To interpret a social situation is to treat the situation as text and then to look for the metaphor that may be seen to govern the text. Ricoeur, in response to Heidegger and Gadamer, returns hermeneutics from ontology (understanding as a mode of being) to the question of epistemology (understanding as human science method). For example, Ricoeur tries to articulate a methodological relationship between explanation and understanding in terms of the problem of distanciation and participation (1976, pp. 71-88).

hermeneutic phenomenology

Hermeneutic phenomenology tries to be attentive to both terms of its methodology: it is a *descriptive* (phenomenological) methodology because it wants to be attentive to how things appear, it wants to let things speak for themselves; it is an *interpretive* (hermeneutic) methodology because it claims that there are no such things as uninterpreted phenomena. The implied contradiction may be resolved if one acknowledges that the (phenomenological) "facts" of lived experience are always already meaningfully (hermeneutically) experienced. Moreover, even the "facts" of lived experience need to be captured in language (the human science text) and this is inevitably an interpretive process.

human science

"Human science" is a name that collects a variety of approaches and orientations to research. The term "human science" derives from Wilhelm Dilthey's notion of *Geisteswissenschaften*. Dilthey (1987) argued that human (mental, social, historical) phenomena differ from natural (physical, chemical, behavioral) phenomena in that human phenomena require interpretation and understanding whereas natural science involves for the most part external observation and explanation. "We explain nature, humans we must understand," said Dilthey. Dilthey sought to develop in hermeneutics a methodological basis for the human sciences. According to Dilthey we can grasp the fullness of lived experience by reconstructing or reproducing the meanings of life's expressions found in the products of human effort, work and creativity.

Hermeneutics and phenomenology are seen to be involved in all the disciplines of the humanities and social sciences that interpret meaningful expressions of the active inner, cognitive, or spiritual life of human beings in social, historical or political contexts. To say it differently, human science is the study of meaning: descriptive-interpretive studies of patterns, structures and levels of experiential and/or textual meanings. Human science research is the activity of explicating meaning. In this respect the fundamental research orientation of all human science is more closely aligned with the critical-hermeneutic rationality of the humanities and philosophy than with the more positivist rationality of empirical-analytic or behavioral cognitive science. This explains the interest of human scientists in the philosophic thoughts of Plato (1961), Aristotle (1941), St. Augustine (1960), Kant (1964), Hegel (1971), Kierkegaard (1983), and Nietzsche (1962), for example. And of special interest for human science are the works of the more explicitly oriented phenomenological philosophers such as Husserl (1913/82), Scheler (1970), Marcel (1950), Sartre (1956), Levinas (1981), Foucault (1977), Ricoeur (1981), Edie (1965), Gusdorf (1965), Strasser (1985), Ihde (1979), and so forth.

In education various human science approaches are practised in fields of study which include curriculum, teaching, administration, psychology, policy studies, sociology and philosophy of education, counselling, therapy, teacher education, nursing education, etc.

intentionality

The term "intentionality" indicates the inseparable connectedness of the human being to the world. Brentano, and later Husserl, argued that the fundamental structure of consciousness is intentional (Spiegelberg, 1982). And every conscious experience is bi-polar: there is an object that presents itself to a subject or ego. This means that all thinking (imagining, perceiving, remembering, etc.) is always thinking about something. The same is true for actions: grasping is grasping for something, hearing is hearing something, pointing is pointing at something. All human activity is always *oriented* activity, directed by that which orients it. In this way we discover a person's world or landscape.

We are not reflexively conscious of our intentional relation to the world. Intentionality is only retrospectively available to consciousness. Or as Merleau-Ponty (1964a, pp. 43-95) said, the world is revealed to us as ready-made and already "there." It is not possible to experience something *while* reflecting on the experience (even if this experience is itself a reflective acting!). For example, our experience of anger dissipates as soon as we try to analyze it while experiencing the anger. We may speak of "specific intentionality" when the intentionality is specific to the act, referring to the directedness of thinking and acting here and now. And we may speak of "general intentionality" when we are being directed to the world in a certain way; the way we choose and find ourselves to be present in the world — for example, as man, as woman, as child, as mother, as father, as teacher, as author, and so forth.

lifeworld

The idea of the lifeworld (*Lebenswelt*), as the world of lived experience, derives from Husserl's last and largely posthumously published text *The Crisis of European Sciences and Transcendental Phenomenology* (1970a). He described the lifeworld as the "world of immediate experience," the world as "already there," "pregiven," the world as experienced in the "natural, primordial attitude," that of "original natural life" (pp. 103-186). Husserl makes a critical historical and phenomenological distinction between (1) our theoretical attitude to life, borrowed from the Greeks, and (2) our natural pre-theoretical attitude to life on which all theorizing is based and from which all theorizing is ultimately derived. Husserl uses the term "natural" for what is original and naive, prior to critical or theoretical reflection.

The theoretical attitude that western intellectual and scientific culture borrowed from the Greeks must be recognized as a new (historically speaking) and distinct style of life. In contrast, the natural attitude of the lifeworld is always "pragmatic," always directed at the world "toward this or that, being directed toward it as an end or as a means, as relevant or irrelevant, toward the private or public, toward what is daily required or obtrusively new" (Husserl, 1970a, p. 281). Plato and Aristotle attributed the origin of the desire to know (philosophy) to simple wonder at things being the way they are. But while wonder is a natural occurrence in everyday life, the modern theoretical attitude tends to turn us into non-participating spectators, surveyors of the world. And even more importantly (or ironically) the theoretical attitude in its modern scientific sense often silences or kills our sense of wonder — a wonder which

Merleau-Ponty (1962, pp. vii-xxi) described as the demand for a certain awareness, a certain kind of attentiveness and will to seize the meaning of the world.

According to Husserl (1970a) each lifeworld shows certain pervading structures or styles which need to be studied. Schutz and Luckmann (1973) elaborated this notion in a sociological direction in their book *Structures of the Life-world*. And Heidegger (1962) gave the idea of lifeworld structures a more worldly, existential thrust by speaking of phenomenology as the study of Being, the study of our modes-of-being or ways-of-being-in-the-world. Wittgenstein's notion of "form of life" and "language games" can be understood as a more linguistic approach to the idea of lifeworld (1982). And more recent formulations associated with the project of phenomenology also seem to have turned toward more semiotic directions.

lived meaning

Lived meaning refers to the way that a person experiences and understands his or her world as real and meaningful. Lived meanings describe those aspects of a situation as experienced by the person in it. For example, a teacher wants to understand how a child meaningfully experiences or lives a certain situation even though the child is not explicitly aware of these lived meanings.

noema

Noema (noematic) denotes that to which we orient ourselves; it is the object referent of *noesis*, the *noetic* act.

noesis

Noesis is the interpretive act directed to an intentional object, the *noema* (or the *noematic* object).

ontic

Ontic inquiry is concerned with the things or entities of the world.

ontological

Ontological inquiry is concerned with what it means to *be*, with the Being of things or entities. Heidegger (1962) calls ontology the phenomenology of being.

phenomenology

Phenomenology is the science of phenomena. The philosopher Kant used the term only rarely to distinguish the study of objects and events (phenomena) as they appear in our experience from objects and events as they are in themselves (noumena) (1964, chapter III). In his *Phenomenology of the Spirit*, Hegel (1977) formulated phenomenology as the science in which we come to know *mind* as it is in itself through the study of the ways in which it appears to us. However, with Husserl phenomenology became a descriptive method as well as a human science movement based on modes of reflection at the heart of philosophic and human science thought.

For Husserl phenomenology is a discipline that endeavors to describe how the world is constituted and experienced through conscious acts. His phrase *Zu den Sachen* means both "to the things themselves" and "let's get down to what matters!" Phenomenology must describe what is given to us in immediate experience without being obstructed by pre-conceptions and theoretical notions. Husserl advanced a transcendental phenomenology. But in his last major work *The Crisis of European Sciences and Transcendental Phenomenology*, Husserl (1970a) formulated the notion of the *Lebenswelt*, the lifeworld, the everyday world in which we live in the natural, taken-for-granted attitude. This notion of the lifeworld has become programmatic in the development of a more existentially oriented phenomenology. Existential phenomenology (not to be confused with the life philosophy of existentialism) aims at describing how phenomena present themselves in lived experience, in human existence. Thus, for Heidegger (1962) phenomenology is ontology—a study of the modes of "being in the world" of human being. Heidegger's professed aim is to let the things of the world speak for themselves. He asks: What is the nature (Being) of this being? What lets this being be what it is?

Phenomenology differs from the various human science approaches such as ethnography, symbolic interactionism, and ethnomethodology in that phenomenology makes a distinction between appearance and essence. "Phenomenology is the study of essences," says Merleau-Ponty (1962, p. vii). This means that phenomenology always asks the question of what is the nature or meaning of something. In the "Preface" to his *Phenomenology of Perception* (1962) Merleau-Ponty points out that the work of phenomenology is as painstaking as the work of artists such as Balzac, Proust, Valéry, or Cézanne. Phenomenology demands of us re-learning to look at the world as we meet it in immediate experience. And it requires of us "the same demand for awareness and the same will to seize the meaning of the world as that meaning comes into being" (p. xxi). In other words, phenomenology does not produce empirical or theoretical observations or accounts. Instead, it offers accounts of experienced space, time, body, and human relation as we live them. In the various disciplines phenomenology has been mobilized to produce a phenomenological sociology (Schutz, 1972), phenomenological psycho-therapy or psychiatry (van den Berg, 1972), phenomenological psychology (Merleau-Ponty, 1962; Giorgi, 1970), etc. In education, phenomenology has been especially productive in the phenomenological pedagogy of Langeveld (1965), Bollnow (1970), Beets (1952), Beekman (1975) in the Netherlands, and in the more philosophy of education oriented writings of Greene (1978) and Vandenberg (1971) in North America.

reduction

Reduction is the technical term that describes the phenomenological device which permits us to discover what Merleau-Ponty (1962) calls the spontaneous surge of the lifeworld. To come to an understanding of the essential structure of something we need to reflect on it by practising a certain reduction. Several levels or types of reduction may be distinguished. First, reduction involves the awakening of a profound sense of wonder and amazement at the mysteriousness of the belief in the world. This fundamental amazement animates one's questioning of the meaning of the experience of the world. Next, in the reduction one needs to overcome one's subjective or private feelings, preferences, inclinations, or expectations that would prevent one from coming to terms with a phenomenon or experience as it is lived through. Third, in the reduction one needs to strip away the theories or scientific conceptions and thematizations which overlay the phenomenon one wishes to study, and which prevents one from seeing the phenomenon in a non-abstracting manner. Fourth, in the eidetic reduction one needs to see past or through the particularity of lived experience toward the universal, essence or *eidos* that lies on the other side of the concreteness of lived meaning. Merleau-Ponty (1964a) stressed that (unlike Husserl perhaps) we should not see the reduction as an end in itself. Rather the reduction is a means to an end: to be able to return to the world as lived in an enriched and deepened fashion. The reduction is "the ambition to make reflection emulate the unreflective life of consciousness."

relationality

Relationality refers to our lived relation to other human beings (see the chapter, "Hermeneutic Phenomenological Reflection," pp. 104-106).

semiotics

Semiotics as the science of signs ("semiotics" in North America and "semiology" in France, Europe) is the application of structuralism to literary studies, semantic anthropology, etc. In *The New Science*, Vico (1725) suggested that humans create themselves and their world (mythically, poetically, symbolically) by structuring the world, society, institutions, etc., in accordance with the mental languages of the structures of mind. The true nature of things is seen to lie not in the things themselves but in the relationships which we construct and then perceive among them. The Swiss linguist Ferdinand de Saussure advanced the notion that the meaning of a word (sign) does not depend upon some substantive correlate but rather he argued that meaning, the signified, is an arbitrary relational quality of differences between signifiers (Ray, 1984).

Texts or signs and their structural relationships are the subject of study for semiotics. According to semiotics, there is no innocent, pure or pristine experience of a real external world. We "encode" our experience of the world in order that we may experience it; there is no neutral text. This encoding produces certain styles. Thus, Barthes has concluded that writing is all style, a highly conventionalized activity (Sontag, 1982). Barthes' critical readings and writings may be interpreted as deconstructive moves to expose, for example, how modern society codifies reality in its own image. And once this reality is thus produced one proceeds to believe that it is the only reality possible.

From a semiotic point of view any social behavior or practice signifies and may be read as a text, as a language. For example, nobody merely talks. Every speech-act displays a complex of messages through the "language" of gesture, accent, clothing, posture, perfume, hair-style, facial manner, social context, etc., above, behind, beneath, beside and even at odds with what words actually say. Similarly, everything around us systematically communicates something meaningful to us, and one can thus speak of "the world as a text." Derrida has provided an influential approach to the semiotics of writing. In his grammatology (science of writing) he argues that our logocentrism and our tendency to treat oral language as primary over written language commits us to a falsifying "metaphysics of presence" (1976). It is based on an illusion that we are able ultimately to come "face to face" with each other and with things. According to Derrida this belief in "presence" expresses a yearning hope that in spite of our always fragmentary and incomplete experience there is reason to insist on the existence of a redeeming and justifying wholeness, an ultimate notion of one-ness, essence, ground, or a faith in objective reality. As reader-interpreter Derrida practises a deconstructive analysis of the text: a double reading which has the effect of showing the ways in which, for example, the argument of a text calls its own premises into question.

spatiality

The term "spatiality" refers to lived space (see the chapter, "Hermeneutic Phenomenological Reflection," pp. 102-106).

symbolic interactionism

Symbolic interactionism is a theoretical perspective in social psychology, originally connected with Mead (1967) and the Chicago School. The foremost proponent has been Blumer (1969). Symbolic interactionists understand social reality as a complex network of interacting persons, who symbolically interpret their acting in the social world. The methodological rule is that social reality and society should be understood from the perspective of the actors who interpret their world through and in social interaction. Its application is in the area of role behavior and perception studies; its interest in empirical research led to the "grounded theory method" of Glaser and Strauss (1967).

From the perspective of symbolic interactionism human beings tend to act on the basis of how they believe other people behave toward them; and their self-perceptions and feelings tend to be mediated by how they think others see and feel about them. In education this principle has been illustrated by now classic studies showing the so-called Pygmalion effect of teachers' perceptions of children and the effect of those perceptions on the children's sense of self and academic ability. In short, symbolic interactionists study the functional relationships between how we see ourselves (self-definition), how we see others (interpersonal perceptions) and how we think others see us.

The *dramaturgical* approach of Goffman (1959) is a variation of the symbolic interactionist method, consisting of a micro-analysis of actors during everyday interaction. He does this sociological work in close analogy to the metaphor of the stage or theatre. Goffman's descriptions of the actor's "self in interaction" demonstrate the precariousness of social relations and social reality (as shown in ethnomethodology as well).

temporality

The term "temporality" refers to lived time (see the chapter, "Hermeneutic Phenomenological Reflection," pp. 104-106).

Bibliography

Arato, A. and Eike Gebhardt. (1978). *The essential Frankfurt School reader*. New York: Urizen Books

Ariès, P. (1962). *Centuries of childhood*. New York: Random House.

Aristotle (1941). *The basic works*. (R. McKeon, ed.) New York: Random House.

Auden, W.H. (1967). A short defense of poetry. Address given at a round-table conference on *Tradition and innovation in contemporary literature*, The International PEN Conference, October 1967, Budapest.

Baldursson, S. (1988). *Technology, computer use, and the pedagogy of writing.* Unpublished Dissertation. Edmonton: The University of Alberta.

Barrett, W. (1978). *The illusion of technique*. New York: Anchor Press.

Barritt, L., A.J. Beekman, H. Bleeker, and K. Mulderij (1983). Analyzing phenomenological descriptions. *Phenomenology + Pedagogy*. Vol. 2, No. 1, pp. 1-17.

Barthes, R. (1975). *The pleasure of the text*. New York: Hill and Wang.

Barthes, R. (1986). *The rustle of language*. New York: Hill and Wang.

Beekman, A.J. (1975). *Dienstbaar inzicht: opvoedingswetenschap als sociale planwetenschap*. Groningen: H.D. Tjeenk Willink.

Beekman, A.J. and K. Mulderij. (1977). *Beleving en ervaring: werkboek fenomenologie voor de sociale wetenschappen*. Amsterdam: Boom Meppel.

Beets, N. (1952). *Verstandhouding en onderscheid. Amsterdam*: Boom Meppel.

Bergum, V. (1986). *The phenomenology from woman to mother. Unpublished Dissertation*. Edmonton: The University of Alberta.

Bettelheim, B. (1975). *The uses of enchantment*. New York: Knopf.

Binswanger, L. (1963). *Being in the world*. London: Souvenir Press.

Blaman, A. (1963). *Verhalen*. Amsterdam: Meulenhoff.

Bleeker, H. and K. Mulderij. (1978). *Kinderen buiten spel*. Amsterdam: Boom Meppel.

Bleeker, H. and K. Mulderij. (1984). *Pedagogiek op je knieën*. Amsterdam: Boom Meppel.

Blum, A. (1978). *Socrates: the original and its images*. Boston: Routledge & Kegan Paul.

Blum, A. and P. McHugh. (1984). *Self-reflection in the arts and sciences*. Atlantic Highlands: Humanities Press.

Blumer, H. (1969). *Symbolic interactionism: perspective and method*. Englewood Cliffs, N.J.: Prentice Hall.

Bollnow, O.F. (1960). Lived-space. *Universitas*. Vol. 15, No. 4, pp. 31-39.

Bollnow, O.F. (1970). *Die pädagogische Atmosphäre*. Heidelberg: Quelle & Meyer.

Bollnow, O.F. (1974). The objectivity of the humanities and the essence of truth. *Philosophy Today*, Vol. 18, 1/4, pp. 3-18.

Bollnow, O.F. (1982). On silence — findings of philosophico-pedagogical anthropology. *Universitas*. Vol. 24, No. 1, pp. 41-47.

Bollnow, O.F. (1987). *Crisis and new beginning*. Pittsburgh: Duquesne University Press.

Bowlby, J. (1978). *Attachment and loss*. (3 volumes). New York: Penguin Books.

Brown, N.O. (1966). *Love's body*. New York: Harper and Row.

Buber, M. (1970). *Voordrachten over opvoeding & autobiografische fragmenten*. Utrecht: Bijleveld.

Burch, R. (1986). Confronting technophobia: a topology. *Phenomenology + Pedagogy*, Vol. 4, No. 2, pp. 3-21.

Buytendijk, F.J.J. (1947). *Het kennen van de innerlijkheid*. Utrecht: N.V. Dekker & van de Vegt.

Buytendijk, F.J.J. (1962). *De psychologie van de roman: studies over Dostojevski*. Utrecht: Aula Boeken.

Buytendijk, F.J.J. (1988). The first smile of the child. *Phenomenology + Pedagogy*, Vol. 6, No. 1, pp. 15-24.

Cairns, H. (1971). Introduction. *Plato, the collected dialogues*. E. Hamilton and H. Cairns (eds.) Princeton, N.J.: Princeton University Press.

Canetti, E. (1978). *Auto Da Fé*. London: Pan Books.

Chesler, P. (1979). *With child: A diary of motherhood*. New York: Crowell.

Dauenhauer, B.P. (1980). *Silence: the phenomenon and its ontological significance*. Bloomington: Indiana University Press.

De Boer, T. (1980). Inleiding. *Edmund Husserl: filosofie als strenge wetenschap*. T. de Boer (ed.). Amsterdam: Boom Meppel.

Derrida, J. (1976). *Of grammatology*. Baltimore, Maryland: The John Hopkins University Press.

Derrida, J. (1978). *Writing and difference*. Chicago: The University of Chicago Press.

Dienske, I. (1987). *Terugkeren en verdergaan*. Unpublished Dissertation. Utrecht: The Rijksuniversiteit van Utrecht.

Dilthey, W. (1976). (H.P. Rickman, editor) *Dilthey: selected writings*. Cambridge: Cambridge University Press.

Dilthey, W. (1985). *Poetry and experience*. Selected Works, Vol. V, Princeton, N.J.: Princeton University Press.

Dilthey, W. (1987). *Introduction to the human sciences*. Toronto: Scholarly Book Services.

Edie, J.M. (1965). *An invitation to phenomenology*. Chicago: Quadrangle Books.

Eliot, G. (1871/1988). *Middlemarch*. New York: Penguin Books.

Evans, R. (1989). *Ministrative insight: educational administration as pedagogic practice*. Unpublished Dissertation. Edmonton: The University of Alberta.

Fadiman, C. (ed.) (1985). *The Little, Brown book of anecdotes*. Boston: Little, Brown.

Flitner, A. (1982). Educational science and educational practice. *Education*. Vol. 25, pp. 63-75.

Ford, J. (1987). *The experience of living with the history of a heart attack*. Unpublished Dissertation. Edmonton: The University of Alberta.

Foucault, M. (1977). *Language, counter-memory, practice*. New York: Cornell University Press.

Freire, P. and D. Macedo. (1987). *Literacy: reading the word and the world*. South Hadley, Mass.: Bergin and Garvey.

Gadamer, H.-G. (1975). *Truth and method*. New York: Seabury.

Gadamer, H.-G. (1976). *Philosophical hermeneutics*. Berkeley: University of California Press.

Gadamer, H.-G. (1986). *The relevance of the beautiful and other essays*. Cambridge: Cambridge University Press.

Garfinkel, H. (1967). *Studies in ethnomethodology*. Englewood Cliffs, N.J.: Prentice-Hall.

Geertz, C. (1973). *The interpretation of cultures*. New York: Basic Books.

Giorgi, A. (1970). *Psychology as a human science: a phenomenologically based approach*. New York: Harper and Row.

Giorgi, A. (1985). Sketch of a psychological phenomenological method. *Phenomenology and Psychological Research*. A. Giorgi (ed.). Pittsburgh: Duquesne University Press.

Glaser, B.G. and A.L. Strauss. (1967). *The discovery of grounded theory: strategies for qualitative research*. Chicago: Aldine.

Goethe, W. (1963). *Goethe's world view, presented in his reflections and maxims*. New York: Frederick Ungar.

Goffman, E. (1959). *The presentation of self in everyday life*. New York: Doubleday.

Greene, M. (1978). *Landscapes of learning*. New York: Teachers College Press.

Gusdorf, G. (1965). *Speaking (La Parole)*. Evanston: Northwestern University Press.

Habermas, Jürgen. (1971). *Knowledge and human interests*. Boston: Beacon Press.

Harlow, H.F. and M.K. Harlow (1965). *The affectional systems. Behavior of non-human primates, 2.* A.M. Schrier, H.F. Harlow, and F. Stollowitz (eds.). New York: Academic Press.

Hart, R. (1979). *Children's experience of place*. New York: Irvington.

Hegel, G.W.F. (1977). *The phenomenology of mind*. New York: Hu-manities Press.

Heidegger, M. (1962). *Being and time*. New York: Harper and Row.

Heidegger, M. (1968). *What is called thinking?* New York: Harper and Row.

Heidegger, M. (1971). *Poetry, language, thought*. New York: Harper and Row.

Heidegger, M. (1977). *Basic Writings*. New York: Harper and Row.

Herakleitos and Diogenes. (1979). *Herakleitos & Diogenes*. (Translated from the Greek by Guy Davenport.) San Francisco, Cal.: Grey Fox Press.

Hintjes, J. (1981). *Geesteswetenschappelijke pedagogiek*. Amsterdam: Boom Meppel.

Hirsch, E.D. (1967). *Validity in interpretation*. New Haven, Conn.: Yale University Press.

Hoy, D. (1978). *The critical circle*. Berkeley: University of California Press.

Hultgren, F.H. (1982). *Reflecting on the meaning of curriculum through a hermeneutic interpretation of student-teaching experiences in home economics*. Unpublished Dissertation. Pennsylvania State University.

Hunsberger, M. (1982). *The encounter between reader and text*. Unpublished Dissertation. Edmonton: The University of Alberta.

Husserl, E. (1911/80). *Filosofie als strenge wetenschap*. Amsterdam: Boom Meppel.

Husserl, E. (1913/82). *Ideas pertaining to a pure phenomenology and to a phenomenological philosophy: general introduction to a pure phe-nomenology*. The Hague: Martinus Nijhoff.

Husserl, E. (1964). *The phenomenology of internal time-consciousness*. Bloomington: Indiana University Press.

Husserl, E. (1970a). *The crisis of European sciences and transcendental phenomenology*. Evanston: Northwestern University Press.

Husserl, E. (1970b). *The idea of phenomenology*. The Hague: Martinus Nijhoff.

Ihde, D. (1979). *Technics and praxis*. Boston: D. Reidel.

Jager, B. (1975). Theorizing, journeying, dwelling. *Phenomenological Psychology*. Vol. 11, pp. 235-260.

Juhl, P.D. (1986). *Interpretation: an essay in the philosophy of literary criticism*. Princeton, N.J.: Princeton University Press.

Kant, I. (1964). *Critique of pure reason*. New York: Everyman's Library.

Kierkegaard, S. (1983). *Fear and trembling, repetition*. Princeton, N.J.: Princeton University Press.

Klein, E. (1971). *Klein's comprehensive etymological dictionary of the English language*. Amsterdam: Elsevier.

Kristeva, J. (1980). *Desire in language: a semiotic approach to literature and art*. New York: Columbia University Press.

Langeveld, M.J. (1965). *Beknopte theoretische pedagogiek*. Groningen: Wolters.

Langeveld, M.J. (1967). *Scholen maken mensen*. Purmerend: J. Muusses

Langeveld, M.J. (1971). *Erziehungskunde und Wirklichkeit*. Braunschweig: Georg Westermann Verlag.

Langeveld, M.J. (1983a). The stillness of the secret place. *Phenomenology + Pedagogy*, Vol. 1, No. 1, pp. 11-17.

Langeveld, M.J. (1983b). The secret place in the life of the child. *Phenomenology + Pedagogy*, Vol. 1, No. 2, pp. 181-189.

Langeveld, M.J. (1984). How does the child experience the world of things? *Phenomenology + Pedagogy*, Vol. 2, No. 3, pp. 215-223.

Langeveld, M.J. (1987). What is the meaning of being and having a father? *Phenomenology + Pedagogy*, Vol. 5, No. 1, pp. 5-21.

Lasch, C. (1979). *The culture of narcissism*. New York: Warner.

Levinas, E. (1981). *Otherwise than being or beyond essence*. The Hague: Martinus Nijhoff.

Linschoten, J. (1953). Aspecten van de sexuele incarnatie. *Persoon en wereld*. J.H. van den Berg and J. Linschoten (eds.). Utrecht: Erven J. Bijleveld.

Linschoten, J. (1953). Nawoord. *Persoon en wereld*. J.H. van den Berg and J. Linschoten (eds.). Utrecht: Erven J. Bijleveld.

Litt, Th. (1967). *Führen oder Wachsenlassen*. Stuttgart: Ernst Klett Verlag.

Maeda, C. (1986). Falling asleep. *Phenomenology + Pedagogy*, Vol. 4, No. 1, pp. 43-52.

Marcel, G. (1949). *Being and having*. London: The Dacre Press.

Marcel, G. (1950). *Mystery of being*. Volume 1 and 2. South Bend, Indiana: Gateway Editions.

Marcel, G. (1978). *Homo viator*. Gloucester, MA: Smith.

McHugh, P., S. Raffel, D.C. Foss, and A.F. Blum. (1974). *On the beginning of social inquiry*. London: Routledge & Kegan Paul.

Mead, G.H. (1967). *The philosophy of the act*. Chicago: The University of Chicago Press.

Megill, A. (1985). *Prophets of extremity: Nietzsche, Heidegger, Foucault, Derrida*. Berkeley: University of California Press.

Mehan, H. (1974). Accomplishing classroom lessons. *Language use and school performance*. A.V. Cicourel, K.H. Jennings, S.H.M. Jennings, K.C.W. Leiter, R. Mackay, H. Mehan, and D.R. Roth. New York: Academic Press.

Merleau-Ponty, M. (1962). *Phenomenology of perception*. London: Routledge & Kegan Paul.

Merleau-Ponty, M. (1964a). *The primacy of perception*. Evanston: Northwestern University Press.

Merleau-Ponty, M. (1964b). *Signs*. Evanston: Northwestern University Press.

Merleau-Ponty, M. (1968). *The visible and the invisible*. Evanston: Northwestern University Press.

Merleau-Ponty, M. (1973). *The prose of the world*. Evanston: North-western University Press.

Milne, A.A. (1979). *When we were very young*. Toronto: McClelland & Stewart.

Mollenhauer, K. (1983). *Vergessene Zusammenhänge*. München: Juventa Verlag.

Mollenhauer, K. (1986). *Umwege: über Bildung, Kunst und Interaktion*. München: Juventa Verlag.

Mood, J.J.L. (1975). *Rilke on love and other difficulties*. New York: Norton.

Nietzsche, F. (1873/1954). *On truth and lie in an extra-moral sense*. Nietzsche. W. Kaufmann (ed.). New York: The Viking Press.

Nietzsche, F. (1962). *Philosophy in the tragic age of the Greeks*. Chicago: Regnery.

Nietzsche, F. (1984). *Human, all too human: a book for free spirits*. Cambridge: Cambridge University Press.

Nohl, H. (1967). *Ausgewählte pädagogische Abhandlungen*. Paderborn: Ferdinand Schöningh.

Olson, C. (1986). *How can we understand the life of illness?* Unpublished Dissertation. Edmonton: The University of Alberta.

Ong, W.J. (1967/81). *The presence of the word*. Minneapolis: University of Minnesota Press.

Ong, W.J. (1971). *Rhetoric, romance and technology: studies in the interaction of expression and culture*. Ithaca: Cornell University Press.

Ong, W.J. (1982). *Orality and literacy: the technologizing of the word*. New York: Methuen.

Perquin, N. (1964). *Pedagogiek*. Roermond: J.J. Romen en Zonen.

Palmer, R. (1969). *Hermeneutics*. Evanston: Northwestern University Press.

Plato (1961). *The collected dialogues*. (E. Hamilton and H. Cairns, eds.) Princeton, N.J.: Princeton University Press.

Polanyi, M. (1958). *Personal knowledge*. Chicago: The University of Chicago Press.

Polanyi, M. (1969). *Knowing and being*. Chicago: The University of Chicago Press.

Pollock, L.A. (1983). *Forgotten children: parent-child relations from 1500 to 1900*. Cambridge: Cambridge University Press.

Progoff, I. (1975). *At a journal workshop: the basic text and guide for using the intensive journal*. New York: Dialogue House Library.

Ray, W. (1984). *Literary meaning: from phenomenology to deconstruction*. Oxford: Basil Blackwell.

Ricoeur, P. (1976). *Interpretation theory: discourse and the surplus of meaning.* Fort Worth, Texas: The Texas Christian University Press.

Ricoeur, P. (1981). *Hermeneutics and the human sciences.* New York: Cambridge University Press.

Rilke, R.M. (1977). *Possibility of being: A selection of poems.* New York: New Directions.

Robinson, M. (1980). *Housekeeping.* New York: Farrar Straus Giroux.

Rorty, R. (1979). *Philosophy and the mirror of nature.* Princeton, N.J.: Princeton University Press.

Rosen, H. (1986). *The importance of story.* Language Arts. Vol. 63, No. 3, pp. 226-237.

Rosen, S. (1969). *Nihilism.* New Haven: Yale University Press.

Rousseau, J.-J. (1969). *Emile.* New York: Dutton.

Rousseau, J.-J. (1980). *The Confessions.* Norwalk, Conn.: The Easton Press.

Sartre, J.P. (1956). *Being and nothingness.* New York: Philosophical Library.

Sartre, J.P. (1977). *Life/situations: essays written and spoken.* New York: Panteon Books.

Schaffer, R. (1977). *Mothering.* Cambridge, Mass.: Harvard University Press.

Scheler, M. (1970). *The nature of sympathy.* Hamden, Conn.: Archon Books.

Schleiermacher, F.E.D. (1964). *Ausgewählte pädagogische Schriften.* Paderborn: Ferdinand Schöningh.

Schleiermacher, F.E.D. (1977). *Hermeneutics: the handwritten manuscripts.* Missoula, Mont.: Scholars Press.

Schutz, A. (1972). *The phenomenology of the social world.* London: Heinemann Educational Books.

Schutz, A. and T. Luckmann. (1973). *The structures of the life-world.* Evanston: Northwestern University Press.

Silverman, H.J. (1984). Phenomenology: from hermeneutics to deconstruction. *Research in Phenomenology,* Vol. XIV, pp. 19-34.

Silverman, H.J. and D. Ihde. (eds.) (1985). *Hermeneutics & deconstruction.* New York: State University of New York Press.

Sloterdijk, P. (1983). *Kritik der zynischen Vernunft.* Vols. 1&2. Frankfurt am Main: Suhrkamp Verlag.

Smith, D.G. (1984). *A hermeneutic of the language of living with children.* Unpublished Dissertation. Edmonton: The University of Alberta.

Smith, S. (1989). *Risk and the playground.* Unpublished Dissertation. Edmonton: The University of Alberta.

Sontag, S. (1982). Writing itself: on Roland Barthes. *A Barthes reader.* S. Sontag (ed.). Toronto: McGraw-Hill Ryerson.

Spiegelberg, H. (1982). *The phenomenological movement.* The Hague: Martinus Nijhoff.

St. Augustine. (1960). *The confessions.* New York: Doubleday.

Strasser, S. (1974). *Phenomenology and the human sciences*. Pittsburgh: Duquesne University Press.

Strasser, S. (1985). *Understanding and explanation*. Pittsburgh: Duquesne University Press.

Straus, E.W. (1966). *Phenomenological psychology*. New York: Basic Books.

Straus, E.W. (1982). *Man, time, and world*. Pittsburgh: Duquesne University Press.

Styron, W. (1980). *Sophie's Choice*. New York: Random House.

Suransky, V. Polakow. (1982). *The erosion of childhood*. Chicago: The University of Chicago Press.

Truffaut, F. (1976/81). *Small Change*. New York: Warner Bros. Video.

Van den Berg, J.H. and J. Linschoten (eds.) (1953). *Persoon en wereld*. Utrecht: Erven J. Bijleveld.

Van den Berg, J.H. (1972). *A different existence*. Pittsburgh: Duquesne University Press.

Vandenberg, D. (1971). *Being and education*. Englewood Cliffs, N.J.: Prentice-Hall.

Van Manen, M. (1979). The Utrecht School: an experiment in educational theorizing. *Interchange*. Vol. 10, No. 1, pp. 48-66.

Van Manen, M. (1979). The phenomenology of pedagogic observation. *The Canadian Journal of Education*. Vol. 4, No. 1, pp. 5-16.

Van Manen, M. (1982a). Phenomenological pedagogy. *Curriculum Inquiry*. Vol. 12, No. 3, pp. 283-299.

Van Manen, M. (1982b). Edifying theory: serving the Good. *Theory into Practice*, Vol. XXI, No. 1, Winter, pp. 44-49.

Van Manen, M. (1985). The phenomenology of the novel, or how do novels teach? *Phenomenology + Pedagogy*, Vol. 3, No. 3, pp. 177-187.

Van Manen, M. (1986). *The tone of teaching*. Richmond Hill, Ont.: Scholastic-TAB.

Van Manen, M. (1988). The tact of teaching. *Human Science Monograph*. Edmonton: Faculty of Education, The University of Alberta.

Verhoeven, C. (1987). *De letter als beeld*. Baarn: Ambo.

Wilson, B.R. (ed.) (1970). *Rationality*. New York: Harper & Row.

Wittgenstein, L. (1982). *Last writings on the philosophy of psychology*, Vol. 1. Oxford: Basil Blackwell.

Wolcott, H.F. (1988). Adequate schools and inadequate education: the life history of a sneaky kid. *Complementary methods for research in education*. R.M. Jaeger (ed.). Washington, D.C.: American Educational Research Association.

Woolf, V. (1932). *The common reader*, Vol. 1. Honolulu, HI: Hogarth.

Zaner, R.M. (1964). *The problem of embodiment*. The Hague: Martinus Nijhoff.

INDEX

Van Manen, M., 6, 91, 136, 137,
    150, 154, 167, 169, 196
Verhoeven, C., 117, 119, 196
Verstehen, 15
Vico, G. 185
Visible and the Invisible, The (Mer-
    leau-Ponty), 96

WILSON, B.R., 15, 196
With Child: A Diary of Motherhood
    (Chesler), 72
Wittgenstein, L., 183, 196
Wolcott, H.F., 138, 196
Woolf, V. 49, 196
writing, 32-33, 111-133, 135-142
    see research

ZANER, R.M., 171, 196

CPSIA information can be obtained at www.ICGtesting.com
Printed in the USA
LVOW060625290812

296445LV00002B/39/A

9 780791 404263